The Legend
of
BEAR BRYANT

The Legend
of
BEAR BRYANT

Mickey Herskowitz

EAKIN PRESS ★ Austin, Texas

Revised Ed. 1993

ISBN 0-89015-910-6

LIBRARY OF CONGRESS CATALOGING-IN-PUBLICATION DATA

Herskowitz, Mickey.
  The legend of Bear Bryant.
  1. Bryant, Paul W. 2. Football — United States —
Coaches — Biography. I. Title.
GV939.B79H47   1987   796.332'092'4 [B]   86-18591

BOOK DESIGN BY PATRICE FODERO

To Clark Nealon, who started me in the writing business and assigned me to cover the Texas Aggies in the Bryant era. For both decisions, he has my gratitude, and a lot on his conscience.

Acknowledgments

The author owes a special debt to Pat Morgan, a classmate of Coach Bryant at Alabama, a friend to both of us, and the developer of the golf course that was one of Bear's favorites and among the country's best, Champions. Without his insistence and encouragement, this book would not have been undertaken.

Jones Ramsey, Bryant's publicity man at Texas A&M, made available his prodigious memory, and his skills as a researcher and interviewer. Charley Thornton, who held that job and others for twenty years at Alabama, was generous with his insights and recollections.

I was fortunate to be able to draw upon the magazine and newspaper coverage of Coach Bryant and his teams by some of the country's ablest writers. The details of the trial of the Wally Butts lawsuit against the *Saturday Evening Post* came from the personal account of Fred Russell of Nashville. Additional thanks are due Alf Van Hoose and Marvin West of Birmingham; John Underwood of *Sports Illustrated;* and Mike Bynum, a resourceful onetime 'Bama student manager who assembled a number of interviews with Bryant's former players in a privately published book called *We Believe.*

Rose Ann French of the A&M athletic department helped locate important files and photographs. Many Bryant disciples contributed stories and impressions—too many to list. They know who they are, and they are appreciated.

Finally, every would-be author should have an editor with the patience and enthusiasm of Tom Quinn.

BRYANT'S RECORD AS HEAD COACH: WON 323, LOST 85, TIED 17

Year	School	W	L	T	Year	School	W	L	T
1945	Maryland	6	2	'1	1964	Alabama	*10	1	0
1946	Kentucky	7	3	0	1965	Alabama	* 9	1	1
1947	Kentucky	8	3	0	1966	Alabama	11	0	0
1948	Kentucky	5	3	2	1967	Alabama	8	2	1
1949	Kentucky	9	3	0	1968	Alabama	8	3	0
1950	Kentucky	11	1	0	1969	Alabama	6	5	0
1951	Kentucky	8	4	0	1970	Alabama	6	5	1
1952	Kentucky	5	4	2	1971	Alabama	11	1	0
1953	Kentucky	7	2	1	1972	Alabama	10	2	0
1954	Texas A&M	1	9	0	1973	Alabama	*11	1	0
1955	Texas A&M	7	2	1	1974	Alabama	11	1	0
1956	Texas A&M	9	0	1	1975	Alabama	11	1	0
1957	Texas A&M	8	3	0	1976	Alabama	9	3	0
1958	Alabama	5	4	1	1977	Alabama	11	1	0
1959	Alabama	7	2	2	1978	Alabama	*11	1	0
1960	Alabama	8	1	2	1979	Alabama	*12	0	0
1961	Alabama	*11	0	0	1980	Alabama	10	2	0
1962	Alabama	10	1	0	1981	Alabama	9	2	1
1963	Alabama	9	2	0	1982	Alabama	8	4	0

*National Champions

BRYANT'S MILESTONE VICTORIES

No. 1   Maryland, 60-6 over Guilford College in 1945
No. 100   Alabama, 19-7 over Tulane in 1959
No. 150   Alabama, 24-7 over Georgia Tech in 1964
No. 200   Alabama, 17-10 over Southern Cal in 1971
No. 250   Alabama, 23-10 over LSU in 1975
No. 275   Alabama, 38-20 over Missouri in 1978
No. 300   Alabama, 45-0 over Kentucky in 1980
No. 305   Alabama, 34-18 over Auburn in 1980
No. 310   Alabama, 38-7 over Mississippi in 1981
No. 314   Alabama, 31-16 over Penn State in 1981
No. 315   Alabama, 28-17 over Auburn in 1981
No. 320   Alabama, 42-21 over Penn State in 1982
No. 323   Alabama, 21-15 over Illinois in 1982

Contents

Contents

Prologue

For me, college football without Bear Bryant is like New Year's without a clock. It surprised me, maybe it shouldn't have, to realize how many other people felt that way.

The day after the news of Bryant's death, the telephone in the home of Johnny Mitchell, a Houston oilman and a friend from his Texas Aggie service, did not stop ringing. "People called from all over the country," he marveled. "They left messages with my wife: 'Tell Johnny we were sorry to hear about Paul.' It was as if they thought he belonged to me."

So he had. In a sense he belonged to all of those who care about the family of sports, about loyalty and excellence, the scriptures according to Paul W. Bryant. Many were the people and places that claimed him: all of Alabama, and parts of Texas, Kentucky and Maryland, where he coached. And Arkansas, where he was born, and whose cotton fields and hardscrabble life he escaped through football.

If one had asked what made Bryant the driven competitor he was, the answer starts here, with the shabby 11-year-old boy who helped his mother sell vegetables from the back of a wagon drawn by mules, enduring the taunts of the town kids. Bryant wrestled with more than a carnival bear in his lifetime. Years later, he wrestled with a win-at-any-cost image that he once courted but came to dislike. Still, you don't win as often or as long as he did, you don't become Paul (Bear) Bryant, and not pick up labels and your share of detractors along the way. The news was sudden and sorrowful and, yes, a little eerie when Bryant's big heart stopped beating at the age of 69. He had done everything he set out to do, and more. He had become the winningest college football coach of all time. Depending on which poll you believed—and he always believed the one that had Alabama first—his teams won six national titles. He retired and helped hand pick his successor, Ray Perkins. And then, six weeks after he announced he was stepping down, 59 days after he coached (and won) his last game, he died.

Eerie? In *Sports Illustrated*, in the end-of-the-year issue, a story by John Underwood began: "I watched the papers last week to see if Bear Bryant had 'croaked.' That's what he said he would do if he ever quit coaching football, and quit he had. A few years ago he told me coaching wasn't as much fun anymore, and I suggested he retire and rest on his abundant laurels. He looked at me as if I'd put my thumb in his soup. 'Quit coaching?' he growled. 'I'd croak in a week.' I've heard him say that three or four times since, and Bryant usually does what he says he's going to do. Maybe he changed his mind about croaking. I hope so."

A lot of people, friends or not, seized on the same thought and concluded that Bryant had virtually prepared for his own death if, indeed, he had not willed it. His wife brought up the subject herself when we talked the day after the funeral. "It makes me mad," she says, "when people act like Papa wanted to die. Papa didn't want to die. Papa had lots of things he still wanted to do."

Unlike most coaches' wives, Mrs. Bryant had to be convinced that her husband's retirement was a good idea. They had met as students at Alabama, where Mary Harmon was a campus beauty (she still was when she followed him into death a year later). Her intuition was not that he would be bored or useless or doomed, but that he might be less happy. Then we were left to ponder the order of things.

Some of us were still adjusting to the idea that football was going to be a little less fun, that it would be strange not having Bear Bryant on the sidelines in the autumn. His friends had been curious about what he would do with himself, and unsure how they should act around him. They spoke of him as though he were leaving *office*, not a job.

Some were still trying to figure out why he retired when he did. It may have been just as he said, that he loved Alabama and felt his old school deserved better than a coach whose team finished the regular season (of 1982) with three straight losses. And no doubt he felt it would be easier for a new coach to come aboard after an 8-and-4 record, than after the less blemished years to which 'Bama fans had grown accustomed.

Our guess was that the reason had more to do with football than with life, unless you accept the proposition that for Bryant they were the same thing. In truth, he had finally reached a point where he no longer wanted to change, as a coach, as he had done for five decades. The day of the wishbone was ending. Texas and Oklahoma, among the teams that perfected it, had already gone another way. One day, in an almost casual remark, Bryant revealed himself: "I'll never teach pass blocking again."

Nothing profound there, or so it seemed. But Bryant knew that the world would belong again to the teams that threw the ball. And pass blocking is mean stuff. It is the least fun you can have on a football field. Every blocker has to get into a rooster fight with the man in front of him. So it was simple, really. His teams had dominated the 1970s with the wishbone, a formation designed for running and passing on the roll. Bryant made a coaching decision. When he felt Alabama might no longer dominate, just winning was not enough. He stepped down.

Yet look at the list of great passers he coached: Babe Parilli, George Blanda, Joe Namath, Ken Stabler, Scott Hunter, Richard Todd. But defense was what he loved and where he insisted games were won. Passing was a science, but defense was heart.

There were contradictions in the nature of Paul Bryant that provided his friends, and even his critics, with endless hours of puzzlement. He seemed as strong as pig iron, and yet he cried without shame: after a bitter loss, or when he learned that one of his former players was seriously ill (as in the case of the dying Pat Trammel), or when the news was good (as on the day he learned that one of his own, Gene Stallings, had accepted his old job as coach of the Texas Aggies). He was like the old-time cowboys, who could brave the hardships of the range and then weep at a painting on a bordello wall.

Maybe this is where we ought to say, flat out, that we hope what will appear on these pages will *not* come off as worshipful. Of course, we may fail. And this mea culpa may be unnecessary. My admiration for Coach Bryant is generally known. When I wrote about him on an almost daily basis for a Texas newspaper, older writers kidded me about being his biographer. But this is not, in the traditional sense, a biography. It is about friendships and loyalties and the tribal rites that form them. Like it or not, I am a character in the story.

It ought to be permissible, in this age of little modesty, false or otherwise, to hide behind another writer to make a point. This is especially so when the writer is a friend, one whose work you have admired, and whose tracks you followed in a mellower time. In 1957, when I was no older than many of Bryant's players, Dan Jenkins was one of the stars of the *Fort Worth Press*. The *Press* had the best sports staff in America, though not many outside of the state knew it, headed by Blackie Sherrod and including Bud Shrake and Gary Cartwright.

These paragraphs are taken from a column Dan wrote in March of that year:

> The second annual edition of a slick magazine titled "Football at Texas A&M" lay open now on the desk, and a number of interesting items have been examined, not the least of which is a photo of John Crow being interviewed by a fellow lodge member named Mickey Herskowitz, who runs out of the *Houston Post* stable.
>
> A thorough reader may find this particular photo the most prepossessing of any reproduced in the handsome 24-page brochure because Herskowitz is the only writer whose li ness appears in it. Nothing could have been more appropriate, actually. Mickey, who, it should be added, is a crackerjack of a phrasemaker, has probably written more words about

the Cadets in the past three years than any living human. A&M is his beat.

And for reasons that were firmly established years ago, a newspaperman generally becomes a part of the thing he writes about regularly, at least in the minds of most followers. I don't know if that's good or bad, but that is how it is.

Well, anyhow, Mickey's in there by himself, and that struck a perversely amusing note with your friend in this department. It also brought to mind a funny remark our foreman, William Forest Sherrod, made one afternoon a couple of years ago, a quip which, incidentally, illustrates the point attempting to be made in the preceding paragraph.

We were in the Memorial Stadium press roost back in 1955, watching the Frogs belabor Texas, and a fellow down the aisle was listening to a near-catastrophe going on in Houston at the same time when A&M was playing Rice.

It had been announced frantically that Rice was ahead, 12–0, with very little time left. Then we got the word that A&M had scored once, but still trailed. When the later announcement was boomed that the Ags had somehow scored again to pull ahead, Sherrod calmly declaimed:

"Herskowitz just ran 80 yards for a touchdown."

There it is. I admired Bryant greatly, sailing far across the line that writers usually establish between themselves and the people they cover. No, I didn't think that he had put down the yard markers in the Garden of Eden, or discovered Joe Namath in the bulrushes of the Nile and driven the Crimson Tide to glory with a series of Sermons on the Mount. But I thought there was something in him that went beyond the scoreboard, and I noticed that his players learned from him, just by being around him. I saw him as a folk hero, long before that was the widely held view.

Many of his friendships lasted a lifetime. He was drawn to people like Johnny Mitchell, whose family built an oil and gas fortune and helped develop the city of Galveston. But they became friends because Mitchell was, and is, an independent character, impulsive, a portly, balding bon vivant with a generous heart. He was a captain in the field artillery in World War II, and served under Patton. The Bear referred to him as "The Old Soldier," an affectionate reference to his war ribbons and his loyalty to the Texas Aggies. It was to Johnny Mitchell's home that Bryant came as a guest on a night in December 1957. They talked and drank until nearly midnight, when Bear put a hand to his chest and said calmly, "Soldier, I think this is it. I'm having a heart attack."

Mitchell rushed him to a hospital, where a physician emerged from the emergency room to tell him: "Don't worry about Coach Bryant. He's strong as a horse."

"What was wrong with him?" asked Johnny.

"Gas," said the doctor.

More likely, Bryant was having a mild anxiety attack. What he had not told his host was the reason he had driven to Houston. In the morning, he was to meet Dr. Frank Rose, the president of the University of Alabama, at the Shamrock Hilton Hotel to sign a 10-year contract as head coach and athletic director.

"If I had known," said Mitchell, later, "I would have left him in my living room, thinking he was having a heart attack."

But they remained close friends. Mitchell was to have met Bryant in Las Vegas in January, 1983, the week of the Super Bowl. He had a plane ticket to leave the day Bryant died.

Since his death, there has been no shortage of attempts to explain Bryant, his success, his place in sports and public life, whatever it was that made him tick. Those with a sense of romance and imagination tried to convince us that he was a sort of Wallace Beery character; that beneath his gruff, gravel surface beat a heart as soft as banana mush. That picture was not entirely wrong. Another old Aggie friend, Clarence Jamail, remembered: "He called me once to help find a job for one of his former Kentucky players, who was down on his luck. He said he could place him in a couple of months, coaching at some high school, but right now the boy needed help. He never forgot one of his players. That's what I remember. His humanness."

But of course his compulsion to win is what most will remember. Some of his most bitter defeats were, in fact, tie games. He hated them. One year Alabama had raced to Tennessee's one-yard line, tied at 7–7 with a few seconds left. A sophomore quarterback named Ken Stabler threw the ball out of bounds to stop the clock. Unfortunately, for Stabler and Alabama, it was fourth down. That was how the game ended, in a tie.

To compound the pain, when they reached the locker room the Alabama players found the old wooden door locked and no one around with a key. They stood there, miserable and impatient and fearful, waiting to see how their coach would react. Suddenly, Bear Bryant stepped back a step or two and slammed his shoulder into the door and with a loud snap it split in two. He led his team inside.

Bryant's position on this issue—tie games—was well put his first year at A&M, when his team lost by three points when he had them try for a winning touchdown in the final minute. He was asked if he considered going for a field goal. He snapped, "Hell, no. A tie is like kissing your sister."

That line became nearly as well identified with Bryant as the immortal "Nice guys finish last" was with Leo Durocher. Later, an admirer asked Bryant how he managed to come up with such a great line.

"Aw," he replied, "I heard Jim Tatum say it once at Maryland."

He was a borrower and a refiner, not an innovator, a master at taking someone else's ideas and making them better. Bryant was willing and quick to seek help and he repaid it many times over. He sought out Bobby Dodd and Darrell Royal when he needed to put in a new offense, and his former players often came back to the campus to offer what they had learned in the pros.

He liked to call himself a field coach, a teacher, as opposed to those who preferred to deal in theory, with the x's and o's. Actually, he could chalk up a blackboard with the best of them. Whatever he was, the record book established him as the greatest of his time, maybe of any time. The years will not turn him into a mythical figure. No need for it. His bloodline can be traced to Amos Alonzo Stagg, whose victory mark he broke, and who practically invented the college game, and to Knute Rockne, of Notre Dame, the first of the great psychologists, of whom Bryant may have been the last.

After Bryant's funeral, Woody Hayes, the Ohio State coach, recalled as a schoolboy reading about the death of Knute Rockne in a plane crash in a Kansas cornfield. "When Rockne died," he said, "there was sorrow on a national scale. I can't recall a sports figure whose death caused the same reaction until Bryant."

A few years ago, ABC used a hidden camera to pick up one of Bear's halftime talks for a television special. He didn't say much until it was time to return to the field, and then his voice was a hoarse whisper: "This is great," he told his Crimson Tide. "We're behind. If we've got any class at all, now is our chance to find out."

Alabama did rally, but the best they could get was a wild 37–37 tie with Florida State. There is no record of what he said after the game. Such outcomes bedeviled him more than losses, but they will not be his legacy.

Winning will.

Chapter 1

The Number

November 28, 1981

A football stadium as it begins to fill is much like a large theater. The early arrivals seem almost a part of the program as they climb over seats, try to locate the correct aisle, and get in the way of the ushers. Stray sounds hang in the air as musicians tune their instruments. You sense, you feel, rather than hear movements backstage.

It is in some ways your last sociable moment, a quiet time to anticipate, to reflect, to remember.

Three hours before the kickoff, the Alabama sky was bright and clear and the first spectators were straggling into the stands. I was already in the press box in Legion Field, in Birmingham, fiddling with my field glasses, watching what little was going on.

At one point, the Alabama team came out for its pregame stroll across the field. This was a ritual Coach Bryant had followed for as long as I had known him. In theory, the idea was to get the feel of the turf, and inspect it for flaws that might influence the game. I suspected it was just as much a way to work off the pregame tensions. But I liked the look of it, the coaches and players fanning out, sending a message: Alabama is here. Alabama is checking things out. Alabama is *ready*.

9

This was the night Bear Bryant's number would come up. The number was 315, and it would establish him as the winningest coach in college football history. The game would have offered a certain fever and tradition without this distraction: it was Alabama versus Auburn.

The Auburn coach, Pat Dye, like so many others in the press box, and in a crowd that would exceed 78,000, had a prior relationship with the Bear. Dye had played at Georgia, but coached under him for eight years. Bryant had recommended him for his present job.

I could not recall having covered any of his other milestones, unless you counted win number 67. Not an impressive number, I grant you. No echo, no glitter, no industries inspired by it. But it was his first victory at Texas A&M, and the only one he would get in 1954, his only losing season in a lifetime of coaching.

Now, in the press box at Legion Field, I bumped into Jesse Outlar of Atlanta, the only other writer in attendance this day who had been there in the cramped, ramshackle stadium in Athens, when the Aggies beat Georgia, 6–0.

In '54 the Atlanta writers had not been able to believe their eyes when Bryant walked on the field for the warm-ups with 29 players in uniform. One of them asked, "Coach, is this all the players you got?"

Bryant snapped, "No, these are the ones who want to play." He knew the wins would come hard and scarce that year. In the locker room after the game, Bryant danced a jig with his trainer, Smokey Harper, white-haired and hard of hearing.

The Alabama-Auburn kickoff was not until 4:00 P.M., but I had decided not to visit the field before the game. The feeling was not one I had to intellectualize. I had seldom done so in the past, and then always at the insistence of someone else, another writer or an old friend of Bryant's. He was often polite at such times, but I didn't think he liked to be bothered before he went to work.

This day there was something else. The story was ending. A victory would mean he had no more goals and the only countdown left would be the one to his retirement. The end of this truly uncommon career was at hand, and I was doing a little mourning for the young coach who spilled his own blood on the field and the teenage writer who could see no bad in him . . . for the times that were gone and wouldn't come again.

I had only recently grown aware of how old he *looked*. Others had dwelled on it, referring not so much to his age as to his antiquity. He was 67, younger than Ronald Reagan, but there was no denying it, the lines, the ridges in Bryant's face went beyond years. His face looked like an aerial shot of a drought area.

I had been told that the previous weeks had been testy ones for Coach Bryant, as the time of the record grew closer. The team was not playing as well as he wanted and he felt frustrated. The record had imposed restraints. If he pushed the players harder, he was afraid it would be seen as selfishness on his part, as a reflection of how much he wanted the record. What he wanted was to get it behind him.

My presence in Birmingham was almost an afterthought. Late in the week, Rick Hinton, the sports editor of the *Houston Post*, asked if I wanted to cover the game. I leaped at the offer. I had not been there the day his Maryland team beat Guilford for his first victory, but I was there when the legend really began, at Texas A&M. I was grateful for the chance to cover the coronation.

It was a gathering of the clan. From around the country they came, his former players and coaches. It was the way you imagined it must be when the gypsies rally around their king. From the Aggies came John David Crow, his Heisman Trophy winner, and Don Watson. There were dozens out of his Alabama past, including Leon Fuller, who was in the press box, scouting for Texas, and Dan Ford, taking a day off from coaching Clemson, and Bud Moore, the ex-Kansas coach. Joe Namath was in the TV booth, working.

Driving to the stadium in a rented car, I spotted the signs planted in front lawns, bearing just the number 315. There were songs about it on the radio, and poems in the paper. People wore badges that proclaimed, in advance, I WAS THERE WHEN BEAR WON 315. Some had painted it on their faces in red lipstick or crayon. They looked as though they belonged to some weird religious cult, and that analogy did not seem too far off. The latest joke was making the rounds: "Did you hear? The Bear got hurt this morning. He was out walking his duck and a motorboat ran over him."

Bryant claimed that his assistants did all the work now, but there was no reason to suppose that his authority had been in any way reduced. Alabama's middle guard, Warren Lyles, had talked about him the day before the game, recalling how closely he still monitored them. That fall, during two-a-day drills, the word had reached Bryant from the cooks in the kitchen that many of his players were skipping breakfast.

"Most of us were just too tired to get up," said Lyles, "so we slept in. One morning one of the guys heard a funny knock at his door at seven-thirty. He shouted and didn't get an answer. He heard the knock again and he got out of bed and threw open the door so he could unload on whoever was there. But it was Coach Bryant. He just said, 'Son, have you been to breakfast this morning?' He said, 'No, sir, but I'm on my way right now.'

"Coach Bryant just walked down the hall knocking on doors. None of us missed breakfast after that."

Football teams do not move well on empty stomachs. Bryant wanted the record and every win it represented and all that such a thing means. It meant more than he would ever admit.

The game started in the glaring sunshine and ended under the lights. And the story I filed to Houston began:

Birmingham, Ala.—After 35 years, all those Saturdays in all those stadiums, it hardly seemed fair to expect that grand, imposing old gentleman in the houndstooth hat to stand out there in the gathering chill of a darkening night and wait until the fourth quarter to learn if The Record was to be his.

But he did and it was. Paul William (Bear) Bryant reached his magic number Saturday as Alabama gave him the 315th victory of his fabled career. The Crimson Tide was fit to be tied, twice, and fell behind once, by a field goal, before subduing arch-rival Auburn. The win came late and tough and hard—exactly the way the Bear says he likes them.

There was certainly no reason to think the War Eagles would make it easy for him. Their defense stopped the 'Bama wishbone cold, and then Auburn's Chuck Clanton returned a punt 55 yards down the right sideline to the Alabama 13. But Al Del Greco missed a field goal attempt.

Two plays later, Alan Gray, one of three quarterbacks Bryant rotated, found a huge hole cleared by tackle Joe Beasley and raced 63 yards to set up a Crimson Tide touchdown. But that run would account for most of the Alabama yardage in the first half. Meanwhile, Auburn moved inside the Tide 30-yard line five times, but scored only once, on a 63-yard run by fullback George Peoples. Del Greco missed a second field goal try and on a third his holder fumbled the snap.

At halftime, the game was tied. In the Auburn locker room, Dye told his players they were better than Alabama and there would never be a better chance to prove it. Across the corridor, Bryant was telling his team they were lucky not to be down by two touchdowns. He addressed himself to the offense: "You're acting like you're playin' your little brothers, or something. Like you're afraid you're going to get hurt, or hurt *them*."

On Alabama's first drive of the second half, moving from the Auburn 26, Bryant sent in the old "whoopee" pass: the quarterback, Ken Coley, dropped back and cocked his arm as if to throw. Meanwhile, end Jess Bendross had pulled like a guard and, as he crossed behind the center, Coley brought the ball down and flipped it to him. Bendross scored.

Bryant may have mellowed but he still controlled a game. Joey Jones, his safety, the son of a former Bryant player, fumbled fair catches twice. After the first one, Auburn's Chuck Clanton dribbled and kicked the ball 38 yards to the Alabama 5, setting up the touchdown that tied the game at 14. The next one gave the Tigers a field goal from 19 yards out and a 17–14 lead with two and a half minutes gone in the fourth quarter.

The next Auburn punt, Alabama had a different safety.

In the press box, the Texas assistant coach, Leon Fuller, a 5'8" halfback on Bryant's second Alabama team, looked fidgety. "Man, I hope Auburn doesn't leave the record for us," he said.

A face mask penalty helped Alabama gain a first down at the Auburn 38. From there, Walter Lewis, their third quarterback, faked a handoff to his fullback, Ricky Moore, and the Auburn defense read the play as a run. But Lewis whipped a pass to Bendross, the split end, streaking for the post. He caught it in full stride and Alabama led, 21–17.

That touchdown would have been enough. But a sophomore

halfback named Linnie Patrick, who carried the ball only once until the fourth quarter, broke off a 32-yard run and then twisted 15 for the final score, 28–17.

Alabama may have done its best blocking of the day in clearing Bryant's path through the mob that invaded the field. His players shielded him and a state trooper tucked the Bear's checkered hat under his arm for safekeeping. Through my binoculars I watched him go. His face showed nothing. His expression had not changed all night.

I made my way down the press elevator and through the stands, elbowing and squeezing past the jubilant Alabama fans. I carried with me very little of the game itself. The Crimson Tide had not exactly delivered up a work of art to lift Bryant past Amos Alonzo Stagg and into that special place in heaven reserved for the coach with the most wins. They had lost four fumbles. The game had been hard-hitting and interesting, but there was nothing, no one memory, you would hold onto for the rest of your life. Just a number. I don't recall ever having so strong a sense of just waiting for a game to end.

Nor had I ever heard a losing coach tell the man who beat him that he was proud and happy for him and that he loved him, as Pat Dye told the Bear that night. Later, Dye was asked how Bryant would be remembered. "As the greatest coach the game has known," he said. "I don't think there is any question about it. If anyone was going to have that record it ought to be him."

In his later years, Bryant was given to references that struck some as obscure. So Dye seemed puzzled when the Bear greeted him with the words, "Governor Jimmy Carter just called me."

It was Bryant's way of needling Dye, who had been an all-American at Georgia, pointing out that he had received a congratulatory call from the governor of his, Dye's, state. The humor was lost on the younger coach, who in reply stammered, "Governor Reagan?"

"Carter," repeated Bryant. "Well, Reagan, too, but Governor Carter. I thought you'd appreciate that."

"Did the president call you?" asked Dye, still trying to get the matter straight.

"Well, sure he did," said Coach Bryant.

After the game they repaired to a trailer that is shipped to wherever Alabama plays, just for Bryant's postgame press interviews. The trailer is carpeted, paneled and lighted for television. There is a podium, almost a pulpit, in front, and folding chairs arranged in neat rows for the press. I walked in and worked my way to the back.

It had taken nearly an hour for Bryant to pull away from his old players and friends and fans and reach the trailer. Even as he began to talk, the celebration was spilling off the surface of Legion Field and onto the parking lots and out to downtown Birmingham and across the state of Alabama.

Bryant squinted into the lights and said, "To turn it around and come back and win, well, if I could have charted it, I'd have wanted to come from behind and win it. That shows our kids have some character and class."

He praised Auburn for "playing their little ol' hearts out," and he accepted the record, as you knew he would, on behalf of all the players, coaches, mamas, papas, ex-students, anyone who might have contributed to a victory somewhere along the way. He didn't appear to miss anyone, except possibly the guys who put the deodorant pucks in the urinals in the locker room.

Then he returned again to Reagan's call: "He recalled that he had been to one of our practices a few years ago in a tuxedo. He had been to something and didn't have time to change. I reminded Mr. Reagan that when we were in the Rose Bowl in 1935, he came to our practices every day. He was out there as a cub reporter or a sportscaster or whatever he was. I appreciated his call very much, and the same with President Carter, except that he didn't come to our practice."

A collective giggle ran through the room and Bryant looked startled. "I wasn't trying to be funny," he said. The noise stopped instantly.

There were long silences broken by a few questions about the game. The day had been tense and strange, but mostly inevitable, and clearly no one could think of anything new to ask. A writer requested that Bryant move closer to the microphone, it was hard to hear him in the back.

"I'm *old*," he replied. "I'm going to sit where it's comfortable for me."

From my seat well in the rear, I risked a question about his quarterbacks: if he had planned to use all three and to use them so early.

His head raised up and he seemed to be looking for the direction of the voice. He said, "Mickey, no one told me you had come up for the game." There were some curious looks thrown in my direction. I mumbled something like, "Wouldn't have missed it for a purty"—a Bryant line, and then I was aware he had ignored my question and the interview had moved on to something else.

Finally, a radio guy asked what his plans were for the Cotton Bowl, and the Bear, faking a little irritation, said, "How the hell could I have plans for the Cotton Bowl, when I haven't even quit shaking yet from the end of this game?"

Then there was the customary mass scraping of chairs and the newsfolk headed for the door, and the long climb back to the press box. Bryant yelled something to me as the troopers gently hurried him out of the trailer. I am tempted to make up a funny or touching line, but the truth is, I have no idea what he said.

I waited until the room had almost cleared before I left. I wanted to remember how I felt, and at that instant what I truly felt was self-conscious, because the record had nothing to do with me. My friendship with the man who set it was based on things that had happened 25 years earlier. And yet, there are not many times in your life that you are so pleased for someone else, and so proud, that their honor seems like yours.

And so, feeling self-conscious, I cut through the stands and trudged back to the press box.

To get a sense of what was involved that night, one needs to consider Amos Alonzo Stagg and his times. Stagg was born in 1862, three years before Abraham Lincoln was murdered. The schools where Stagg gained his fame, Chicago and College of the Pacific, dropped football 20 or 30 years ago. A.A. was in his prime in those lilac days before the First World War, a time of candy-striped shirts, gaslights and horse-drawn streetcars. In the game Stagg knew best, the players wore helmets they could fold and stuff in a pocket.

Stagg's teams were the first to huddle, to quick-kick, to place-kick, to use a man in motion. He was a head coach for 57 years, retiring at 91. He died in 1965 at 103.

Bryant may have felt as old on certain days, and may have looked as old to some of those in the Oil of Olay generation. But he beat

Stagg's mark in two-thirds the time, coaching through his 38th season. That he lasted as long in today's meat-grinder game was a small miracle in itself.

Similar comparisons were made between Roger Maris and Babe Ruth, between Pete Rose and Ty Cobb. But the planet has changed since the heyday of Stagg. With each passing week, Bryant had to endure more cameras and tape recorders, more people bearing pads and pencils. When Stagg won his 314th game he was not chasing a goal. His record was probably of great interest only to Pop Warner, who was on his heels. Warner coached 44 years and finished with 313 wins.

Many of the coaches who were riding high when Bryant began his career—Frank Leahy, Earl Blaik, General Bob Neyland, Red Sanders—were no longer living. The championship coaches who came along at about the same time, Bud Wilkinson, Duffy Daugherty, Bobby Dodd and Woody Hayes, were gone. And even the young turks who came along years later, Darrell Royal, Frank Broyles and Ara Parseghian, had been off the job since the mid-1970s.

It was Broyles who had said: "I think it is paramount to the future of college football that Coach Bryant set the record. His doing so would be a tremendous boost to the sport. He is the only one who can . . . he has been more willing to give of himself and his talents than, maybe, the rest of us. Then I'll say this: After he sets the new record, his will never be broken. The man was made to coach. We will not see one like him again."

That forecast turned out to be true, and not so true. Bryant's victory total would be surpassed as early as 1985. The coach was Eddie Robinson and, no, he was not like Paul Bryant. He was black, and he won his games at an all-black school, Grambling College, in a little town in Louisiana that no one ever heard of until Eddie Robinson began sending players to the pros, in greater numbers than Alabama or Notre Dame. It was a reassuring sign of the times that no controversy developed as Robinson caught and passed the Bear. The NCAA recordkeepers and the wire services quietly moved Coach Robinson to the top of the list. I believe Bryant, who did not recruit a black player until 1971, would have approved. He was no racist, but he tolerated the policies of the schools that hired him.

It should be noted that when the policies got in the way of winning, he tolerated them no more.

Everyone agreed that Robinson was probably the last coach who would pass Bryant. Times have changed. You don't get a head coaching job at 22 anymore. And once you have it, you are more likely to get fired, or come down with that new disease, occupational burnout.

They first met at a coaches' clinic years ago, and after that Robinson traveled all over to hear Bryant lecture. They visited each other's spring practices. There was respect and affection between them, two old boys from the rural South who knew what sacrifice meant. Above all, both were winners.

"The greatest thing about Coach Bryant," said Robinson, "was that he could talk to kings and queens and the man in the street." They had talked about scheduling a game, coaching against each other, but time ran out on them. "I loved the man," said Robinson. "No one replaces the Bear. Anyone who met him would tell you, he just had that power."

Among those who shared that opinion was Steve Mott, who played center on Bryant's last team. "He had such influence over people," said Mott, "it was amazing. He could have walked into a shopping mall, told everybody to leave, and the mall would have been empty in minutes."

In March 1982, Bryant was honored with a testimonial dinner in Washington, D.C. I flew up with a planeload of Texas Aggies.

One was struck again that night how often, lately, Bryant had talked, or joked, about dying. When it was his turn to speak, he said he was "sick and tired" of hearing about Bear Bryant. He sounded as if he meant it, and one could hardly blame him, not after five hours of speeches, awards, gifts, a movie of his life and table favors that included a commemorative Coca Cola bottle with his picture on it. (I saved mine. Still has the Coke in it.)

"All I been hearing is Paul Bryant this and Bear Bryant that, 315 this and 315 that," he growled. "But I'll say this, you did something for Mary Harmon. I've always said I wanted the biggest funeral in Alabama." He cast a sideways glance at his wife and went on, "Mother, if I croak now all you have to do is just lay me out."

It was acceptable to talk about dying, which we would prefer to think of as a distant and impersonal thing. What no one talked about, out loud, in all those hours of what was called "America's Tribute to Paul (Bear) Bryant," was that shapeless monster of a thought: what Alabama would do when Bryant retired. By the end of the long and reverent night, when I noted to the guests at my table that the subject of his retirement had been avoided, one of the wives said drily: "I got the impression they were going to let him coach posthumously."

The banquet had been organized by a United States senator, Jeremiah Denton of Alabama, who said he envisioned it as a national tribute, in the nation's capital, to honor a national record. If you are a senator from Alabama, giving a party for Bear Bryant is like wrapping yourself in the flag.

If I sometimes fretted that I took things like football too seriously, or may have been misdirected in my admiration for Coach Bryant, such company reassured me. Denton had been a Naval captain, later promoted to admiral, who spent seven years in a prisoner-of-war camp in Vietnam.

Seldom has a city so divided seen a room so filled with universal devotion. The guests were from Maryland, Kentucky, Texas and Alabama, from the left and from the right, joined by their enduring loyalty to one man. "Coach Bryant would have been number 1 at whatever he wanted to be," Charley Milstead said. "I'm just glad he wasn't a Communist."

The Reverend Billy Graham prayed, President Reagan telephoned, ABC's Keith Jackson narrated and Bob Hope joked. "I don't know where Bear gets his players," Hope said, "but he gets his hats from Ralston Purina. He's so tough that the inside of his hats are lined with real hound's teeth."

A thousand tickets were sold at $125 each, and 50 sponsors paid a reported $10,000 each to have their company signs slide across the room on a string trailing a replica of the Goodyear blimp. There were delegations from each of the schools where Bryant had served and, at our table, when Dennis Goehring spoke for the Texas Aggies, he announced, proudly, "There are fifty-four of us here and we're having a helluva time."

Some of his former players were white-haired and wrinkled and looked older than the man they came to honor. They called him Coach Bryant. Not Paul and, heaven forbid, not Bear. Said Jerry Claiborne, who had returned as head coach to the old Kentucky home where he began as a player: "If I live to be ninety, I'll still call him 'Coach.' "

There was a short, touching film of Bryant's life that included some priceless scenes, such as the grain store where he worked after school as a boy in Fordyce, Arkansas. The storekeeper fondly recalled, "If he didn't tear it up or mess it up, he fell over it. That's how clumsy Paul was."

So the world of commerce lost a klutz and football gained a giant. Who could have guessed? Certainly not Paul Bryant, who played in the first football game he ever saw, for the Fordyce High School Redbugs.

Among those in the ballroom, living proof that Bryant had chosen his field well, were Jackie Sherrill, Dan Ford, Pat Dye, Ray Perkins, Claiborne, Bill Battle, Gene Stallings and Jimmy Wright, some of the 47 head coaches who played or worked under him. Dye sat at the head table, under a re-creation of the scoreboard of the game that put Bryant in the history books. It had to be the least bit unsettling for Dye, the losing coach, to have that score literally hanging over his head.

Perhaps the tribute the Bear appreciated most happened before the banquet. In twos and threes his former Aggie players came to visit him—Milstead, Goehring, Roddy Osborne, Buddy Payne, Joe Munson, Marvin Tate, Carter Franklin, Bobby Lockett, Loyd Taylor. The group included Elmer Smith, who coached there, and Jones Ramsey, his publicity man, by then in his 20th year at Texas, but still a keeper of the Bryant flame.

I received a call in my room to come join them. The stories and the laughter rang out far into the night, about Junction, and the nearly winless team of 1954 and the nearly perfect ones of 1956 and 1957. Many of those stories are repeated in these pages. But what I remember best is the curious sight that greeted me when I got off the elevator and walked down the long corridor to Coach Bryant's suite. Every few feet, cocktail glasses were perched on potted plants and decorator tables the length of the hallway. They were left there by Bear Bryant's former players, reluctant to be received by their old coach with drinks in their hands, 25 years after their eligibility had expired.

Chapter 2

The Junction Boys

September 1954

The impression Paul Bryant made on Texas A&M, and vice versa, was oddly out of proportion to the years he spent there. Four years out of 38. Yet so many of his memories were rooted in the Aggie experience.

The answer is partly in the nature of the school and the people it produces. The Aggies seem to choose up sides faster, yell louder and stay mad longer than those from other places. The rest of the answer could be found in Bryant, who went there as a coach still young, and left there knowing that he would never have to give that much again. When he arrived, A&M was still a military school—"Sing Sing on the Brazos," the cadets called it—a cold, colorless, womanless world, perhaps the toughest recruiting challenge in all of college football. When I once suggested as much to Bryant, he shot me a look you would expect to get from Noah if you tried to tell him about the flood.

A good deal of what he felt about A&M, and the image that followed him, had to do with a place called Junction. Hardly anyone outside of the 2,400 citizens who lived there had heard of the town in 1954, when Bryant hauled his first Aggie football team out there to train.

No one could remember a college team ever holding fall practice away from its own campus. It happened that way once but will never again. The next year, the NCAA made such trips illegal.

The decision to take the team to Junction was made after Bryant had a chance to observe his material in the spring. What he saw depressed him powerfully. He saw how much work he and his staff had ahead of them, and he did not like the idea of getting that work done in front of strangers. The alums were excited by the arrival of Bryant, and eager to drop by the campus and watch him shape up the winning team he had been hired to build.

So the Aggies were going to take a field trip and Bryant asked for suggestions. One of his coaches, Willie Zapalac, who had played at A&M, remembered that A&M had acquired an old army base at Junction, called the Annex. It was used as a summer training facility for physics and geology majors. The housing was a cluster of Quonset huts, with cement floors, plywood walls no thicker than a partition, tin roofs, and screens for doors and windows.

In 1954, Junction was just a dust bowl 300 miles from the Aggie campus. All of the Hill Country and most of West Texas was in the grip of a seven-year drought, the worst of the century. There was little or no grass on the grounds. Bryant had the rocks cleared from the most level patch of earth he could find and had it marked off for a practice field.

A quarter of a century later, I wrote in a sports column that Junction was an hour from the nearest neon sign. A former native of the city wrote an angry letter, pointing out that such signs were visible at the City Cafe, Kimble Courts, Sun Valley Ranch Motel, the Mountainview Lodge and the Texas Theater. "I think the funeral home had one, too," my critic wrote, "but I'm not sure about that."

Gene Stallings, then a skinny sophomore end who would captain the team as a senior and return 10 years later as coach, had the definitive line about the camp Bryant conducted. Someone asked if Junction had been as tough as the stories about it claimed. "All I know is," he replied, "that we went out there in two buses and we came back in one."

Stallings remembers returning to school after the summer break, and reporting for a team meeting. "Coach Bryant told us to pack a couple changes of clothes," he said, "a towel or two and a pillow because we were going to take a little trip. He said we should be packed in 10 minutes. We were packed in five and waiting in front of our dorms when the two buses rolled up. We climbed aboard and moved off and nobody knew our destination. And nobody *asked*. It was that kind of feeling."

Nearly 10 hours after they pulled out of College Station, the buses passed through Junction and stopped at a campground three miles west of town. Coach Bryant made a short speech, explaining why they were there—to learn football *his* way—and then he gave them the next day off. Most of them went swimming in the creek that ran behind the property.

I arrived the next afternoon, in time to watch the Aggies scrimmage on what was officially the first day of fall practice. Jones Ramsey met me at the airport in Kerrville and we headed for the camp, a 45-minute drive through the twisting, rising hills that kept me staring nervously at the steep drop outside my window. Ramsey, the Aggie publicity man, shared his hut with me, directly behind the room where the coaches held their meetings.

In his autobiography, which covered his career up to 1974, exactly 20 years later, Bryant recalled: "We practiced early in the morning, at 5:00 A.M., and late in the afternoon, to beat the heat, and there was a little swimming hole they could go to, but there wasn't any entertainment outside of having Mickey Herskowitz there."

If no one else understood that reference, Ramsey and I did. I dictated my story over the pay phone outside the meeting room. On a day that most teams set aside for photographs or filling out forms or touching their toes, the Aggies had worked out in full pads. Excitedly, I dictated a story that included some descriptive phrases about the crunch of bodies coming together, and the constant thunk of helmets crashing.

Before I began talking, the raised voices of the coaches could be heard through our common wall, arguing the way coaches do. I wasn't aware that the voices had grown quiet until I noticed Ramsey, sitting on one of the beds, nervously tapping his index finger against his thumb.

By the time I hung up the phone, a student manager was standing there. "Coach Bryant would like to see you," he said, coughing slightly.

The other coaches had cleared out. Bryant explained, softly, that he wasn't eavesdropping, but he could not help but overhear parts of my phone call. He was disturbed, he said. He frowned and asked, "Did I hear you say something about bones getting mangled?"

His face darkened and he looked at me, waiting for an answer. I could feel myself freezing. I thought, *Holy shit! I've made him mad.* My heart was calling Kong to the gates. Up to then I don't believe I had talked with him, alone, for more than 15 minutes. I had been on the A&M campus maybe twice in my life and had covered one football game there. I had no obligation, no loyalty, no reason to feel guilty. But I was on my first important assignment for the *Houston Post*—important to me, anyway. Until that year, no paper in the state had covered the Aggies on a regular basis. On our staff, writers who had been there longer were assigned to the local teams, Rice and Houston, or busy with golf. The interest in Bryant had prompted Clark Nealon, then the sports editor, to put someone on the Aggies. My credits up to then had been high school football, Little League baseball, and backing up Clark when the Buffs, our team in the Texas League, played at home. For me this was a career move, an expression no one ever used at that time.

Bryant was still waiting. I could no longer stare at the corrugated ceiling of the hut. "It does sound familiar, Coach," I admitted. "But I think I said crunched, not mangled."

He had no difficulty in being understood in those days. He convinced me that I was wrong, that I had not seen a full-scale scrimmage, and that a lot of mamas and papas would be upset if they thought he was up there in the hills, grinding their sons into the unforgiving earth. With great difficulty, I phoned the office back and edited (softened) my story.

Okay, freedom of the press is a flaming sword and all that, but I was younger than some of the players, and smaller, and it was not easy to say no to Bear Bryant. Nor would it get any easier through the years. Which is one reason why the Junction Boys survived, and nine of them as seniors played on a team that went undefeated and won the Southwest Conference title. And why the rest of their lives they would tell stories about Junction, the scene of their happiest suffering. Stallings, Jack Pardee, Don Watson, Dee Powell, Bobby Drake Keith, Lloyd Hale, Dennis Goehring and Bobby Lockett were the ones who went out as champions.

Of course, I had been right. Bryant had worked their asses off, worked them like mules, or like Chinese coolies laying down the railroad tracks to the west. I watched them practice twice a day and just soaked it up, the constant movement, the contact, the coaches shouting and whistles blowing. Sometimes, to make a point, Bryant would get into a stance and go one-on-one with a player. He wore baggy khaki pants and a white T-shirt and a baseball cap, and now and then he would leave the field with spots of blood on his shirt.

As far as I knew, this was college football the way it was played and coached everywhere. And during the 10 days the Aggies trained at Junction, I formed an impression that was never to change. People can watch a football practice day after day, for hours, and never know what is going on. There is no way to tell if a team is good or bad, if the talent is anything special, or which players are in or out of position. Most writers are at the mercy of whatever the coach tells them. If he tells you, "We worked on blocking and tackling," you can either go off and interview the equipment bag or you can put in the paper, "They worked on blocking and tackling."

The only reason I knew the Aggies were a terrible team that year and might not win a game was because Coach Bryant kept saying so. They had no size, no speed, and no talent, he would say, sometimes mixing up the order, and he was still trying to make up his mind if they had any guts.

His trainer, a colorful, white-haired old character named Smokey Harper, had already made up his mind that the Aggies were lacking in that department. Smokey had been with Bryant at Kentucky. One day he said, "These folks here are curious. At Kentucky, we'd have four or five fights a day during practice. These folks don't get mad. They say 'excuse me.' "

The one thing everyone in that camp seemed to have in common that summer was fear. Fear of Bryant. The players were motivated to get through each day without screwing up, without forcing Coach Bryant to look right at them. For one thing, he was a big man, bigger than just about anybody on the team, and when he stood in the middle of the field the players walked around him as though he were a swamp.

Recently I looked it up, and was startled to realize that A&M's starting line that year averaged 182 pounds a man. Today you see lines bigger than that in junior high school.

But in at least two things Bryant was consistent all his life. He preferred quickness to size and he built his teams from the defense out. He would give the offense the ball on the one-yard line and bark at the defense, "Heart! If you got any now's the time to show it." He would yell at them, over and over, "speed-speed-speed," as if the repetition of the word would make them go faster.

One day was not much different from the next. Sometimes I would work at my portable typewriter between practices and the clacking of the keys would be the only sound you could hear. The players were up each morning before dawn and worked out once before breakfast. Then they would fall back onto their cots, exhausted, and nap until lunch. They came to dread the afternoon practice.

"Heat, dust, no grass, lots of cactus," said Stallings. "Any time you got knocked down you had to avoid the prickly sandspurs."

The radio station in Junction, KMBL, was a year old, the signal so weak that unless the wind was blowing just right you could not pick it up at the camp three miles away. A young couple owned the station and did their own announcing and engineering. The arrival of Bryant and the Aggie football team was a major news story, and they poured all their resources into covering it, meaning that they placed a telephone call every day to Jones Ramsey. Asked what had taken place the first day of practice, Ramsey replied, "Oh, the usual things. They worked on offense and defense."

Anybody get hurt?

"Naw, it was just routine," said Jones. "A few guys tossed their cookies, that was all."

Later, driving into town with Ramsey, I tuned into the nightly newscast on the car radio. ". . . And out at the Annex," we heard him say, "the Texas Aggies went through the first day of fall football drills in the usual way. They worked on offense and defense and a few of the boys tossed their cookies."

I came to know the players and, gradually, to understand what Bryant was doing. He kept moving players around, looking for a place to use their talent or, if they had none, a position where he could hide their weakness. He moved a halfback named Elwood

Kettler to quarterback, and he lined up Jack Pardee, a redheaded product of six-man football, at a new spot every day, finally settling at end. The next year he made him a fullback, and Pardee went on to become an all-American.

Kettler said he hated going to bed at night, because he knew he would have to get up before daylight and put on his pads, and they would still be wet from practice the day before.

One of their biggest linemen, Bill Schroeder, lost 17 pounds, missed a week with a mild heat stroke, and had to play the season at 197 pounds.

Bryant had hauled the team away from the campus because he wanted privacy, no distractions, and he got his wish. Some candidates fainted, some were dragged off by the heels, some packed their bags and disappeared in the night. The defections started right away, after the first practice, but they did not seem serious or even newsworthy until the players considered A&M's two best walked out.

Joe Boring had made the all-conference team as a safety the year before, and Fred Broussard, the center, was the only pro prospect they had. Broussard quit one day in the middle of a workout, while the players waited, hands over ears, for the loud noise that seemed sure to come.

The custom was for a player to quit in the dead of night, without facing Bryant, slipping off to the highway to thumb a ride to his home, or back to College Station.

Bryant was stunned. He had never had this happen before, a player just checking it in right there in broad daylight, in front of his very eyes. "Young man," he said, "where you going? You better think about it now."

There was a gate at one end of the practice field and Broussard was headed for it. Bryant called after him, "If you go through that gate, you're gone." He hesitated for an instant, then opened the gate and kept walking.

That night Bryant spotted him in the dining room, a word that doesn't fully describe the place where the team ate. Bryant ordered him out of the chow line, explaining that, "You must be making a mistake. Only A&M football players eat here."

When the captain of the team, Benny Sinclair, stopped by Bryant's hut and asked the coach to take back the rebellious player, the Bear refused. As thin as the Aggies were, this was a loss that hurt, but this was no time to compromise. "I won't take him back," he said. "We've got a long way to go and we want players we can count on. I won't take him back, but I *will* help him pack."

When Ramsey asked what information he should give to the Associated Press, given Broussard's status as an all-conference center, Bryant replied: "Just say Broussard quit. Q-U-I-T. That's all."

Broussard was a tall, intense young man who had tested the coaching staff of Ray George the year before, and was always welcomed back. Now the Aggies knew they would have discipline. Ramsey had known it since the spring, when he had lunch one day with Bryant at the White Way Cafe, on Highway 6, across from the campus. The cafe was a beer joint, really, but it served a nice blue plate special and Bryant was partial to their greens and cornbread.

The coaches had been breaking down the films of the games from the year before, and Broussard had been graded in the 60s, which is not a passing score on the football field, either. During the meal he looked up from his plate and said, "Jones, if Broussard makes all-conference this year, playing like he did last year, your ass is fired."

Bryant had a point to make at Junction, a philosophy to instill, and he did it. After Broussard left, all the remaining centers, five of them, quit the next day in a group. The Bear just walked past the line, shaking their hands. "Good-bye, good-bye, bless your hearts, good-bye."

For all his forcefulness, it was a depressing time. No matter how much talent you have, and the Aggies had precious little, no matter how creative your offense, and Bryant believed that more than five plays constituted a circus, your chances of winning are very limited if you cannot snap the ball to your quarterback.

Lloyd Hale, a sophomore guard, volunteered to play center. By his senior year he made the all-conference team, and Bryant would later rate him with Paul Crane, of Alabama, as one of the two best he ever coached at that position. As Bum Phillips would note later, "Bryant didn't coach football. He coached people."

Herb Wolf, a reserve fullback, moved in behind Hale. But the only fellow in camp who could snap the ball deep for punts was one of the student managers, Troy Summerlin. Hale learned the position quickly, but as a security measure, Bryant kept Summerlin on call for the team's early games. He wore football shoes, shoulder pads under a jersey, and maroon shorts.

Elwood Kettler bruised every knuckle on both hands, while Hale and his backups practiced their snaps. In retrospect, it is clear that the Aggies were not getting a great deal better at Junction. But they were getting tougher. Stallings and Don Watson and some of the other sophomores could hardly wait each morning to see who was missing. They would watch the players brave enough to face Bryant sip slowly from the water fountain between the huts, then knock on the coach's door. When Summerlin had a carload, he would pile them into an old black sedan and drive them to the bus station.

There were not many high spots at Junction, but Marvin Tate, a senior guard who weighed around 170, provided one of them. He delivered a hit one day that just echoed over the field. Bryant blew his whistle and stopped practice. "Manager," he ordered, "get this boy a lollipop." He had found a hitter.

It was Tate who came to Bryant later that season and told him that the profanity of the coaches bothered some of the players. On the practice field, the language was sometimes rough enough to make a Southern sheriff blush. But Bryant did another of his unexpected things. He called a team meeting, apologized, and announced a system of fines for swear words: $10 for him, $1 for his assistants and a quarter for the players. The money went into a pool and at the end of the season they used it to finance a barbecue.

Over half the players who made the long bus ride from College Station dropped out. As more names were released each day, coaches and writers around the country, and possibly a few parents, began to wonder what was going on in the Texas hill country. Ramsey's phone started ringing with regularity. And to my surprise, the attention didn't annoy Bryant. He was, in fact, delighted to learn that the Southwest Conference press tour would stop at Junction, one day after visiting the Texas Longhorns, in Austin.

That comparison made Bryant dry-wash his hands. He didn't exactly invent the art of poor mouthing, but he advanced it considerably. He was at his best with teams he considered to be underdogs, and he wanted the writers, fresh from interviewing Texas, with 100 players in uniform, to draw that contrast with his scrawny little beat-up Aggies. They were all walking around with scabs on their noses and foreheads and elbows.

When the writers stepped out of their custom-made motor home, Ramsey was ready for them. By then the Aggies were down to just 29 players. Blackie Sherrod, the Dallas humorist, said Ramsey was the only college publicity man in America who could type his roster sideways, double-spaced, on a single sheet of 8½-by-11 paper. And that was how Jones greeted them, with his roster sideways on one sheet of paper.

Football writers are accustomed to getting rosters in a form called the three-deep; a breakdown by positions through the first three units. Texas, and most other schools in the conference, could have listed their players down to the seventh or eighth string. The Aggies did not have enough for three.

But something else happened at Junction, besides attrition. Out of the dust and broiling heat and the rock patch that served as a practice field grew an extraordinary fellowship. Hemingway called it the bonding of men. For many reasons, including the runt-of-the-litter syndrome, the players who survived that camp, and a 1-and-9 season, would become the team closest to Bryant's heart.

No one knew what to expect when the Aggies opened their first season under Bryant at home, on Kyle Field, against Texas Tech. In spite of their shrinking numbers and the poverty of their recent seasons, the presence of Bryant had raised Aggie hopes. That night they turned the ball over half a dozen times and the Red Raiders blew them away, 41–9.

In Athens, Georgia, two of his coaches, Elmer Smith and Pat James, were scouting the Georgia Bulldogs, a team they would meet in two weeks. Unable to learn the A&M score, they located a pool hall that had a Western Union sports wire. Most of the ticker tape had spilled onto the floor, and Elmer and Pat got down on their hands and knees to dig through it. When they found the score— 41–9—Pat James, who was 25 and had played under Bear at Kentucky, looked at the older coach and said, "Elmer, what are we going to do?"

Smith shook his head and said, "Pat, we've got to go back home. That's the only place we can go."

The next morning they were in the film room waiting for their daily meeting with Bryant. "We got the surprise of our lives," recalled Elmer. "Coach Bryant said: 'Now, listen, I don't want to hear one of you raising your voices at these players. I'm the cause of their not playing well. I took it away from them in practice.' "

The loss to Tech was the only game all year the Aggies did not have a chance to win going into the final minutes. "That was an insight into Coach Bryant," said Smith. "It was the opposite of how we expected him to react. But he gained the respect of those players."

The Aggies nearly beat a better Oklahoma State team the next week, falling 14–6. Still, looking at their schedule, there was reason to doubt that they would win a game all year. Then they flew to Athens to meet Georgia.

Elmer Smith had spent endless hours looking at Georgia game films. But it paid off. He noticed that the Bulldogs' quarterback tipped his plays, placing his feet a certain way for a pass and another for a run. Jack Pardee called the defensive signals that day, and he hardly took his eyes off the quarterback's feet. The undermanned Aggies shut them out, and Kettler passed for the game's only touchdown and a 6–0 win, the only one they would get that year.

(The Monday after the game, Bryant telephoned the Georgia coach, Wally Butts, and tried to tell him about his quarterback's habit. Wally brushed him off. The story had a strange sequel. It would figure again in a libel suit brought by the two coaches against the *Saturday Evening Post* eight years later.)

As the losses began to pile up, one near miss after another, Bryant drew more attention to himself. He did it partly by calculation, to deflect the heat from his team, and partly just on the sheer color of his personality.

When Kettler threw away a pitchout on the goal line, and cost them a win over Baylor, Bryant pulled me aside before he met with reporters after the game. "I want you to ask me a question," he said.

I said, "Okay, Coach. What's the question?"

"Ask me who called that play on the goal line."

In a few minutes he was encircled by writers, and after the first wave of questions, I called out: "Coach, do you mind telling us who called that play on the goal line?"

Bryant poked his chest with his thumb and said, "I did. What of it?"

He did that sort of thing all year. At midseason there were rumors of dissension on the team, and Clark Nealon sent me to College Station to check them out. You have to know I was not overjoyed at the prospect of implying that the Bear had lost control of his team. Ramsey went into his office with me for support. I said, "Coach, I hate to ask you this, but you've lost five in a row and my editor has heard talk there may be dissension up here."

I learned another lesson that day. Bryant could make you feel like a bug if you asked something stupid, but he enjoyed a question he could get his teeth into. He leaned across his desk and said, with almost measured politeness, "Mickey, you can write this down. I don't think there is any dissension on this team. But if I see anybody out there who's not giving 150 percent, there's going to be some and I'm going to cause it."

The next week, the Aggies lost by a touchdown to an Arkansas team that was on its way to the conference championship. If there had been anybody left on the bandwagon, the last of them had fallen off. The wire services wanted a reaction from Bryant to his team's losing streak. When Ramsey gave him the request, he said, "Well, I'll tell you, Jones. When you're winning, all the alumni will come around glad-handing and telling you how great our team is doing. But when you're losing, they all want to tell you how lousy *your* team is doing. Just tell the AP that this is *my* team now and I'm proud to have 'em."

Ramsey looked at him with awe. "Coach, that's the greatest thing I ever heard. How'd you think of that?"

And Bryant said, "Aw, I heard Frank Howard say it one time." He had a fine memory, and he never minded giving credit to the original author.

Every week he seemed to be ready with fresh and colorful quotes, some of them printable. When I asked him about the passing of Elwood Kettler, the ex-halfback, he answered, "Kettler throws the ball like he's slinging shit off his hand."

When they were getting ready to play Arkansas, he did his best to fatten up the opposition. "They're quick and mean and looking for blood," he said. "Us? Why, compared to Arkansas, we're Peaceful Valley."

When SMU dealt them another loss from the razor's edge, 6–3, Bryant took consolation in the game story written by Tex

Maule, then with the *Dallas Morning News*, later to become the pro football authority for *Sports Illustrated*. Tex had noted that the Aggies were blowing SMU's bigger specimens off the line of scrimmage. He described how their defense stopped the Ponies, only to lose the game on mistakes by the offense. "He wrote a story," Bryant said, "the way a coach would."

Make no mistake, the Bear had an ego, a colossal ego. He never seemed to miss a word anyone had written about him, and he would startle you years later by bringing up some forgotten reference.

Patience was not then one of his virtues. He was quick to divide people into winners or losers, into those for or against him. This is not an attractive trait, but it was offset by the fact that Bryant did not resent having someone prove him wrong.

Dennis Goehring, a chunky, curly-haired guard, was one of those he didn't think was big enough or mean enough to help the team. He encouraged Smokey Harper, his resident headshrink, to agitate Dennis and drive him off, if he could.

About the only thing Smokey ever said to Goehring that fall was, "You'll never make it, boy," usually without looking up as he taped his ankles. One day, Goehring had taken enough. "Smokey," he snarled, "I'll be here long after you and Bryant are both gone."

When that word got back to the Man, as the players called him, he knew he had a football player. Goehring made a couple of all-America teams his senior year. Later, he opened a bank in College Station, and one of his stockholders was a fellow named Paul Bryant. They do not make many cornball stories like that one in sports any more. It is our loss.

Goehring may have been the only player who ever won Bryant's approval after getting a penalty for playing dirty. He was in and out of the lineup in 1954, as a sophomore, and aching to win a starting job. Against SMU, he played part of the game at defensive tackle. At 180 pounds, he was badly outmatched by the fellow across from him, who weighed 235.

"I didn't get into the game until the third quarter," he recalled, "but the instant I lined up across from this guy I knew I had to do something smart or desperate, or both, in order to beat him and keep Coach Bryant from yanking me. So I deliberately charged offside on the first play. With that old forearm cure. Took him by surprise and caught him right in the chops. Knocked him into his own backfield. It did the trick. It made that big ole tackle respect me right away and made him gun-shy the rest of the game.

"When I got to the sidelines later, Coach Bryant chewed me out for being offsides. I explained to him I thought it was the only way I could beat my man. He stood there for a moment, his face blank, and then he gave me a pat on the head. 'Son,' he said, 'I always did like a lineman who could think in an emergency.' "

After the season ended with defeats by Rice and Texas, I wrote a story that focused on the exploits of a touted freshman group. Noting the loss of 16 seniors from a squad that was beaten nine times, I described the Aggies as "the team most improved by graduation."

On my next trip to College Station, Bryant saw me cutting across the campus and waved to me. I joined him on a bench. He cupped an arm around my shoulder and said, "Little buddy, I read what you said in the paper about my seniors. I didn't think it was funny, and I'm going to tell you why."

Which he did. How hard they had worked, the sacrifices they made, the class they showed in never giving up. What Bryant had done was put up a wall in my mind, and in the future I would toss ideas against it like a pelota. I would still be flippant at someone else's expense from time to time, but I gave up a few, too.

That was Junction, the year of losing dangerously. I had no feeling then that this would be one of the most remembered of college football teams.

Twenty-five years later, in May 1979, they came back for a reunion. The idea was born during an interview with Bryant at the Sugar Bowl. He was asked if there was anything else he wanted to do in his long and legendary career, besides breaking Amos Alonzo Stagg's record for the most victories.

The announcer probably dropped his mike when Bear said, "Yeah, I'd like to go back to Junction, Texas, and see how much the town has changed."

And so the plans were made to entertain Bryant and the hardy Aggies he had led into the hills, giving him the chance to gaze fondly on the players who gave him his only losing season in 38 years of coaching.

The town had changed dramatically. A lush green lawn was

visible where the Aggies once scuffled in the dust. The trees were tall in the pecan bottom, where the ground sloped toward the south fork of the Llano River. When the long-awaited rains began to fall in 1956, the valley, like the Aggies, was restored to former glory. But you would have had a hard time convincing the Junction Boys that it was not their sweat that made the grass grow and the desert bloom.

The population had increased in all those years by only 600. But brick school buildings, a modern summer campus now owned by Texas Tech, had replaced the concrete blocks that once supported the huts where the '54 Aggies slept.

The tree-shaded courthouse square was even quieter, since most of the traffic bypassed the town on Highway 10. The townspeople remained pretty much the same. They had seen the arrival and departure of drought, floods, webworms, Aggies, Bear Bryant and wearisome big city sportswriters.

On the surface, you would have to say this class reunion was an unlikely one. It was as if a bunch of stockbrokers had gotten together to celebrate the Crash of '29. Although the irony was clear, no one had to wonder why they were there. If any football coach in America seemed to symbolize the winning-is-the-only-thing ethic, it was Bryant. So it stood to reason that if the Bear wanted to toast a losing season, the best time to do so would be 25 years later.

They looked at each other with eyes that seemed to paraphrase Tevye's line from *Fiddler on the Roof*:

I don't remember growing older—when did they?

Of the 29 who had stuck it out, 22 showed up. There was a banker, Dennis Goehring, and a lawyer, Bill Schroeder. Some, like Joe Schero, owned their own companies. Most of the rest seemed to be football coaches or petroleum engineers. Richard Vick flew down from his oil company office in New York. Herb Wolf had just gotten back from Nigeria when he heard about the reunion.

Some had not seen each other since they had left college. Kettler, a country boy, then coaching at Texas City, once had doubts about Herb Wolf, a city boy from Houston. "There is no one I admire more now," said Kettler. "When he came to A&M, Wolf wore suede shoes and a ducktail haircut. But he was a battler. Now he's a success. They're all so successful I can't hardly talk to them."

Of course, Junction didn't do that. But it was a bar of the music that made the man.

Bryant talked about how proud he was of them, of the men they had become and of the unbeaten season they had given him in 1956. And as for Junction, "Well, if I had to do it over again, and the circumstances were the same, I wouldn't change a thing."

A few of the Junction Boys turned in their seats and exchanged glances and they didn't seem quite so sure. But it was nice, they agreed, that Coach Bryant thought so.

Chapter 3

Out of Arkansas

September 11, 1954

Keeping track of Coach Bryant's birthday was never hard. It was September 11, always just before or after the first week of each football season.

He turned 41 at Junction and I spent part of the day with him, watching his 10-year-old son, Paul, Jr., splash around in the creek. I had asked Bryant for an interview and he invited me to sit with him while he kept an eye on young Paul. We just stretched out on the grass and felt the midday Texas sun on our faces.

It was the first opening I had found for a private and unhurried session with him since he had taken the Aggie job. Even before I could peek at my notebook and refer to the questions I had prepared, he started asking me about myself. I think he knew that I was a sophomore at the University of Houston. So I slipped in the fact that I had joined the Marines at 17—actually, I was in a Marine Reserve unit that had been called to active duty—and was attending school on the G.I. Bill. I told him I had known since I was in the second grade that I wanted to write. An English teacher had read an essay of mine aloud to the entire class, and bragged on me.

Writing about sports just seemed so much more appealing than working for a living.

Not only did I want Bryant's respect, I knew instinctively it would be essential in any kind of dealings I hoped to have with him. Without turning his head—his eyes were still on the creek—he said, "You were a Marine? What were you, one of those guys who slit throats?"

He wasn't making fun of me. But his voice had a little banter in it, a quality I would get to recognize quite well. He had been in the Navy during the war. The Marines he knew then were probably in underwater demolition work. Frogmen. I was once stationed at a base where they trained, and when I was getting up in the morning they were coming in from maneuvers, in their wetsuits. They were exotic looking figures, with knives on their belts, sometimes carrying spear guns. They were also the most beat-up bunch of people I had ever seen . . . faces scarred, arms in slings, walking with a limp.

I watched Bryant light a cigarette, a Chesterfield, unfiltered. He wasn't a chain smoker yet but he was getting there. I figured him for someone who wasn't ready for filters.

I guess I expected him to roll his own. Years later, a publisher asked me to work with the actress Bette Davis on her autobiography. The first day we met, Bette kept dipping into a silver bowl supplied with unfiltered Chesterfields. She'd finish one and start another, but her secret was she never inhaled. Bryant took long, deep draws and the smoke seemed to stay inside him.

We sat there on the creekbank without talking until I began to get uncomfortable. I didn't want to ask him the usual football groupie journalism questions. What I wanted to do was impress him with my technical knowledge of the game. But I didn't know how to start.

Finally, just to get the conversation going again, I nodded at the water and said, "Is Paul Junior going to be a football player, Coach?"

Bryant snorted. "Hell, no," he said. "He'll probably play in the band. When I was his age I was pushing a plow."

That didn't mean he loved Junior any less. But Papa Bear had been pushing a plow at 10. He surely did.

*   *   *

Fordyce had always been referred to as his birthplace, and when he corrected the record one day I misunderstood what he said. "Moro what?" I asked.

"Bottom," he said. "Like your ass. Moro Bottom."

The distinction seemed mighty thin, since Fordyce was the nearest town with a school and that was where he gained his reputation as a young football player. But they must have been worlds apart to the adolescent Paul Bryant. Moro Bottom was in the backwoods, on Moro Creek, a few miles north of Fordyce. There were six families spread over a two-mile area. There were timberland and wild hogs for hunting and the Bryants farmed cotton and vegetables on 260 acres. The land was cheap and Bryant, years later, referred to it as no more than a truck farm, by modern standards.

He was born in 1913, the 11th of 12 children, the youngest son of Wilson Monroe Bryant, out of Georgia, and Ida Kilgore, from a family of Texas farmers. Three children had died in infancy. There were no paved roads, just dirt and gravel. His older brothers sometimes earned a dollar hitching up the mules and pulling a passing car out of the mud on rainy days.

He went barefoot most of the time, and he was 13 before he owned his first pair of new shoes. His mother took him into town, to Mays' General Store, and he wound up with a pair a size too small. If you wanted to describe the Bryant of his later coaching years, that perpetual frown, the way his eyebrows would knit, you would have been tempted to say he looked like a man whose shoes pinched.

Fordyce, with a population of around 3,000, was where the city kids lived. They were the ones who hooted and laughed when Paul rode into town on the back of the vegetable wagon, with his mother driving the mule. Years later I tried to imagine what it must have been like for Paul Bryant to hear anyone laughing at him, and I knew he must have held in a lot of anger over a lot of years.

There is no point in doing a heavy analytical number on his childhood. It was pretty clear from what he said, the way he talked about his mother, that he was a mama's boy. I mentioned this once to a lady psychologist and all she said was, "I'm not surprised."

I don't believe there was any connotation in that statement that would have embarrassed Coach Bryant. In fact, he used it, his boyhood hardships, as he used whatever experiences he had, in an effort to reach his players.

One day I was just standing around outside the locker room at Texas A&M, when a team meeting broke up. One of the players dropped onto a folding chair nearby, a look of puzzlement on his face, and I asked him what had been said inside.

"Coach Bryant told us," he confided, "that we were going to have to work harder than his other teams, we would have to give more of ourselves, because we were war babies. He said most of us were raised by our mothers while our fathers were in the war, and we might have missed out on some discipline."

War babies. Bryant used that term before it became fashionable among social behaviorists. It had nothing to do with the baby boomers, those born just after the war. His reference was to the boys who were without a father's hand, firm or otherwise, during the critical preteen years. His Aggie freshmen would have been 12 years old, or thereabouts, when the bombs fell on Pearl Harbor. This was all he meant by the phrase, which echoed so oddly in the ears of young athletes not given to self-reflection. But another message came across. At a key point in their lives, they may have been deprived of discipline. And now Paul W. Bryant was going to supply some. In fact, it was going to be a case of overcompensation.

Which brings us back to Moro Bottom, Arkansas.

As the last boy still at home he had to do all the hard chores around the farm. He plowed and chopped wood, drew water for the cows, and was up at four on the days his mother made her selling trips, getting the wagon ready. High blood pressure had made his father an invalid. His mother was a tall, handsome woman, gray-haired from his first memory of her.

Some people turn their childhoods into a fantasy, and they grow nostalgic over the Depression and bathing in washtubs. Not Bryant. He hated making those rounds in the wagon, and he never let go of the pain he felt. Before he started school, the rounds would take them past the schoolyard as the kids were getting out for lunch. Even in his 60s, he remembered the names of the ones who laughed at him and made fun of the elderly mules hitched to the wagon.

Later girls giggled at his clothes and a fifth- or sixth-grade teacher, big on personal hygiene, made him trade his seat in the front of the classroom for one in the back. He was big for his age, and not much of a student, but he became the first in his family to attend college. His mother dropped hints that she wanted him to be a preacher. The Bryants belonged to the Church of God, didn't smoke or drink or attend picture shows, and never saw a football game, even the ones Paul played in.

There was a strong religious base to Bryant's character, but not until late in his life was it generally accepted as sincere. When he said he didn't know who his starting fullback would be, "but I'm praying on it," or when he thanked "the good Lord" for this or that, it came off as the kind of false piety all too common in sports. Or else one accepted such references as harmless, just folksy, good-ole-boy language, unrelated to anyone's religion.

On that score, Bryant never tried to change anyone's mind, never waved his beliefs like a flag. But he fiercely disliked the walking-on-water jokes, the Bear as a kind of Dixie Christ in cleats. All you had to do was watch his expression when someone dropped that kind of remark.

The Depression came early and stayed late in Arkansas, and hit hard, as it had in Oklahoma. In his school years, which spanned the '20s, there wasn't much difference between being an Okie or an Arkie. The times were mean and money short. Bryant earned 50 cents a day working in the fields on a farm his brother Jack was sharecropping.

There isn't much doubt, not in my mind, that in the first quarter of his coaching career, maybe half, Bryant measured the desire of his players against his own. He thought adversity was good for the soul, and the more you sacrificed the less likely you were to give it all back in the fourth quarter. It took him a long time to realize that a generation had arrived to whom football was not the most important thing. "All I had was football," he said. "I hung on as though it were life or death, which it was."

Among those who knew him in Fordyce, there were no glowing predictions of future success, not in coaching or anything else. A high school teammate named Ike Murry, later a lawyer who became the attorney general of Arkansas, once said: "If I had been writing the class prophecy for our senior class, I'd have written this about Paul: 'He'll be lucky to stay out of the penitentiary.' "

Bryant described himself as a hell-raiser who felt his mother's switches—made from the limbs of a cherry tree—at home and the paddle at school. He was a little vague about an incident that led to his spending a night in jail, but apparently it had to do with getting caught riding a freight train. He was frequently involved in fights and, at 13, beat up a grown man who refused to pay him for the groceries he delivered. He was "a trial," as he put it, to his parents and coaches.

But, mostly, what endures from those years is the story of his nickname, details of which have been volunteered by everyone but the circus bear he wrestled one night at the Lyric Theatre.

"I don't remember who won," said his friend Ike Murry, "Paul or the bear. But I do remember that half the crowd was pulling for Paul, half for the bear."

It was his self-confidence and a willingness to challenge the unknown that put Bryant in the ring with a bear that night. And those were among the assets that would account for his success, and his longevity, as a coach.

When I was to meet Bryant for the first time, Jones Ramsey counseled me on two things: "Don't call him Bear. He hates that name. And don't ask him how he got it. He's tired of talking about it."

By that afternoon on the creek I knew the outlines of the story, but I was curious to hear his version. So I asked. And with no apparent reluctance, he gave what I took to be a fairly practiced recital of the event:

"A carnival came through town and they had this little ole scraggly bear. A man was offering anybody a dollar a minute to wrestle it. Somebody dared me to do it. I said I would."

The rest of that day, the circus people paraded through the streets with a sign that said, PAUL BRYANT WILL WRESTLE A BEAR TONIGHT AT 8 AT THE LYRIC THEATRE.

He was 14 years old and even then he knew he needed a game plan. He intended to charge the bear and take him down, keep him from rolling over on him. "I got the bear pinned, holdin' on real tight. The man kept whispering, 'Let him up. Let him up.' He wanted action. Hell, for a dollar a minute I wanted to hold him till he died.

"The bear finally shook loose and the next thing I knew his muzzle had come off. I felt a burning sensation behind my ear and when I touched it I got a handful of blood. The damned bear bit me. I jumped from the stage and fell into the empty chairs in the front row. Still have the marks on my shins. Then I ran up the aisle and out the theater. When I came around later the man from the circus was gone. I never did get my money. All I got were some scars and a name."

Sometimes when he told the story he mentioned that he did it to impress a girl. There was a fair amount of ham in young Paul Bryant, a need to attract attention. He found the perfect showcase when he discovered football. It was a license to commit mischief set to music: crowds, bands and pretty girls.

Ike Murry was the center on the state championship teams at Fordyce in 1929 and 1930. Bryant lined up at tackle on defense and end on offense. "Bear was a showman even in those days," said Murry. "Crowds loved him. He never caught many passes. His best play was when he went downfield to block a halfback. We played on a field that was half-grass, half-dirt. Bear would rumble down and put a rolling block on that halfback. I don't think he ever blocked him, but he'd always raise a cloud of dust, kicking and scrambling around the guy's feet. The crowd would roar. People loved it."

Bryant played in the first football game he ever saw, in the eighth grade. He was invited to join the team the week before, and a cobbler nailed cleats onto his street shoes. He went on to Fordyce High, and was all-state as a sophomore for the Fighting Redbugs. He was no early bloomer, but he had size and the meanness to go with it. He started free-for-alls in two sports, and after one basketball game he wound up fighting every boy on the Camden basketball team. A police escort was needed to get the Fordyce team out of the gym and onto their bus. It was years before the two schools played each other again.

Bryant managed to look sheepish when he recalled those episodes. What bothered him was the fact that he took advantage of his coaches. He was just young and stupid, he said, and he knew he got away with behavior he would not tolerate later from his own players.

By his senior year he was 6'3" and weighed 190, and football was going to be his ticket out of the briar patch.

The rugged, hungry kids of Arkansas had always attracted scouts from the University of Alabama. Bryant was working at a summer job in a meat market, as a butcher's helper, when an assistant coach named Hank Crisp stopped off in Fordyce. Crisp recruited him for the Crimson Tide, and later that summer piled him into the rumble seat of his coupe and drove him to Tuscaloosa.

Under the relaxed standards of that era, Bryant spent a year getting housing and aid from Alabama while he made up math and Spanish credits at Tuscaloosa High. At one point, he thought about doing what he would never countenance in the players he coached. He considered giving up, leaving Alabama and heading for Texas to work in the oilfields. He wrote a letter to his cousin, Collins Kilgore, telling about his plans, and Kilgore fired off a telegram: GO AHEAD AND QUIT. JUST LIKE EVERYBODY SAID YOU WOULD.

Those words struck a nerve. After that, nothing could drive him off. He was 17 that fall of 1931, practicing with what is now called the redshirt team. His father had died that year from food poisoning, partly because his parents' religious beliefs did not sanction doctors. He was self-conscious about how he dressed and talked. He missed the father he had never known as a well man. But he concealed those feelings by adopting a pose. He cultivated the slow walk and the slow talk and the long stare. And people mistook it for confidence, well before the confidence was real.

Bryant would become known as "the Other End" at Alabama, a description he never resented. The more significant *other* was Don Hutson, also an Arkansas product, out of Pine Bluff, rated by many as the greatest pass-catching end ever to play football. He went on to pro stardom with the Green Bay Packers.

As opponents in high school, Fordyce and Bryant had beaten Hutson and Pine Bluff two years in a row, the second time by 50–12. Hutson had caught touchdown passes for Pine Bluff's only points.

They were roommates, best friends, and the starting ends on Alabama's unbeaten, untied team in 1934. They even got into a few off-the-field business ventures, including a laundry. None were very enriching, but Bryant's ambitions even then went beyond the life-style football alone would provide.

Hutson and Dixie Howell, the tailback, were to win recognition as one of the sport's most remembered combinations. Howell was a triple threat, a fine runner, kicker and passer. Bear admired Hutson too much to mind being overshadowed by him. He did catch the pass that set up Alabama's first touchdown in the Rose Bowl, and helped the Tide come from behind to upset Stanford, 29–13. But his reputation would come in other ways.

The next season, 1935, without Howell, Hutson and Bill Lee, an all-America tackle, Alabama started shakily, getting tied in its opener by Howard and losing two weeks later to Mississippi State. Bryant came out of that loss with a fractured shinbone in his right leg. He suffered the injury in the first quarter, went to the bench and returned in the third quarter to finish the game.

Injuries were treated more casually in those days. Teams rarely had a doctor on the bench and one of the coaches usually doubled as the trainer. Bryant was in pain, but no one suspected the leg was broken until the Monday after the game. Tennessee was next on the schedule, and Bryant made the trip by train to Knoxville with his leg in a cast, and on crutches. Before the kickoff, the team doctor removed the cast and told him he could suit up for Tennessee, even if he didn't play.

Chances are, the thought had not crossed his mind until Coach Thomas invited Hank Crisp, who worked with the defense, to speak to the team. "I don't know about the rest of you," Crisp challenged them, "but I know one thing. Ole thirty-four will be after them. He'll be after their asses." He walked over and put his arm around Bryant's shoulder. He should have put it under him because, for a moment, Bear thought he might faint. Back then schools changed the numbers every week to sell their programs. Bryant had been 26 the week before. He looked down at his jersey and realized he was ole number 34.

On the sideline, Coach Thomas turned to him and asked if he thought he could play. Bryant started the game and in the first few minutes caught a pass that led to one touchdown, and moments later caught another and lateraled to Riley Smith, who took it in for a score. Alabama stunned Tennessee, 25–0. The team's historians called it the finest game of Bryant's college career.

An Atlanta sportswriter named Ralph McGill, who later would become better known as a front page columnist, greeted the broken-leg story with skepticism. The next week, before the Georgia game, McGill made a trip to Tuscaloosa to check it out, saw the X rays, and filed a story that began: "As far as this season is concerned, Paul Bryant is in first place in the courage league."

The Georgia fans gave him an ovation when he stepped on the field. Alabama won that one, 17–7.

Bryant gave it his best aw shucks, John Wayne treatment. "It was just one little bone," he said. Red Drew, who coached the ends, countered: "Well, how many bones do you need for a broken leg?"

Frank Thomas had succeeded Wallace Wade as head coach at Alabama, Wade having quit to take the Duke job the day before Paul Bryant arrived on the campus. This was to be his first indication of the vagaries of the coaching profession.

But he idolized Coach Thomas, and one incident explains why. When Bryant was still taking classes at Tuscaloosa High, and working with the redshirts, Thomas singled him out one day. The varsity was scrimmaging the freshmen, and having no luck trying to block a punt. The exasperated Thomas motioned to Bryant and instructed his varsity players to "let this little high school boy show you how." Bryant brushed aside an end with a forearm and threw himself at the kicker. The ball went one way and the kicker the other. Calmly, he did a U-turn off the field and returned to the redshirts on the other side of the running track.

Thomas had bragged on him and Bryant responded. It was a technique Bryant would master in his own career.

Bryant's commitment to football was total. He had interests off the field, but he couldn't finance them. He could afford a date only when Coach Hank peeled a few bills off a roll he carried and told him to buy some toothpaste. It was not much more than milk-and-cookie money, and if there were rules against it no one paid any notice.

If Bryant gave his coaches any reason to worry, it had to do with the time he spent romancing the coeds. They didn't stop worrying until June 2, 1935, when he married Mary Harmon Black, a campus beauty.

The story of his broken leg was widely circulated, but Bryant attracted little attention from the pro scouts. Of course, there were a lot fewer pro scouts in 1935 and the money, for most of the players, was not much more than a teacher earned. Frank Thomas offered to take him on as an assistant coach and he grabbed it.

In the spring of 1940, after four seasons under Coach Thomas, he joined the staff of Red Sanders at Vanderbilt. They had a program to rebuild, and Sanders took Bryant with him on a recruiting trip across the state of Arkansas, into East Texas, Alabama and Florida, back up to Georgia and home to Tennessee. When they ended their dragnet, they had the makings of a football team.

Although Vanderbilt's record improved only marginally, Alabama, which had romped the year before, 39–0, had to rally in the fourth quarter to beat the Commodores, 25–21.

Sanders was stricken with appendicitis the week of the Kentucky game, and made Bryant, then 27, the acting head coach. Kentucky had to score late in the game to escape with a 7–7 tie. It was just one game out of hundreds he played in or coached, but the memory still pained him years later. He said Vandy had it won, but he coached them into that tie.

One of his duties was to make the evening curfew check at 10:30 each night. He would walk up the center of the stone steps at Kissam Hall, and the players nearest the door would alert the others, setting off a stampede to their rooms. Bryant would make a slow, ominous walk down the hall. The players dreaded it. Anyone caught in the hallway had to run the stadium steps the next morning at six.

The next season Vanderbilt went 8-and-2, and after an upset of Tennessee the players gave him the game ball. The gesture was not one that endeared him to the tightly strung Sanders, and Red fired him. No one ever knew it, however, for two reasons.

First, he interviewed for the head coaching job at Arkansas, and Bill Dickey, the great Yankees catcher, put in a word for him with the governor, Homer Adkins. Driving back to Nashville, Bryant knew the job was his.

Arkansas was his home, and he would have been a head coach at 28, except for the second thing. The date was December 7, 1941, and listening to the radio in his car he heard the news that the Japanese had attacked Pearl Harbor. The day after his return, he kissed Mary Harmon good-bye and reported to Washington to join the Navy. He received his commission in early 1942, and later that year was on a troop ship that got rammed in a convoy, and was dead in the water for three days. Two hundred were lost at sea when the captain gave a premature order to abandon ship. Bryant stayed aboard.

He later sailed on a tanker to North Africa, but spent most of his three and a half years in Commander Tom Hamilton's fitness program. He wound up coaching the football team at North Carolina Pre-Flight, at Chapel Hill.

After the war he did not return to Vanderbilt. There was no job waiting for him there, but he and Red Sanders were about the only ones who knew it. He didn't want it anyway.

During his first season at Vanderbilt, he turned to another member of the staff, Norman Cooper, and said: "Slim, assistant coaching is for the birds. I'm gonna be a head coach, be my own boss, or I'm not gonna coach."

He had met George Preston Marshall, the owner of the Washington Redskins, when he was still working for Coach Thomas. He wound up sending Marshall scouting reports on players in the Alabama area. At Christmas, Marshall sent him a check for $500, almost half his starting salary at Alabama, $1,250. He kept on scouting. And when he landed in North Carolina, during the war, he stayed in touch.

He was waiting for his discharge in August 1945, when he traveled to Chicago to watch Hutson and the Packers take on the College All-Stars. At a press party he bumped into Marshall, who immediately offered him a job as an assistant coach with the Redskins. Bryant told him he had already turned down two offers to work as an assistant. What he wanted was a head coaching job.

Marshall snapped, "Why the hell didn't you say so." He left, returned in a few minutes and told Bryant to go to his room to wait on a phone call. When the call came, the voice on the other end of the line belonged to D. H. (Curly) Byrd, the president of the University of Maryland, and the school's onetime football coach.

Byrd offered him the job over the phone, sight unseen, on the recommendation of Marshall. Bryant said he could be there the first thing on Saturday, the day after the all-star game. Byrd told him if he wanted the job to be in his office the next morning at eight. He was there on the dot, and this was an era when the time it took to make a flight sometimes depended on the size of the bugs that hit the windshield.

Bryant signed his contract on September 7, 1945, before he had been officially discharged from the Navy. Those were wild and makeshift times. Bryant returned to Chapel Hill and polled the squad to see how many of his players wanted to go with him. He hand-picked

17, including his quarterback, Vic Turyn. "It was unbelievable," recalled Turyn. "We were discharged on the eighteenth [of September], enrolled at Maryland on the nineteenth, and opened the season on the twenty-seventh." Bryant was not even sure his veterans would be eligible. Curly Byrd told him not to fret. Byrd made the rules at Maryland.

The confusion was so rampant, and the structure of college football so loose that year, that Sid Gillman, at Cincinnati, sent one of his assistants across the country to scout their opening foe, the University of Washington. The assistant, Jack Faulkner, later a coach in the pros, simply enrolled in school, went out for the team, and took part in the first week's practices. Then he flew back to Cincinnati with his scouting report. (Cincinnati lost, big.) Faulkner tried to hide in the press box during the game. His face had shown up in the Washington team photograph that was plastered on store windows all over town.

The Maryland opener was against tiny Guilford College, and Don Hutson came down to lend moral support to his old teammate. Bryant worried himself sick, and spent most of the night before the game throwing up. On the sideline before the kickoff, Hutson tried to calm him. "Paul," he said, "if you're this nervous about playing Guilford, you're in the wrong business."

Maryland won, 60–6. It was the first victory in a collection that would establish, among other things, that he had picked the right business.

Chapter 4

The Roads Taken

What seems clear from the start was that no one taught Paul Bryant how to coach: not Frank Thomas or Hank Crisp at Alabama or Red Sanders at Vanderbilt, the last boss he would ever have on a football field.

Bryant knew. Out of whatever had driven him, whatever insights he had gained from the hard process that shaped him, came a philosophy. He believed that football was simple: you pushed, the other fellow pushed back, and whoever pushed harder won. He didn't think, as a young coach, that football had to be fun. Winning was fun. So his practices were a form of physical punishment. His players were in shape and they were motivated. Some met his demands because they wanted his approval—this was a gift and there is no point in trying to explain it. Others responded out of fear and others because they had no choice. Football was their ticket through school, as it had been his.

Some of them actually seemed to enjoy his methods or, at least, this was what they told themselves later.

A receiver named Sammy Behr (rhymes with *Bear*; we might as well toss in a little symbolism here) caught a screen pass from Vic

Turyn and scored Maryland's first touchdown in the win over Guilford College. It was, of course, the first of Bryant's career, but that distinction has been fairly well lost among the honors and records that were yet to come. After all, who remembers the salesman who sold Henry Ford's first car?

But Sammy Behr has an almost benevolent memory of the young Paul Bryant: "If you gave Coach Bryant a nickel as a player, he would give you a dollar in return. For about an hour, the first day of practice, he did nothing other than give us a lecture and demonstrate how to block and tackle. He mixed it up with us. He was a young man [32], a big man, and he had beautiful people working with him." He had four assistants: Carney Laslie, Frank Moseley, Ken (Tuffy) Whitlow and Herman Ball.

Laslie, a senior at Alabama when Bryant was a freshman, helped coach his team in the service and their friendship would last a lifetime. Moseley had coached at Kentucky before the war. Whitlow was a star center from Rice and briefly a pro. Ball was a holdover from the old Maryland staff.

Sammy Behr probably did not understate the case when he said that the team opened the season with three basic plays. "We worked on them tirelessly at practice and executed them pretty darn well in the games. It was apparent right off that he was special. I'm proud I had the chance to play for him, even if it was only one year. I'm proud our team was the one that got him started."

Not all his players were so respectful, especially those who had served with him in North Carolina, and felt that their presence on the Maryland campus was a quid pro quo. Turyn, for one, had a sassiness Bryant liked in his quarterbacks. Turyn recalled an example of the Bear's taste for contact. On one play, Turyn and Harry Bonk, a fullback who had already played at Bucknell and Dartmouth, were to double-team the end. They spread him over the field like apple butter, while Bryant ranted that he (the end) wasn't trying. "We told Bryant to go over there and try to stop us," said Turyn. "So he did. He tore us apart with his elbows." Their younger teammates watched, in amazement, as the early good humor faded and the competitive tempers flared. "We worked on him as hard as we could," added Turyn. "But we couldn't get through him. He just flat enjoyed taking us on."

He won their respect the old-fashioned way; he beat it out of them. And that may have been the key to his original success. He convinced his players that it would be easier to face that week's opponent than their own coach. "He had us believing," said Turyn, "that regardless of our size, we were so good we couldn't lose. The guys would do anything for him. He had a soft spot in his heart *off* the field. He would do anything for you."

The Terrapins won their next two, struggled through two losses and a tie and finished strong, with three straight wins. VMI fell, 38–0. The next two were upsets, both by 19–13 scores, over Virginia and South Carolina. They scored in the last 65 seconds on a Hail Mary pass—off a reverse—to end Virginia's 14-game winning streak. A reverse! A moment of madness we can only attribute to Bryant's youth.

He had begun the year as a virtual unknown. In the victory over Virginia, he gained the notice of his peers, not exactly in the preferred way. A boiling Frank Murray, the coach of the Cavaliers, made a beeline for Bryant after the game, wading through the spectators to congratulate him—on "your team having played the dirtiest game I have ever seen."

What Bryant said in reply, if anything, was never recorded. He turned and walked away. The accounts of the game leave unclear whether Murray had a case. Most likely, the Maryland players, with their hard core of war veterans, treated Virginia's students with the same impartial roughness they dealt every other foe.

That year, 1945, was one of transition in America: the winding down of the war and the first joyful confusion of the peacetime economy. The Detroit Tigers defeated the Chicago Cubs in baseball's World Series, the last matchup of teams whose rosters had consisted largely of players spared by the draft—the young, the old, the afflicted.

There was a good deal of talk about life "returning to normal," whatever that was. A boom was coming, but the demand would outstrip supplies for the rest of the decade. For now, the country had a shortage of everything but returning war veterans.

G.I. benefits would finance schooling and tract houses and cars. Words that sounded new had entered the everyday language: suburbs and patios and barbecue pits. Mary Harmon and the two children—Mae Martin was nine and Paul, Jr., a year old—joined Bryant in the middle of the season, and they were invited to the home of a rich ex who had the first wall-to-wall carpeting the Bryants had ever seen.

There now occurred one of those negative episodes that, for the chosen, take a fateful and positive spin. The category is known as falling into a mudhole and emerging with a bottle of Arpege in each hand. Or, as Bryant would put it so earthily in some of his locker-room chats, it was the art of making chicken salad out of chicken shit.

A few weeks after the Christmas holidays, Bear Bryant resigned as the Maryland football coach. Just like that. Flat gave the job back to them, his first head coaching job, the one he had been craving ever since he walked away from that vegetable cart in Moro Bottom.

What had happened was the one thing he would not tolerate, not then, not ever, from anybody. Curly Byrd had stuck his nose into Bryant's football business. Twice.

The night before the Virginia game, the Bear had bounced from the team a big tackle who had been spotted in a beer joint. The player turned out to be the son of a Maryland politician. After Christmas—Bryant had spent the holidays with his family in Birmingham—he returned to College Park to discover that Byrd had reinstated the big tackle and fired Herman Ball, without so much as consulting the Bear.

At a banquet honoring the team and its 6–2–1 record, Dr. Byrd had announced that Paul Bryant had a lifetime contract as Maryland's football coach. Not on paper, he didn't. He had no contract at all, except for the season just past, and now he didn't want one. Byrd had been the school's coach for 23 years, starting in 1912, and Bryant admired him, his style, his poise, his connections, the sense of power he projected. Not many people said no to Dr. H. C. (Curly) Byrd. No one seemed surprised that when he needed a toastmaster for the football dinner, he lined up his friend Sam Rayburn, the Texas congressman, and speaker of the house, the man who made Lyndon Johnson president. Bryant liked the way he got things done. He just didn't want him as a co-coach.

He had taken a team that had lost all but one game the year before, and had no recent football reputation, and given it instant respectability. Still, he had been a head coach for nine games and you would not exactly describe him as established. You grope for an answer to explain Bryant's action. Was he principled, or merely impulsive? The qualities that would let him endure for 40 years now enabled him to risk it all in one: he had an abundance of self-confidence, conceit, independence, security and stubbornness.

Bryant could not have his authority challenged, not only because it was bad for his ego, but because it was bad for the team. This may be a closer call than it appears: was the Bear moved by personal considerations, or did he give himself up for the team?

We may be on shaky ground here. It is risky to ascribe unselfish motives to anyone involved in sports, which by their nature are the stuff of narcissism. Bryant was seen by many as an opportunist, each time he left a comfortable and secure position for a depressed one. But at Maryland, and later Kentucky, he believed he was defending the concept, his concept, that the team is bigger than any individual. This is the team-as-fortress school of coaching. He may not have been right, but there is little doubt that he believed he was.

Bryant always claimed that he cried when he made up his mind that Curly Byrd's interference left him no choice but to quit. And maybe he did. For a big, gruff man who struck so many people as fearsome, he was never embarrassed at the idea of shedding tears, and at times did so to great effect. Whatever his reaction in that moment of communion, this much we do know: that he picked up a bunch of telegrams sitting on the desk at his office and carried them to the home he had rented near campus just before the Christmas holidays.

Among the telegrams was one from the president of the University of Kentucky, Dr. Herman Donovan. All it said was, IF YOU WANT TO BE HEAD COACH AT KENTUCKY CALL ME COLLECT.

Bryant called and almost immediately accepted the job. The salary was $8,500 a year. The announcement was to be made in two days, and you have to wonder if his heart was really in it. Kentucky had won two games out of ten that season, had never won a conference title, had not enjoyed a winning record in five years and last went undefeated in 1898. And he still had to tell his coaches, his players and Dr. Curly Byrd that he was leaving.

Byrd tried mightily to persuade him to stay, but, true to form, neither man would give up any ground. The big tackle was back on the team, the assistant coach was fired, and Bryant was bound for Kentucky.

Now came the totally unexpected twist that would make Bear

Bryant almost overnight a national sports figure. When the news was announced on Tuesday, 2,500 Maryland students walked out of their classes and staged a strike. All over America, students protest for a variety of creative reasons: wars, civil and social injustice, poor cafeteria food. But no one had ever heard of a strike inspired by the leaving of a football coach, much less one who had been on the job for one season.

The students picketed in front of the administration building for two and a half hours, until Bryant appeared at a 1:00 P.M. rally. He told them their strike was "senseless," that Dr. Curly Byrd was the best friend any of them had, Maryland had been swell to him, and he was moving only because he owed it to his family. He urged them to return to their studies.

Questions were shouted out of the crowd, wondering what would happen to the players Bryant had recruited. "They'll all stay," he promised.

Sammy Behr, who had scored that first touchdown, wept when Bryant broke the news to the squad. He was not alone. "I begged him to take me with him to Kentucky. He told me, 'Sammy, I found you here and I have to leave you here. This is where you belong.' "

The veterans who had followed him from preflight school might have felt betrayed, but they tried to understand. "He told us we had a commitment to the university," said Turyn. "We were upset to see him leave, but he left because of a principle." Turyn stayed, graduated and joined the FBI.

The uproar at Maryland assured the Bear of a warm reception at Kentucky. In that strange American quirk for creating celebrities out of events that amount to nothing more significant than a traffic accident, he had emerged as that coveted article—a big-name coach.

Kentucky was where Bryant earned the name "the Great Rehabilitator." He turned around the Kentucky team as quickly as he had Maryland, and his methods began to attract more attention.

His work habits astounded his players and put enormous pressure on his coaches to keep up. Some of the wives bitched about the hours and the commitment. Mary Harmon wasn't exactly thrilled, either. During the season, Bear left home before first light and returned after the kids were asleep. He was no better a parent than most coaches and, in truth, was more aware of his players' problems than those of his son and daughter. But little Paul and Mae Martin felt neither neglected nor unloved, and no one ever heard Mary Harmon complain—in public. Their consolation was the state itself.

Lexington was bluegrass country, rich, rolling pastures, shady lanes, rows of burly mansions nestled among towering oaks and maple trees. And, everywhere, the echoes of history. So much of the past survives in the land of bourbon and fine horseflesh. Along the Paris and Winchester Pikes—where else in America are roads still called "pikes"?—gray stone walls bordered the open fields. They are called "slave fences," as they were built by slaves who picked the stones from the earth and fitted them into fences of useful beauty.

There was a feeling of continuity in Kentucky, echoes of a more leisurely time when horses were loved not so much for themselves as for a way of life they represented. It was not farfetched to say that in parts of the state, horses lived—and maybe still live today— better than people.

This was tradition. This was society. Bryant had arrived at the right time, at a perfect age, at a place where he was to enjoy the fullness of his coaching and personal powers. He began to feel more at ease around the very rich and the life they led. It was a nice life if you had time for it, this world of good spirits, fine horses and pretty faces. A winning coach at Kentucky could write his own ticket. Women were powerfully attracted to him, and if Bear resisted certain temptations, he did not always act out of moral convictions. Rather, he had a code to establish and he wanted no backlash when he told his players: "Enjoy how warm and soft that little hand you're holding is when you walk across campus, because the memory of it is going to keep you company on the bench on Saturday."

At Kentucky, he was more convinced than ever that his way was right. Pain and discipline were the fish he peddled.

A 17-year-old coal miner's son from Youngwood, Pennsylvania, had just finished his freshman season when Bryant held his first team meeting. When Bryant walked into the room, George Blanda thought to himself: "This is what God must look like."

Blanda may have been the first of what became known as the Bryant type of player: tough, stubborn, dedicated, durable. As a pro, he played quarterback and kicked until he was 49, cut by three teams in three different decades. He was with the Oakland Raiders when he appeared in his last training camp. They had brought in a

22-year-old soccer-style kicker from Boston College to replace him, a kid named Fred Steinfort. On the first day of camp, Steinfort walked up and introduced himself. "I know who you are," said Blanda. It was the last words they spoke to each other.

How much of that grit came from Bryant isn't clear. George was a competitor when Bear found him, a tough Slavic kid driven by a desire to stay the hell out of the mines of Youngwood. His father worked below the ground all week, swinging a pick. Someday someone may want to do a book on the environmental influences on athletes, and the research can begin within 25 miles of where Blanda lived. They grew some terrific specimens, fellows named Stan Musial, Johnny Lujack, Arnold Palmer, Chuck Knox, Johnny Unitas.

A year after he retired, George and I collaborated on a book about physical fitness. It was a riot. By then he smoked a pack or two of cigarettes a day and had a potbelly. My idea of exercise was catching a taxi.

But George had something to say about motivation. He said he remembered how it was, growing up watching the football studs go off to college, "and within a year they would be out of school and back home, for one reason or another. It always struck me that they were quitters. They couldn't stick it out. I made up my mind that if I went to college I was going to play football and graduate and there was no way I was going to be embarrassed by running home."

That vow was sorely tested during the 11 months that Bryant required the Kentucky football team to practice in 1946. "I don't know if that was legal," says Blanda of the nearly year-round practice schedule, "but you could get away with it. Coach Bryant would scrimmage us in the late summer heat, and then everyone who was still alive had to go through another hour of special drills."

Bryant found out that Blanda was a competitor before he realized he was a quarterback. For the 1946 season, he decided to install the Notre Dame box, and on the depth chart Blanda was listed as a quarterback. In the Notre Dame box, his duties were to call signals and block. To make matters worse, George was a third-string blocking back. One of the people ahead of him was Jerry Claiborne, who in the 1980s returned to Kentucky as head coach.

On defense, George was a linebacker, a position he liked even less than blocking back. He expressed his feelings in practice one day by wiping out half a dozen teammates. "You could see he got results," said Blanda. "We won seven games that first year and eight the next. He convinced me that hard work would get you someplace. Bryant laid the groundwork for my whole life."

During the final spring scrimmage, Blanda made up a play in the huddle. The play failed, and before George could call another Bryant was in his face. He had been watching from the press box. "You can't believe how quick he got there," said Blanda. "He grabbed my jersey and said, 'You shithead. I'm the coach of this team. Until you're smart enough to get your own football team, don't go making up any plays for mine. Or your ass will be back in that little town in Pennsylvania so fast you'll think you never left it.' "

Bryant would not tolerate such free-lancing, yet he had seen what he needed of George Blanda. The next year he put in the T-formation, with Blanda running, passing and kicking. The team struggled for much of the season, Blanda's last. They were 3-and-3 after six games, and trailed Villanova, 13–6, with 44 seconds left, the ball on their side of the field. On the last play of the game, with a tackler hanging onto him, Blanda dropped off a pass to a halfback for a touchdown, then kicked the tying extra point. The Wildcats didn't lose another game.

The Bear's best Kentucky teams were ahead of him, but he had begun to recruit and develop players who would become the most decorated the school ever had. Bryant used to get a laugh out of a story he told on the banquet circuit, about a freshman who reported in the fall of '48.

"His appearance literally stopped practice," he remembered. "He had on a zoot suit with the trouser legs pegged so tight I couldn't figure out how he got his feet through the bottoms. His suspenders drew up his trousers about six inches above his waistline. His coat came almost to his knees. He had a ducktail haircut and he twirled a long chain around his finger. One of my assistants asked him if he wanted something.

"He said, 'Yeah. Where's the Bear?' He found me in a hurry. We gave him a uniform, but I figured he wouldn't have the heart for our type of football. To help him make up his mind, I told the coaches to see that he got plenty of extra work. The boy's name was hard to pronounce so we started calling him Smitty.

"Well, I was wrong. Smitty had the heart of a competitor and the desire to be a great player. His senior year, he was voted the outstanding player in the Sugar Bowl, when we ended Oklahoma's winning streak. He made it to the pros and was a fine defensive end for the Giants."

Smitty's real name was Walt Yowarsky, and that story followed him through his later career as a player, coach and scout in the pros. When the yarn was repeated one more time to Yowarsky, he said, "With all due respect to Coach Bryant, who was a great man, someone I loved, I may have dressed funny and I'm sure I looked funny, but I never wore any zoot suit. And I was a tough kid, but I never thought I was tough enough to call him Bear, not then, not ever."

No matter what his players heard about him—how hard the work, how long the hours, how fierce the competition—they never seemed prepared for the way he took over their lives. And not all of them went quietly into the night.

Not the closest, but one of the most interesting of Bryant's relationships was with Bob Gain, the tackle who would become the most honored lineman in the school's history. Gain was a freshman in 1946, rawboned and rough-edged, a man-child on a team loaded with ex-servicemen nearly as old as their coach.

Gain was from an inkspot of a town in West Virginia, and by his senior year in high school he was rated the best football prospect in the history of the Steubenville Valley, which included parts of Ohio. He had lost his father at 11 and worked in the coal mines at 16. He worked one summer in a strip mine owned by Jimmy Snyder, who would later gain national fame as Jimmy the Greek, oddsmaker and sports wizard. Bryant knew Jimmy.

Late one night the doorbell rang at the Greek's house in Steubenville. It was a Kentucky assistant coach, Mike Balitsaris, who happened to be Greek, sent by Bryant to enlist Jimmy's help in recruiting Bob Gain. No school was going to sign him, and maybe 80 had shown an interest, without Snyder checking them out. "We got to have him," said Balitsaris. "Coach Bryant said it's my ass, if I come back without him."

In his own mind, Snyder had narrowed Gain's choices to Georgia and Kentucky. His reason wasn't especially flattering to those institutions. "I knew he was only going to major in football," said the Greek.

Bryant's next move was to send in Carney Laslie, whose snow-white hair gave him the look of a Roman senator. Snyder was impressed. Bob Gain was impressed. But there was a problem. His mother was a widow, with no money, and another school had offered him a bonus to sign. The figure Snyder remembered was $5,000.

The Greek matched it, as a gift from a friend, so Gain would not base his decision on the highest bid. "This was a terrific kid," said Snyder, "a straight shooter, and I cared about him. I told him I'd give him the money, no matter where he went. 'You don't have to be obligated to anybody.' "

So Gain signed with Kentucky, and when he played with the varsity his first spring, in the blue-white scrimmage, Jimmy was there with a friend of his, a bookmaker from Lexington. He got the bookie to give him odds of 50-to-1 on a $100 wager that he could pick a player on the field who would be an all-American before his junior year. The bookie stipulated that he had to be picked by one of the major wire services, and to the first team. The bet was struck and the bookie said, "All right, which kid do you want?"

Snyder said, "His name is Bob Gain, and remember it because that's $5,000 if you lose."

Gain made the second all-America team as a sophomore, and then swept the board as a junior. The Greek had broken even on his recruiting gift, or so he thought. Actually, he wound up with a small profit: "After he retired from his career with the Cleveland Browns, in the early sixties, Bob got word from home that I was in financial trouble. He didn't call. He didn't write. He just sent a check for $2,500."

Getting Bob Gain to Kentucky was one story, keeping him was another. Time would not add any romance to the memories of the raw recruit from West Virginia. "Bear Bryant wanted a winner and here I was, a 17-year-old kid, and he had me going against guys 24, 25, 26. I got worked over pretty good that first year. He overpracticed and overworked the players because he was trying to get the old-timers in shape. In the meantime, he was killing us younger kids."

Many quit, but that was not Bob Gain's style. He didn't want to get out, he just wanted to get even. "There were days when he was tired and I was tired and, well, I just wanted to punch him out. Not Coach Bryant. Just the man who was responsible for all my pain and agony."

After Bryant had tongue-lashed him during a practice in 1950, Gain smoldered, pacing his room in the dorm, his anger boiling, swearing revenge. "He was talking about how he would whip Coach Bryant for what he said to him," recalled Dude Hennessey, who played end at 5'8" and later coached for the Bear at Alabama. "We egged him on. Naturally, everybody started placing bets on the fight, and everybody put their money down on Coach Bryant. Gain had no choice but to try him.

"We piled into two or three cars and drove over to his house and Gain walked up to the door. Coach Bryant answered his knock and said, 'What the hell do you want, Gain?'

"And we could barely hear him from the curb: 'Coach, I was just wondering if I could go home for Christmas this year.'"

In the summer, Bryant took his players on what he called a "retreat, actually a farm near Lexington." In the strange logic that often governed college football, it was legal then for players to attend a summer camp, provided they did not take a football with them. (You may, if you wish, suspend disbelief and picture the Wildcats running their plays without a ball.) To punish a player late for practice, Bryant would hand him a shovel and send him into a nearby cow pasture to shovel cow chips for an hour or so. One day Bryant overslept and arrived 15 minutes late. At the end of practice, Pat James stepped forward and handed him the shovel.

Without a word, he walked out into the pasture. He had to take his medicine, too.

Pat James was a guard, a good-natured fellow who occupied the other end of the scale from Gain. Pat idolized the Bear, and feared him, even after he had been on his coaching staff for years. Somewhere in between fell Charley McClendon, a rugged, hard-bitten country boy who later had a successful run as a head coach at Louisiana State. Charley Mac was usually the one Bryant chose for his demonstrations, when the spirit moved him, and he could not resist making a point by banging heads with his players.

Bear would be sporting a T-shirt and a baseball cap, but he delivered a good blow and often sent the player, in a helmet and full pads, sprawling. One day, Bryant settled into his stance, looked up and saw something in McClendon's eyes he hadn't seen before. He straightened up, brushed off his khakis and said, "Aw, hell, you get the idea."

For most of his career, the Bear had a fair sense of how far he could push and how hard he could press—his players, his opponents, himself. But Bob Gain was clearly a holdout.

Later that summer, Bryant took some of his veterans on a fishing trip. As Gain tells it, the Bear wound up in the water, somehow, and the big lineman held him . . . and held him . . . and held him. Finally, he let his coach surface and climb back into the boat.

Bryant was sputtering and spitting water as he said to Gain, "You tried to drown me."

"I didn't," said Gain, drawing out the words, unable to resist a smile, "but I could have."

Gain, a thoughtful and analytical fellow, was always the one at team reunions who did not genuflect. He regards those as the formative years for Bryant, a testing time for his theories and methods, when the desire to win was just a perpetual flame inside him.

After he graduated, Gain went into the army and then on to a great pro career in Cleveland. The way Bryant told it, the night before Gain's unit was to see action in Korea, he scribbled a short letter to his old coach. The Bear ranked it right up there with one he received, under similar conditions, from Steve Meilinger, who wrote: "Tonight we love you for the things we used to hate you for."

While he never disowned the sentiments he expressed, the references to his letter made Gain mildly uncomfortable. For one thing, he remembers being in the states at the time. And it wasn't a battle he had on his mind but a party. Bryant had invited him to be his guest, the night before Kentucky played Tennessee. An assignment from his commanding officer prevented him from attending. "We were getting to be pretty good friends by then," said Gain, "and I didn't want Coach to think otherwise. That's when I wrote him the letter."

What caused the clash of wills between the two is not hard to define. Even in his late teens, Gain asked only that he be treated as a man. Given his record, it was not too much to ask. He was one of the few, among those who stayed, who would not adapt themselves meekly to Bryant's requirements.

He won much more than the Bear's respect; he would not have lasted without it, no matter how good he was. He became the yardstick by which Bryant would measure all his great linemen to come—

Charlie Krueger at Texas A&M; Lee Roy Jordan, Billy Neighbors and John Hannah at Alabama. Before he ended his career, Gain would negotiate an unlikely treaty with Bryant.

But first there were scoreboards to be stormed. In 1949, Vito Parilli, another Pennsylvania kid, succeeded Blanda at quarterback and led the team to a 9-and-2 season. They called him the Sweet Kentucky Babe. He was an early version of Joe Namath, without the white shoes and temperament.

Parilli had visited the campus the year before with Skip Doyle, the star tailback from his high school team. Parilli was brittle-looking and quiet, and the coaches ignored him. The tailback signed with Ohio State, and the Kentucky staff began to hear that the same school had another prospect, a halfback who could throw.

One day, Carney Laslie swung a sedan into the driveway of the Parilli home in Rochester, Pennsylvania, and Paul Bryant climbed out of the passenger seat. They moved into the living room and Bear made his stock recruiting speech and invited Babe to visit the Kentucky campus.

Babe gave him a startled look and said, "Coach, I've already been there."

There was an awkward pause, the Bear thinking fast now, making the connection: uh-oh, the kid we brushed off, the one who tagged along with Skip Doyle. "Well," he said, recovering his pulse, "this time we'll *know* you're there. I'd like to fly you and your daddy down to see us."

Parilli flew to the campus and worked out with some of the Kentucky players. He had the arm, and the moves, and Bryant envisioned him right off as a quarterback. Of course, he envisioned a few others, too. When Parilli reported in the fall, he was shocked to find that he was one of 11 freshman quarterbacks.

But Bryant must have had a feeling about Babe. He sent Carney Laslie to fetch him in a limo, along with a tackle from Virginia named John Nestoskie, and they drove to Lexington in 17 hours, stopping twice for gas and eats. It was not, technically, a kidnapping, although Carney told the players they were going to Pittsburgh to see the Pirates play.

Bryant would never again spend as much time with a player as he did with Babe Parilli. They would meet in Bear's office, or in the dorm, and play "the quarterback game." The coach would throw out a situation, the down and yards, the score and quarter, the weather, what the defense was. Babe would call a play, and another quarterback would referee, rule it a gain or a loss. They would take turns, but the game was designed for Parilli. And he learned from it.

Their nine wins in 1949 did not satisfy Bryant, mainly because they lost to an inferior Santa Clara team in the Orange Bowl, 21–13. He blamed himself for overworking them, leaving their game on the practice field.

Years later, when he would be aw-shucking it and talking about how inflexible and hardheaded he was, and how his impatience drove away talented players and cost him games, it took a while to realize he wasn't always pretending to be humble. The record backed him up.

Bryant was still boiling about the defeat when he was introduced at the banquet after the Orange Bowl. The audience expected at least a word of congratulations for Santa Clara. Instead, Bryant grumped: "I'm a win man, myself. I don't go for place or show." And with that he sat down.

They loved that kind of talk around the horse farms of Lexington. But to a football crowd it seemed graceless, and he earned some critics he needed a lot of years to shed.

The 1950 season opened with what should have been a breather. North Texas State was flattened, 25–0, but Parilli was kicked in the groin, and had to undergo surgery to relieve the pressure from internal bleeding. Bryant visited him twice a day, monitoring his progress. At midweek he dropped a playbook on his hospital bed, the game plan for that week's game against LSU. "Learn it, Babe," he said. "The game depends on it."

Parilli remembers nearly freaking out. "I couldn't walk," he said. "I could barely move. And Coach Bryant was telling me, in so many words, that he expected me to be the quarterback against LSU."

Actually, what we have here is another of those interesting, conflicting accounts from eyewitnesses. As Bryant often recalled, and described in his 1975 autobiography, ". . . I counted him out. He said he'd play."

What a guy.

But Parilli did play. Bryant had put in the shotgun formation for him, lining him up 10 yards behind the center and taking a direct snap. Before the kickoff, Pat James called a meeting of the offensive line, and threatened to maim the guy who missed his block if Parilli so much as got his pants dirty.

During the warm-ups, Bryant put his arm around his quarterback and said, "Bigness is in the heart, Babe." Then he sent him onto the field with these words: "Get in there and start throwing, and throw until I tell you to stop."

LSU never laid a glove on him. Kentucky went the length of the field on its first drive, keeping the ball for 17 plays, every blessed one a pass. With his drop, Parilli was 15 yards deep, and the LSU linemen wore themselves out just trying to find him.

Kentucky scored twice in the first half and made it stand up for a 14–0 win. Later, Parilli said, "I could have played in a tuxedo." The next week he was near full speed. The miracles of healing that took place on a football field would make Oral Roberts weep.

The toughness of the Wildcats' defense, and the imagination of their game plan, may not have justified the risk taken by their quarterback. Parilli said he always assumed that Bryant had consulted the team doctor. And, given the attitude toward sports injuries in the 1950s, we can assume that the doctor gave him at least a 50-percent chance of surviving.

One can conclude from this incident whatever one wishes. It is understood that some will consider Bryant a heartless tyrant who disregarded the danger to an ailing player. Our view is that in his recollection of these moments, the Bear was not protecting himself. Rather, he saw his players as heroes, Parilli on the field, Bob Gain in the trenches. This was, and is, the pick-up-your-bed-and-walk school of sports mythology.

The circumstances made that game, and the season's last, among the most remembered in Kentucky football lore. When he arrived, Bryant had promised a championship team in five years. (He talked in terms of a five-year plan, but his teams always won sooner and he sometimes left early.) The fifth season was 1950 and he delivered. To this day, it remains the best the school has known. The Wildcats won their first 10 games, not allowing a point in the first four, and warmed up for their finale against Tennessee by slaughtering North Dakota, 83–0. The mismatch was so awful that Bryant pulled his first three squads at the half, and sent them to the practice field to scrimmage against each other. His reserves finished the game, sitting on a 76–0 lead.

North Dakota was on the Kentucky schedule because it ran the single wing, and Bryant wanted his team to see the formation before they met Tennessee, the leading practitioner of that attack. The single wing was considered horse and buggy stuff, even then, but General Bob Neyland was still winning with it.

As matters developed, North Dakota did not do a very good impersonation of Tennessee. With a chance to challenge for the national championship, ranked second in the polls behind Oklahoma, the Wildcats ran into an arctic chill in Knoxville, where the student body had to be called out on Saturday morning to clear the snow off the tarp. The temperature at game time was eight degrees.

Parilli couldn't throw, and Tennessee shut them out, 7–0, in an upset and a bitter one for Bryant. He had never beaten Neyland, in five games, and Kentucky had failed to score in four of them.

"Coach Bryant always had trouble with those folks in the orange jerseys," his trainer, Smokey Harper, once said. "He had a helluva time beating Tennessee, and it was the same thing later with Texas."

The answer was at least partly in Bryant's nature, and he knew it. He thought Tennessee, and later Texas, had better players, and he tried to make up for it by overcoaching and overworking his own, in the process taking away their best chance to win.

In 1950, an unbeaten season had been left on a frozen field in Knoxville. The gloom was thick as giblet gravy when the Wildcats shuffled into the locker room. For one thing, Bryant had just about maneuvered his team out of a bowl game. With a national title in his sights, he had been holding out for the Rose Bowl.

He knew he had some hard pitching to do. Oklahoma had accepted the Sugar Bowl, and Kentucky's loss to the Vols had spoiled a pairing of unbeaten teams. The Bear asked the players to vote on which bowl they wanted, and to his amazement they voted for "none of the above." They took their cue from Gain, one of the co-captains, who kept his hand at his side. Out of 44 players, 3 raised their hands.

Bryant was stunned, enough that he did not object when Gain asked if the players could meet in private. The coaches left the room. Gain climbed onto an equipment trunk and told his teammates they couldn't end the season with a loss. He figured they all felt as he did; if they were going to play it ought to be against number-1 Oklahoma. But he wanted to bargain with Coach Bryant: one practice a day, not two. One scrimmage a week. And three days off for Christmas. Heads nodded. This was a small and nervous mutiny, but they were going with it.

A suspicious Paul Bryant walked back into the locker room to be told by Bob Gain what the players' terms were. The Bear must have bottled some strong emotions, but all he said was, "What if I can't get Oklahoma?"

"Then we don't play anybody," said Gain. He called for a vote, and 44 hands shot up.

Bryant left to find a telephone and returned ten minutes later. Most of the players were still in their uniforms, grimy and sweaty, the fumes filling the room. The Bear just stood there and looked at them, milking the moment, and giving them a little payback. Finally, he said, "We got Oklahoma . . . in the Sugar Bowl."

A roar went up that must have baffled the crowd still milling around outside, a roar you did not expect from a team that had just been beaten, 7–0. Bryant kept his word in the weeks before the game and there were no reprisals. He could tolerate that one confrontation. He might have been amused by it. In the end, the result was what he wanted, and he had already decided to change his tactics of a year earlier.

His players didn't know that the Bear had clinched the Sugar Bowl bid, in his 11th-hour phone call, by assuring the sponsors, "We'll beat their ass." One of his protégés, Joe Namath, would gain fame nearly 30 years later by guaranteeing a win in public, but Bryant did not make such commitments lightly.

Oklahoma was as close to a dynasty as college football had at the time, replacing Notre Dame. Bud Wilkinson had perfected the split-T, and the Sooners had won 31 straight games behind an array of talent headed by Billy Vessels, Eddie Crowder, Buck McPhail, Leon Heath.

To stop Oklahoma's relentless ground game, Bryant devised a defense that used four tackles. Gain and Jim Mackenzie were joined by Walt Yaworsky, who replaced an end, and John Ignarski, a middle guard. He brought up his cornerbacks and created a virtual nine-man line.

Meanwhile, to compensate for their lighter practice schedule, he had the squad watching hours of Oklahoma game films, an exercise not yet common among college teams. The players could not believe their eyes. It wasn't Oklahoma's talent that impressed them. "We were looking at the film of their Nebraska game," said Gain, "and we see the Nebraska tailback go down, their best player. He's sprawled on the ground with an arm stretched out, and an Oklahoma defensive end walks over, steps on his hand and pivots on it with his cleats.

"We pick out three or four of their guys and we see everything. Elbows, knees, a little sneak punch. In the film room we're yelling at each other, 'See that! See what that sonuvabitch did? Run that back.' "

The day before the team was to leave for New Orleans, Bryant was picking up strange vibrations. He called in the seniors and told them: "I've got news for you people. I know what's going on, and we're not going down there to have a brawl. Now, whatever you guys want to do within the rules, okay. Just don't forget why you're there."

The loss to Tennessee had dropped Kentucky to seventh in the polls, but for the first time since the Associated Press had published the rankings, the school was in the Top Ten.

The game caught on, and a sellout was assured three weeks before the kickoff. Hundreds of Kentucky horsemen and cattlemen paid scalper's prices to see their team take on mighty Oklahoma.

The defense worked just as Bryant had diagrammed it. Parilli completed 13 of 15 passes in the first half for two touchdowns, to Shorty Jameson and Al Bruno. Bear played it close to the vest in the second half, and the Wildcats held on to win, 13–7. They had beaten the national champions and ended the longest winning streak in college football.

Walt Yaworsky, who would not have started without the four-tackle defense, was voted the player of the game. He twice threw Oklahoma's quarterback, Eddie Crowder, for losses on the goal line.

The win, the recognition that came with it, and a gesture by Wilkinson may have begun the conversion that made Bryant more bearable (no pun intended). "Wilkinson taught me something that day," he said. "He showed me the class I wish I had. He came into our dressing room afterward and shook hands with me and as many of the players as he could reach. I had never done that before, or seen it done."

From then on he did it himself, paying the ritual visit to the locker room of any team that had beaten him. At times, he had to choke down a lot of pride to do it.

Suddenly, Bear Bryant was the hottest coaching property in America. Southern Cal called. Arkansas offered to make him coach *and* athletic director. LSU exes asked him to name his price. Alabama kept a candle burning in the window, but Red Drew was still under contract and he didn't want to replace one of his old coaches.

Bryant had no intention of leaving Kentucky, where he and Mary Harmon had put down roots, had become friendly with the richest families in the state, and where the governor, Lawrence Wetherby, kept a room for him in the mansion. He returned to Lexington thinking what a perfect week it had been. Then he opened a drawer in his desk and found 64 Sugar Bowl tickets, bought out of his own pocket, that had gone unused.

And there was a cloud hanging over his head in Kentucky that would not go away, a cloud about the size of a basketball.

Chapter 5

My Old Kentucky Home: The Exit

There is a cycle in sports, and sometimes even in life, in which the weak become strong and enemies become friends. This was the saga of Paul Bryant in Kentucky, where he took a downtrodden football program and made it a national power, and where the oversized shadow of Adolph Rupp finally drove him from the state.

On the day he made that impulsive phone call from his desk in Maryland, he knew that Kentuckians loved horses and they loved basketball. What he did not know was that they loved them more than football.

He was a long time in concluding that an error had been made in a survey somewhere, or that, if those feelings were true, they could not be changed. To Bryant, football was only a little more precious than air. Long before anyone gave credit for the line to Vince Lombardi, Bryant had a sign on his locker-room wall that read, WINNING ISN'T EVERYTHING. IT'S THE ONLY THING.

Now, we can get into a lot of grief, and chew up a lot of space, debunking myths as we go along. But the fact is, the origin of that saying probably goes back to the Duke of Wellington. Bryant and Lombardi both borrowed it from a more modern source. On the eve of the Army-Navy game in 1944, a telegram was received by the West Point coach, Earl Blaik, quoting that deathless phrase about winning. It was from the Philippines, signed by General Douglas MacArthur.

In 1949, Bryant nearly left Kentucky to accept an offer from George Preston Marshall to coach the Redskins. Pro football did not even have a national base at the time, but the sport would boom in the decade of the '50s, bringing on the era of the big stadium, big television and big bucks. It might have been the perfect spot for the restless Bear. For a fellow who enjoyed the company of governors, the White House was just a few blocks away.

For the record, Bryant always sort of glossed over the offer, as though it had been a casual and fleeting moment. But when he retold the story one night in Birmingham, many years later, he had the pen in his hand and the contract was on the table. Then he had a flash of doubt.

"All the arrangements were made," he said. "Then I turned to Marshall and said, 'George, I'm one of the greatest admirers of Sammy Baugh around, but what if something came up and I felt it was better for the team to trade him, or one of those other stars, or let them go?'

"Marshall said, 'Oh, you wouldn't do that,' and he just kind of waved it off.

"So I said again, 'But what if it came up, how would you feel about it?'

"He said, 'Paul, there isn't any point in our worrying about something that isn't going to happen, so just sign the contract.'

"I knew right then I couldn't coach for George Marshall. I put down the pen and went home."

In truth, leaving had been on Bryant's mind almost from the moment he checked his hat in Lexington, and discovered it was a size smaller than the one worn by Adolph Rupp. Bryant stayed, turned down dozens of offers, because he had made a commitment and he didn't feel he had kept it until 1950, when his team gave the school the first Southeastern Conference title it had ever won in football.

By now, of course, he wanted to stay. There was nothing about Kentucky not to enjoy, except the presence of Adolph Rupp. It was not a clash of personalities, a case of loathing someone or not understanding each other. Bear understood the man they called the Baron only too well. "All Rupp wanted was to be number 1 and win everything. Not just basketball games, but everything. He was just like me."

There was a basketball hoop over nearly every garage in Kentucky. No coach had won more games or championships than Rupp, and with his plump looks and cranky voice he looked the part of a lovable small-town judge. Bryant was jealous of him and his success and readily admitted it. He went to a booster-club meeting one year at a roadstop outside of Lexington, where earlier Rupp had drawn hundreds and received the key to the city. Twenty people showed up for the football coach and the master of ceremonies told him, half-jokingly, when he had won as many games as the Baron he might get a key, too.

Bryant shot the booster a look that would cure head lice. He got up and said he didn't want their key, when he had won as many games as Rupp—and he would—he'd buy the damned town. And he sat down.

The Bear had not picked on a pygmy. Rupp was held in the kind of fear and awe and fascination that would come to Bryant in his own time. If a feud existed, it was clearly one-sided. Rupp felt unthreatened by Bear and did not go out of his way to torment him, other than by being himself.

Bryant insisted on his players maintaining a C average, hired tutors for them and tried to charm the faculty. Then a faculty committee called on Rupp to register a complaint, and through the doors Bryant heard Adolph cackle: "By gawd, come on in here! I been waiting for you bastards to show up! I wanta know what the hell happened to my basketball player over there in your English class," and he threw out a name while some anonymous department head cringed.

"By gawd," Rupp continued, "you expect me to take these pine knots and make all-Americans out of them and I send you a B student and he's making a hot-damn D!"

When Bryant was older, closer to the age of Rupp when Bear had come to Kentucky, a great deal seemed clearer and simpler than it had then. "I should have gone in there and asked Rupp to do something for me," he said. "He'd have liked that and he would have done it and he would have been my friend."

In 1950, Kentucky won the conference title in both football and basketball. The admirers of Rupp pitched in and bought him a new Cadillac. Bryant always claimed that his gift was a cigarette lighter. The story may or may not be true, or complete, but later he repeated it at a few banquets and always got a nice laugh. The fact is, he did have a lighter, a silver one with a Kentucky logo, and he would pull it out of his pocket for effect.

Whatever the details, or the irritants, the times were never going to be quite as good again for Bryant and his Wildcats. The 1952 team lost four in a row, the longest such streak he had ever suffered. That was the year Steve Meilinger played tight end, quarterback and halfback, and rallied them to a 5–4–2 season. One of the wins was a squeaker, at home, over Texas A&M, 10–7.

Meilinger was, for that time, a splendid specimen, 6'2"and 200 pounds. But he had been expelled from high school one year, and was said to have an attitude problem. His attitude clashed in a hurry with Bryant's fist, more or less. It was his sophomore year and the descendant of German immigrants, from the rich recruiting grounds of eastern Pennsylvania, encountered the customary culture shock.

It was the Bear's pattern, then and later, to single out the players with the most potential, and to demand more and test them harder. Meilinger ran his wind sprints with the linemen, and it became clear that at 50 yards he was faster than any of the backs. The player who led the wind sprints was the first to be excused from practice. It was a privilege he might have enjoyed if he had been less exhausted. "When anyone left the practice field," he recalled, "you had to run eighty yards up a hill that led to the dressing room. When you got there, you had to lay on the floor for thirty minutes before you had the strength to undress and shower."

In the spring of his sophomore year, Meilinger wised off to one of the assistant coaches. He had just finished dressing after practice when a student manager told him Coach Bryant wanted to see him.

"He had showered and just finished dressing when I walked in. He was knotting his tie in front of a mirror behind his desk. With his back to me, he said: 'We recruited you as a football player and not a smartass troublemaker . . .'

"Then in one motion he turned and swung a forearm that knocked me clean across the room. I slammed against a wall and sagged into a chair. It was just like in the movies. I never moved. I was a big, tough kid but I knew if I twitched a muscle he would be all over me. Then I heard him say, very calm, in that deep voice of his, 'Get your ass out of here. Turn in your suit and be out of this building in five minutes and off this campus by tonight. We don't want you around here any more.'

"I can still see me picking myself up out of that chair and heading down the hall. My head was spinning. I got about forty feet when an assistant coach, Carl Samms, called after me: 'Come back here. The Man wants to see you again.'

"So I went back into his office. He was sitting there with his hands folded on a can of film. 'I'm gonna give you one more chance,' he said. 'If you screw up one more time, if I just *point* toward the gate, you better be gone or I'll be on your heels, kicking your butt every step you take.'

"What I have never doubted is this: He knew exactly what it would take to knock me across the room. He knew exactly how to tell me I was through. And he knew exactly how far down the hall he should let me walk before he called me back.

"After that I never questioned his methods or how he handled me. I think I could have been a helluva problem for another coach at another school and never made it." He made it big at Kentucky, of course, and came to regard Bryant as "a father away from home. And I was the kind of kid who needed one."

Kentucky won eight games in '51 and polished off TCU in the Cotton Bowl. Then came the slump. It was after a loss to Cincinnati, their third in a row, that he decided to move Meilinger to quarterback, giving him a week to learn the plays. He had never played the position in his life. But Bryant's other quarterbacks were small, and lacked the quickness to make the running game go in the split-T.

He told Steve: "You're big and faster than any back we have. All you need to do is learn to handle the ball and how to hand it off and I think we can win some games . . . if you can cut it. I think you can, or I wouldn't be asking it of you."

Meilinger rarely attempted a pass, even in practice. The idea was to let him hand off, throw some blocks and turn him loose on the quarterback keeper.

The game that Saturday was in Miami, on Halloween night. Bryant had worked them out in secret, and kept the change out of the papers. Miami was unprepared for it when Meilinger opened at quarterback, with Herbie Hunt, the starter, on the bench. It was just pure old foot-in-the-face football, but with the Wildcats ramming the ball right at them, Kentucky scored three early touchdowns. Later, Hunt passed for one and Miami went down, 29–0.

Meilinger was another Bryant disciple who went into law enforcement—the stats on how many did might be interesting, compared to how many chose coaching. It must have been a little like the Marines. Of those who serve their two or three years, many stay in the corps, and some return home and run for sheriff. Steve served with the FBI and became a chief deputy United States marshal.

By 1951, the Kentucky basketball team was in hot water over recruiting violations, and whispers of a larger scandal had begun to be heard. The school, the boosters, the fans rallied behind the Baron. To Bryant, the outpouring of support for Rupp around the state confirmed his belief that football would never rate top billing. Furthermore, he feared that his own recruiting would be damaged by the investigation.

It is hard now, in an era of constant rapid-fire disclosures of misdeeds in college sports, to measure how devastating was the news of the basketball scandal that broke that winter, eventually sweeping entire lineups into prison.

Rumors began to spread like toadstools. The first arrests involved big names on such ranking powers as City College of New York and Bradley University. By the purest of chance, it happened that in the midst of the furor, with big-city kids being hauled off to the slammer, Adolph Rupp was scheduled to appear at a luncheon of the New York Basketball Writers.

The man who had flogged and driven Kentucky to the top of the roundball world deplored this betrayal of the game he loved. But he glared icily at his Eastern audience and assured them, "Gamblers couldn't get at my boys with a ten-foot pole. Our boys are under constant and absolute supervision while they are on the road, especially in New Yawk." Within days, three members of the Kentucky team, Ralph Beard, Alex Groza and Dale Barnstable, had admitted conspiring to fix games.

Within the week, a mysterious package was delivered to Adolph Rupp's office, long and slender in shape, leaving little to the imagination. It was an 11-foot pole, courtesy of the New York Basketball Writers.

Kentucky's fans were in shock as the basketball team went on probation. Meanwhile, Bryant had turned down the coaching job at Minnesota, and was talked out of another offer from Arkansas by Dr. Donovan, who renewed his contract for 10 years and raised his salary to $12,000. More important to Bear, he thought he had been promised by the school president that Rupp would retire, when it could be done gracefully, after the sentence was served.

When the Texas Aggies played at Kentucky in September 1952 their publicity man, Jones Ramsey, escorted a group of writers to Bryant's office for an interview. Rupp was then preparing to open practice, and he poked his head in the door on his way down the hall: "Don't fo'get, boys," he sang out, "the *big* show starts Monday."

No one who saw the look on Bear Bryant's face that day was surprised when he later announced his departure from Kentucky.

The 1953 season opened with the loss to the Aggies at College Station. The irony was stretched a bit thin. The Aggies had four wins and a tie in their first five games, then lost all the rest to cost Coach Ray George his job. Bryant was impressed with the corps of cadets, their noise and spirit. That was the only impression he carried with him, except for the memory of getting beat.

Kentucky rallied to finish with a 7–2–1 record, including a season-ending win over Tennessee. Bryant thought that next year's team might be his best.

But there would be no next year at Kentucky for the Bear. The first week of February 1954, he was on a recruiting trip to Birmingham when he picked up the papers and read that the university had given Adolph Rupp a new contract. Dr. Donovan was quoted as being pleased, and expressing his confidence in the Baron, and his ability to overcome certain recent unpleasantness.

On the spot, just as he had in Maryland, Bryant made up his mind to go elsewhere. He had been deceived, he felt, and, perhaps just as distressing, he would still have to contend with Rupp if he stayed.

He had given Kentucky nine good years, every one of them a winner, and had established himself among the country's coaching elite. But in one respect he would be replaying a tape of his Maryland decision. The best offers were gone. The schools that had been after him with all their resources, and their pools of talent, Alabama, Arkansas, LSU, Minnesota, USC, had hired their coaches.

The only job unfilled, and the only offer he had, was the one he accepted: from Texas A&M, and he did it over the phone. The decision was a kind of fluke, made while his players were on spring break. They might have made the competition with Rupp seem unimportant, and talked him into staying.

Dr. Donovan and the regents announced that they would not give Bryant his release. They intended to hold him to the contract he had signed a year ago. The Bear took his case to Governor Wetherby, whose control of the state was reflected in his license plate, which read X-1. The governor heard his side with a sympathetic ear, picked up a phone and ordered the regents to let him go.

Once again, Bryant had built a new house he would never fully enjoy. This one had an air conditioner in the master bedroom. That night he and a couple of his closest friends, including Bull Hancock, the horseman, sat on the bed, with the cold air blowing on them, and killed a fifth of whiskey.

There had been no public feud between Bryant and Rupp and, in fact, no angry words exchanged in private. The news of Bryant's resignation therefore was not only a shock, but to many a mystery. It was suggested that he would not have left if he had not lost Paul Hornung, the best player in the state, to Notre Dame. Hornung, a triple threat who had been a sensation at Flaget High in Louisville, went on to win the Heisman Trophy in 1956 for the Irish and enjoyed a legendary career with the Green Bay Packers. It was taken for granted that Kentucky would land him. But his mother wanted her son to attend Notre Dame.

Years later, long after feelings had cooled, and on a night when Bryant figured one theory was as good as another, he introduced Hornung at a banquet as "the reason I left Kentucky."

Hornung did not want to seem untouched, but later he told Coach Bryant, "I would appreciate it if you didn't say that. I still have to live in this state."

Once his decision was made, Bryant reacted as he always did. By taking charge. He flew to Dallas for a secret meeting with members of the A&M athletic board to negotiate his contract.

A room had been set aside at the airport and when Bear walked in he noticed all the drapes were closed. He and the board talked for an hour before he even raised the question of money. The first thing on Bryant's mind was how quickly he could win there.

He asked one of his hosts, Jack Finney, how many players A&M could sign, out of 20, if they offered the same scholarship as Texas. Finney told him half. Bryant was pleased. He knew he could win if he could compete for talent with the state's biggest school.

He did not then know about the Aggie spirit, and the kind of enthusiasm and optimism and self-delusion it sometimes inspires. "You couldn't get ten," he wrote later, referring to the recruiting contest with Texas. "You would be lucky to get one. The chances were you wouldn't get any. Not then."

The Aggies had not given a coach more than a one-year contract since the ex-students had to pay off Homer Norton's last three years in 1947. Norton had given them great teams, including a national champion in 1939. Fifteen years later, the Aggies were still reliving that season, and the heroics of players like John Kimbrough, the all-American fullback, and a future all-pro linemen in Martin Ruby. Two of their stars had died in the war, Joe Routt and Herb Smith. A good part of it was sentiment, but the Aggies had celebrated little else in the years after the war. They were hungry and they were hurting.

They were able to give Bryant the control he had never had: the title of athletic director as well as head coach. He wanted to be paid the same salary as the department heads, until he heard the figure— $15,000. They knew it was not enough money to justify the move from Kentucky, and the hitch was quickly cleared by one of the committee members, a Houston oilman named W. T. (Doc) Doherty. He agreed to put Bryant on his company payroll for another 10 grand. He would have his own television show, and an attendance clause in his contract, a practice then unheard of in college sports.

Bryant's hiring sent shock waves through the Southwest Conference, where the trend at that time was to promote an assistant or sometimes to bring in a popular high school coach. Bryant was going to shake up the system, about that no one had any doubt.

Bryant's reception by A&M, the state, the press, was wild and almost feverish. A crowd of 3,000 students waited nearly four hours for him at the tiny airport in College Station, Texas, unaware that he had been bumped from his flight in Cincinnati. Jack Gallagher, a veteran writer with my paper, the *Houston Post*, had flown to Kentucky to get the jump on the competition, and wound up with the last seat. True to the instincts of the profession, Jack refused to give up his space. "You don't think I'm going to stay behind," he said, "and let all the other writers from Texas greet you when you land?"

Bryant arrived on the next flight, around 8:00 P.M., and most of the crowd followed the school car that carried him to the Memorial Student Center on the campus. When Bryant registered, he hesitated at the line that requires an address. He was, of course, between homes. With school officials and students peering over his shoulder, he finally wrote down, in heavy strokes, "Paul W. Bryant, Texas A&M, College Station, Texas." A cheer went up in the lobby.

From the Student Center, Bryant was led to an outdoor theater called the Grove, where special events are held, including Aggie yell rallies. Nearly 6,000 cadets were waiting for him, at that time nearly half the school's enrollment.

Jones Ramsey had given Bryant a short briefing on the campus customs and traditions. A speaker, he said, was expected to remove his jacket. Now the showman in him took over. The Bear walked on the stage, removed his jacket, flung it to the floor and stomped on it. Then he took off his tie and stomped on it. The cadets were coming unglued. Next, rolling up his sleeves, he walked to the microphone and announced:

"I'm Paul Bryant and I'm ready to go to work."

That did it. The place was in a frenzy. The Bear had flat won their hearts. All he had to do now was win some games. That would come, but not instantly and not painlessly. His Aggie years were going to be difficult and daffy and grand. He would dominate the conference and the headlines. There would not be a time or a place quite like it again.

His contract was impressive enough as he dictated it, but the speculation made it out to be even richer than it was. An undercurrent of resentment greeted Bryant among the A&M faculty, and to help defuse it he appeared on a radio debate with a professor of English, Tommy Mayo. He was no anti-sports egghead and, in fact, had once roomed with Dana X. Bible, whose great coaching career included stops at Nebraska, A&M and Texas.

But Mayo was concerned about the kind of emphasis on winning that he felt the hiring of Bryant represented. Not a new angle, even then. The topic of the debate was: "Is College Football Over-emphasized?"

What listeners remembered of the show was one exchange. Bryant asked the professor, "Sir, how many people are watching when you give a final exam?"

Mayo replied, "About fifty."

Bryant said, "Well, I have fifty thousand watching me when I give mine—every Saturday."

After the initial excitement and freshness wore off, what Bryant was left with was the reality of Texas A&M. It has been, and is, a superb university, whose graduates in engineering, geology and science have made contributions around the world. The Aggies are famed, even notorious, for their pride and fellowship and undying allegiance to their teams. The former students have been described as "invincible in defeat, insufferable in victory." Not a bad description. Then or now.

The Aggie spirit was the subject of a wartime film called *We've Never Been Licked*, a rather forgettable work except for the debut of a young actor named Robert Mitchum. The cadet corps was at the soul of most Aggie traditions, including the Twelfth Man, the bonfire before the Texas game, and the marching band. But none of the things that made A&M so distinctive were especially helpful in recruiting football players. Notably unhelpful was the absence of coeds.

Tradition is at the soul of what it meant, still means, to be an Aggie. When A&M teams first appeared on national television, viewers unfamiliar with the school were amazed to learn that the student body stood throughout every home game. The students are the Twelfth Man. You conclude that the first requirement of an Aggie is good feet.

The tradition started on January 2, 1922, when the Aggies were playing the Praying Colonels of Centre College in the Dixie Classic, the parent of the Cotton Bowl. Centre College was then a national power, their nickname given them by the patron saint of sports-writing, Grantland Rice, who had observed them one day in a pre-game prayer. (Whenever he was in the vicinity, a player would shout,

"Quick, down on your knees, here comes Granny Rice." It might have been a gag.)

The game was bruising, the rosters thin, and so many Aggie players were injured that Coach Dana X. Bible sent a student manager into the stands to find a former squadman named King Gill, who had paid his own way to the game. Gill had dropped off the team a few weeks earlier to concentrate on basketball.

The Aggie bench was nearly empty when the manager brought Gill to the field. "Boy," said Bible, "we may not have enough players to finish the game. You may have to go in and stand around for a while." Gill replied with a crisp, "Yes, sir."

Several players held up a blanket so that King Gill could change into a uniform on the sidelines. The Aggies went on to win, and Gill never was needed, but his readiness to serve became the inspiration for the Twelfth Man.

The school would endure as one of the last bastions of male dominance for another 15 years. Then the barriers would come tumbling down. A&M would be fully integrated and girls would be allowed on the campus even in daylight. Membership in the cadet corps, once mandatory, would be optional.

Bryant and his staff were everywhere in those first months. It was the darnedest manhunt the conference had ever seen and, of course, the Aggies would run afoul of the NCAA's watchdogs. They dropped a dragnet across the state and brought in 120 recruits for their first freshman team.

The first time I laid eyes on Paul Bryant was at an A&M booster club meeting in Houston, during that time. The signing of several widely sought prospects was to be announced, one of them Kenneth Hall, a running back from nearby Sugar Land who had rewritten the high school record book.

A tailback in the single wing, Hall had rushed for over 4,000 yards—in one season. He had rushed for over 11,000 in his career, almost never playing in the second half. Thirty years later, he still holds the record for touchdowns in a season, 57, and a career, 127.

As the prospects were introduced, each would stand and the crowd would politely applaud, with a sprinkling of howls and cheers. Then it was the turn of the alum who had brought in Hall, and after a fairly long recital of his accomplishments, he concluded with, "and

I'm proud to announce that Kenneth Hall has decided to be an Aggie."

The room erupted, as the exes gave Hall, and each other, a standing ovation. I was in the back, already standing because the restaurant was unable to provide seats for all those who wanted to get a glimpse of this messiah who was going to resurrect Aggie football. The noise was worth two Excedrins, at least. It went on for minutes. Then the room quieted down and it was time for Bryant to speak.

He made his way slowly to the podium and he just stood there, looking at his audience. Then he said, without a smile, "I'm damned happy to hear Kenneth Hall is coming to A&M. I hope he goes out for football."

The Aggies roared and I saw Hall blush and duck his head. It was a funny line, but I got the notion that Bear was not entirely joking. He was telling the exes, I thought, that it was swell to whoop it up in a bar or a restaurant, but it was a little early for cheers. Paul Bryant wasn't real big on taking things for granted.

Then came Junction. It is hard, but by no means impossible, to imagine now how fresh and unpredictable Bryant appeared to us. Toward the end of his career, it must have seemed that everything had been said or written until our eyes and ears glazed over; indeed, if he had a new thought you wouldn't have understood him anyway.

But that year, and the three to follow, he had the capacity to surprise us weekly, sometimes daily. His language dripped with color, even the parts you could actually put in a family newspaper. He never sent a writer away hungry.

At bottom, he was the most human of coaches. The poses, the calculation, could be interesting. But just when you thought you had him pegged, he would disarm you with his honesty or vanity. Jones Ramsey was walking with him across the campus, taking a coffee break, two weeks after Bear had suddenly landed at A&M. Jones confided that it was his thirty-third birthday. Bear looked at him with undisguised envy. "Goodness, I'd give anything to be thirty-three again," he said. At the time, he was 40.

Noted Ramsey: "He was so handsome then, he must have hated the idea of growing old."

It took me a while to realize what a quick study he was. His instincts were uncanny. He could look at a film, or hear a scrap of conversation, and arrive at the right answer faster than anyone I have ever met. We had an early glimpse of how well he read people, including coaches, on the press tour that fall of '54.

Bryant, who was new to the conference, asked the writers to jot down on a sheet of paper their choice to win the championship. After he collected the picks he read them out loud. Only one person selected Arkansas, the eventual winner, and that was Bryant. Not even the respected sports editor from Little Rock, Orville Henry, had guessed the Hogs would sneak off with the title in Bowden Wyatt's first (and only) season as coach.

But Bear had been interested in the Arkansas job, knew their material, and reckoned that Wyatt would outsmart some of the coaches and outwork the rest. He planned to do the same as soon as he had the livestock.

The 1954 season was going to be an exercise in reality therapy. When it was over, the conference would slap the Aggies with a two-year probation, the first time, Bryant noted, "that a school got put on probation after winning one game." The penalty would cost A&M trips to two bowl games and came as a stunning blow to Bryant, who thought he had been punished enough by losing nine times. He thought he had been bushwhacked, done in by athletic directors and coaches whose own purity was not above suspicion. He thought they were trying to sit on him and apply some damage control, before he got on track.

The action was announced at a spring meeting in Houston, at the Rice Hotel. When reporters asked for a press conference, Bryant gave them a time and suggested they come to his room. Then he slipped down to the drugstore, checked out the rack of paperback books, and made a purchase.

When the writers drifted out the door, they could not help but notice a book that Bryant had casually left on a table at the entry. The title was: *Prisoner in His Room.*

Bryant had good cause that first year at A&M to question his judgment, if not his sanity. The Kentucky team he had left behind won eight games under Blanton Collier.

That winter he had an unlikely encounter at a coaching clinic in Utah. Adolph Rupp was there, and in the middle of his talk, with newsmen in the room, the Baron pointed in Bear's direction and said: "I want to tell you gentlemen something. Paul Bryant over there was at Kentucky, and he left us for a lot of money. You think he's down a little bit now, but I'll tell you, he will win. He *will* win. And you gentlemen in Texas who are playing him, he will run you right out of the business. Five, ten years from now he will be the top man, make no mistake about it, and don't forget that Uncle Adolph told you."

You recall the classic final scene from *Casablanca*. Humphrey Bogart, as Rick, puts his arm around Claude Rains, the French Vichy captain, and, as they walk into the mist, tells him: "Louie, this could be the start of a beautiful friendship." Yeah, that was the kind of look Bryant gave Adolph Rupp. They wound up as friends. After Rupp retired, and did not have long to live, Bryant sent a private plane to fetch him, and flew him as his guest to an Alabama-Kentucky game.

Chapter 6

Up the Down Elevator

Two minutes are missing from my life that I can never recapture. I spent them in an elevator, riding from the press box to ground level at Rice Stadium, in Houston, in November 1955.

A slice of college football history happened during those two minutes, and I became a kind of local celebrity for having missed them. I have looked at the films and read the accounts of what took place, so that the events are more real to me now than if I had actually observed them. Some years, as the anniversary of that day approached, I have received requests for interviews. It is almost as though I had suffered from a rare form of amnesia, instead of a slow elevator.

By being in the wrong place, I became a part of the story and now, all these years later, I do not regret either minute of it.

The Texas Aggies had bused down to Houston to meet the Rice Owls, bringing with them a record of seven wins and a tie in their last eight games. They had opened the season by losing to UCLA, the defending national champions.

The turnaround had come more quickly than even the most ardent Bear Bryant fans had predicted. Loaded with sophomores, the Aggies had climbed to ninth place in the weekly polls. So sudden was the Aggie ascent, they were uncomfortable in the role of favorite, as they were over Rice by two touchdowns.

The decline of Rice seemed even more hasty. The Owls had two more chances to win a conference game, including this one. Two years ago, they had tied for the title, gone to the Cotton Bowl and bombed Alabama, 28–6. That game became the most historic of all Cotton Bowls, when a player named Tommy Lewis jumped off the Alabama bench to tackle Rice's Dicky Maegle, who had broken loose on an apparent 94-yard touchdown run. The officials awarded Maegle the touchdown, ejected Lewis from the game and penalized 'Bama on the kickoff.

The Owls were coached by Jess Neely, a flinty son of the South, who disliked Bryant and resented the publicity given his hard-nosed approach to football. Neely was no wimp himself. While Maegle was still sprawled on the grass, shaken by the unexpected tackle, Neely raced past him and confronted Alabama's Red Drew on the sideline. He pointed to a now miserable Lewis, who seemed to be shrinking, trying to lose himself among the other players on the bench. Neely's shrill, almost metallic voice carried to both sides of the field: "Red! Red!" he demanded, "what in the world was that piss-ant thinking?"

In spite of Rice's off year, nearly 68,000 fans had packed the stadium to see the Owls engage the resurgent Aggies, who had lost the last 10 games in this series. This one did not figure to be high-scoring. Both Neely and Bryant preached defense.

But what the fans got for three quarters was no scoring. Rice shut down an Aggie ground game that had gained more respect by the week. Bryant had borrowed a page from his Kentucky playbook, making a split-T quarterback out of a player from another position, this time Roddy Osborne, a sophomore fullback. Lined up behind him were John David Crow and Jack Pardee.

Rice had one drive stopped at the 10-yard line, and that was the only scoring threat by either team until the middle of the fourth quarter. Then Rice took advantage of a short Aggie punt and scored on a pass play to lead, 6–0. A fumble on the kickoff gave the ball right back to the Owls, 31 yards from the goal. They stayed on the ground, kept the clock running, and scored again as Paul Zipperlin went wide from the 5.

A&M's Dee Powell blocked the extra point try, but it hardly seemed to matter. Rice led, 12–0, and the clock was winding down to less than three minutes. In front of the Aggie bench, Bryant huddled with his starters. All he said to them was, "There is still time. You can still do it, if you believe you can."

If the Aggies believed, theirs was definitely a minority opinion. The crowd had begun to vote with their feet, heading up the aisles in droves, most of them disenchanted Aggie fans. In the press box, it was time for the writers assigned to the dressing rooms to head for the elevator. I lingered at my seat, my chin resting on my crossed arms. Clark Nealon, then the *Post* sports editor, who had been watching these games since the 1920s, turned and asked if I was feeling all right. "You're pale as a ghost," he said.

"Clark," I confided, "I'm just thinking about having to face Coach Bryant in the locker room." I was, in fact, preparing myself mentally, in the way of a man who has done his duty and knows he will catch hell for it. My assignment was to write a postgame story— a sidebar, as they are called—on the Aggies, and it did not figure to be a glad experience. A feature story of mine had appeared in the paper that morning, entitled: "The Bear of the Brazos: A Man of Many Moods."

There was little about the headline, or the story, that would strike anyone as offensive. But if the Aggies lost, as they seemed in the certain process of doing, I knew Bryant would be a man of just two moods: angry and suspicious. He would believe that my story had hexed him.

We had been through this once, when his heralded freshmen were beating up the varsity in practice and stirring the juices of old Aggies. I had driven to College Station on one of my weekly visits, and Bryant learned that I had interviewed John David Crow. I had heard the coaches raving about Crow, the best running back in Louisiana his senior year in high school. He could block and play defense, too, and his progress was even ahead of Kenneth Hall's.

Bryant asked me what I was doing, and I told him I had been assigned to write a story about the freshmen. His face clouded up immediately. "Well, hell, isn't there anything else around here worth writing about? You put their names in the paper and they'll all get swelled heads."

He really thought that way. I explained I had no choice, and later that week, on the day the story ran, the Aggie freshmen were clobbered by Baylor. Bryant was waiting for me the next time I stopped by his office. His voice had a needle in it. "Oh, hello, Mr. Crow," he said, "and how's your dream backfield today?"

I caught the elevator on its last locker-room run. It stopped on each floor, picking up new passengers, while one or two always fought their way from the back to get out. Inside the elevator we heard the roar of the crowd, three distinct roars. When the door finally opened, there was a stampede to cover the 20 or 30 yards across the concourse. The writers stumbled and pushed and wedged their way through the stands, upsetting the popcorn vendors and blind-siding old ladies, trying to catch a view of the scoreboard on their way to the field.

What I saw bewildered me. The scoreboard lights spelled out: A&M 14, Rice 12. And even as the numbers sank in, on the field Don Watson of the Aggies was diving across the goal from three yards out. The curious thought struck me that they had put up the touchdown before it happened, and the Aggies had just taken the lead. Then the numbers blinked, and it was 20 to 12.

In exactly two minutes and nine seconds, the Aggies had scored three touchdowns to produce what was then the greatest rally in college football history. It must still rate among the most dazzling two-minute drills ever executed. Here is how it happened:

The teams had exchanged punts, after Rice's second touchdown, and with the ball at the Aggie 42 Bryant sent into the game Loyd Taylor, a stubby halfback from Roswell, New Mexico. Taylor veered to the left sideline and fled 55 yards before he was knocked out of bounds at the Rice 3. On third down, from the 1, he wiggled across for the score, kicked the extra point, and cut Rice's lead to 12–7.

Now came the game-breaker, one of the most remembered plays of this rivalry. Neely pulled his entire team off the field to warn them of an attempted onside kick. And here it came. The Aggie kicker, Jack Powell, spun one to the left that bounced around at the Rice 40. Players on both sides lunged and clutched at it, but Gene Stallings smothered it for the Aggies at the 43.

Bryant had inserted Jimmy Wright, another soph, and his best passer, at quarterback. On the next play, Wright unloaded a bomb, over the head of Paul Zipperlin, the defender, and into the arms of the streaking Taylor. His kick was good again, and in a span of 46 seconds Taylor had accounted for all 14 A&M points.

The Rice fans were so stunned as to be almost catatonic. And to this day, thousands of Aggies can recall exactly where the ball was when they turned on their car radios in the parking lot, and listened to the storybook finish.

When the Owls got the ball back, they went to the air, and on first down Jack Pardee intercepted a pass and returned it 37 yards. A&M was threatening again at the Rice 8. A penalty moved the ball to the 3, and from there Watson scored.

I watched the final minute and nine seconds from the field, behind the Rice bench. When I made my way up the tunnel and reached the door of the Aggie dressing room, I found Bryant sitting nearby on the bottom step of a concrete stairway. I blurted out, "Coach, I got caught in the elevator and missed most of it. What happened?"

"Damned if I know," he said. "I was too busy praying."

When I returned to the press box to work on my story, I explained to an amused Clark Nealon what had happened. After several false starts, with little balls of crumpled paper beginning to pile up around my ankles, I said to Clark, "I've never seen anything like it."

"Except," he corrected me, "that you didn't see it."

Of course, in my mind's eye I have. I saw it even more clearly, the details sharper and the color fine-tuned, as the years passed. It remains the greatest rally I was ever told about. And I learned something about Bear Bryant and how he coached, an insight that was valid for all the games to come.

He shrugged off most questions about what he did, or why. He said he recruited pretty much like the next guy, his practices and drills were not so different, and he ran an attack that looked the same as most others. He also allowed some plays to be called by people in the scouting booth. "But one thing I control," he said, "is the substitutions. Most games are decided by five or six plays. The secret to winning in football is having the right players on the field when those five or six plays happen."

Bryant had that touch, and this was why he usually referred to himself as a game, or field, coach, as opposed to the theorists whose pleasure was in the equations they worked out on a blackboard. He was not soft on the science of the sport, although he sometimes gave that impression. He could scribble x's and o's with the best of them, and many a waiter froze at the sight of what he had done to their table linen. But reacting, moving the chess pieces, this was the part he loved.

There is a line from an old Broadway musical, *The Fantasticks*, that goes: "You have to die a little to be born again." It was written then, and I still believe, that Bryant performed the finest pure coaching job of his career in guiding the Aggies to nine losses his first season there. He did so by keeping the scores respectable, and refining the players who would lead his winning teams.

On the A&M campus, and among their booster clubs across the state, the wait for the 1955 season was an impatient one. The Aggies were to open at Los Angeles, in the Coliseum, against a UCLA team that had been number 1 in the nation the year before and was coached by Red Sanders. The Bruins were three deep at every position, with five or six all-America candidates, including end Rommie Loudd, fullback Paul Davenport and guard Hardiman Cureton.

You would have expected Aggie hopes to be minimal, given their record and the preponderance of sophomores on their roster. But these were no ordinary sophs. They had been, at that time, the most publicized recruiting crop any Southwest Conference school had harvested. They were A&M's Team of Tomorrow, and the old grads dry-washed their hands in anticipation.

Some of the names were already familiar and would become more so: John David Crow and Kenneth Hall. Jim Stanley, out of Kentucky, an unsmiling guard already labeled by Bryant as "the meanest player" on the team. Bobby Marks, a rangy end from Louisiana. Charlie Krueger, only 17, but a 6'6" tackle who would draw comparisons to Bob Gain. Bryant had reached out to New Mexico for Loyd Taylor, and close to home had reeled in prize schoolboy backs in Bobby Joe Conrad, Roddy Osborne, Jimmy Wright.

It was like watching a 13- or 14-year-old girl, wobbly on her first pair of high heels, looking into a mirror and discovering she is pretty. The Aggies had been waiting a year for this team. No, they had been waiting all their lives.

The Aggie practices were sharp and lively and the players were looking forward to their trip to California. One day, William Bendix, the actor, who had played Babe Ruth in a movie about the home-run king, joined the team at the training table and made a brief pep talk. It was never clear what brought him to the campus, or why he had stopped by to visit the team. He was just there.

Bryant was oddly relaxed when the press buses dropped off the writers on the annual preseason tour. We adjourned to the country club for the coach's interview and lunch, and I tried to find a shortcut through the recital of the three-deeps, one of the all-time pointless exercises football writers ever invented. It was the custom then to ask the coach a few general questions, before he turned to his roster and read through the players at each position on his first three units, offering a comment or a description if he ran across a name he recognized.

Bear had covered the starters when I broke in and asked a question about his plans for UCLA. Before he could answer, Dick Freeman, with the *Houston Chronicle*, an old-timer and a legendary drinker, spoke up. "Just a minute, young man," he chided me, "we haven't finished the three-deep yet."

"Give him hell, Dick," said Bear, with a big grin.

When John David Crow's name was mentioned, Freeman asked, his voice both curious and sympathetic, "Bear, what's wrong with Crow's face?"

One side of the young halfback's face had been paralyzed at birth, as Bryant explained it, by a problem during the delivery. Freeman sort of clucked his tongue and said, softly, "That's a shame. If not for that he'd be handsome."

Bryant came right back: "Oh, Dick, to me he's handsome *right now*."

The result was a slight droop of the eye and mouth, but as Crow grew into his permanent look the distortion seemed less, and if you knew him well you tended not to notice at all. Bear was right. Crow was handsome, a big blond, blue-eyed, with a great heart. The team doctors talked about correcting the problem with surgery after he finished his football career. John David never bothered.

At the end of the interview that day, as the writers moved into the dining room for lunch, Dick Freeman passed out, just falling stiff as a board into the arms of a startled Willie Zapalac. They dragged Dick over to a couch and left him there, sleeping peacefully.

It was a moment of comic relief for Willie, the only assistant coach Bear had retained from the previous Aggie staff.

Ramsey flew out to Los Angeles a week before the game to advance the crowd, and made his headquarters at the Palm Room of the Ambassador Hotel, just off the famed Coconut Grove. The charter flight from College Station was full, and I recall someone saying that of the players aboard only two had ever flown.

The underdog Aggies played UCLA on even terms most of the night, and lost on three touchdown passes thrown by Ronnie Knox, a heralded tailback who later dropped out of school. In the dressing room after the game, Mel Durslag, a Los Angeles columnist whose irreverent style would win him a national following, asked Bryant if he actually had thought his young team would win against UCLA.

Bear did a double take. "Hell, yes," he said. "Why do you think we came out here?"

No matter how unrealistic that hope should have seemed, or what a powerful team you knew UCLA had, the gloom was thick on the plane heading back to Texas after the game. Somehow I got involved in a minor episode that did not lighten the mood, at least, not then.

I had purchased tickets to the game for friends in Los Angeles, the Kabaker family, whose son Orrin I had known since my early teens. They were waiting for me at the airport as I boarded the flight, having hastily written and filed my story back to the *Post*. To thank me for the tickets, they had brought a five-pound box of chocolates, and I tucked it under the arm that was not carrying the typewriter, waved good-bye and started up the steps. Happily, there was a seat in the middle of a row at the back of the plane, well away from the coaches up front.

While I was getting myself adjusted, and catching my breath, I passed the box of chocolates to a player in front of me and told him to help himself. I didn't figure to finish five pounds of chocolates alone.

I was just sitting there, waiting for the plane to move, still wound tight from the game, the pressure to bang out my story and the rush to the airport. Then I saw it. The box of chocolates was weaving its way from player to player, from row to row, across the aisles, heading irreversibly toward the front of the aircraft. Toward Bear's seat. My box of chocolates.

That memory comes back to me every time I see some fools start a wave in a stadium.

It did not take long for the explosion that I knew was coming. Suddenly there was Bryant running up the aisle, the box in his hands, shouting, "Who brought this crap on the plane?"

Several of the players around me turned in their seats and looked in my direction, but no one spoke. I did the best I could to make myself smaller. The exit door was still open and Bear walked up to it, cocked his arm and sent my five pounds of chocolates flying out over the tarmac.

No one spoke as he returned to his seat. The trip home began and ended in utter silence.

At this point, I choose, as modesty or discretion sometimes makes necessary, to hide behind another writer. We jump forward in time some six years, and a column in the *Arkansas Gazette*, by Orville Henry:

> The years came and went and the bond between the writer and the coach grew. No one could write more or better about Bryant, a fascinating subject, and no one could get away with more stuff on the subject than Mickey.
>
> Bryant moved to Alabama. Once established there, he returned to Houston to make a banquet appearance. Mickey's editor, acting out of sentiment, assigned him to mosey over to the coach's Shamrock Hilton suite and bring everybody up to date on the celebrated coach. So Mickey did and they re-hashed all the old times and talked about Alabama as well. The writer left.
>
> "You know," Bear turned to a friend in his room, "it was great to see little Mickey again, but he didn't really seem at ease. Something seemed to be bothering him."
>
> About that time, the door, not completely closed, swung open.
>
> "Coach," said Mickey, hoarsely, "that was *my* box of candy." Then he turned and let the door shut behind him.

I only know that I never disclosed that story, so it must have been Bear who talked.

*   *   *

The shut-out loss to the Bruins had silenced the Aggie exes, and the soaring expectations of August had taken a dive. They had now lost 10 out of 11 under Bryant and their celebrated sophs had been unable to put a point on the scoreboard.

The coaches studied the game film so hard they all but plugged their eyeballs directly into the socket. They came away with even more respect for UCLA and less apprehension about their own personnel. Bear reevaluated a few positions and looked ahead to LSU, a game scheduled for the Cotton Bowl in Dallas.

One of the players who emerged from the opener with low grades was Ken Hall, the beginning of a misjudgment that would injure both player and coach. This was the era of two-way players, and in Bryant's scheme Hall's positions were fullback and linebacker. Most teams used the same system, which would seem to defy the idea of aptitude testing. Kenneth had been a safety in high school, when he was called on to play defense.

Bear watched Paul Davenport run right through Hall in the film, and fumed, "Twice he didn't even touch him. Didn't even wave to him as he went by." Sarcasm was then one of Bryant's customary tools. But Hall was a talented fellow playing out of position, in an atmosphere alien to him, for a coach whose roughness troubled him.

It was a muscle game the colleges played in the mid-1950s: one-platoon, the split-T, three-yards-and-a-cloud-of-dust, survival of the meanest. That was John David Crow's game. Against LSU, the school from his home state, Crow scored twice and the Aggies breezed, 28–0. The win was a turning point for Bryant and his team.

One of Crow's touchdown runs was so special that Bear would recall it in detail 20 years later:

"We ran a trap play and both guards pulled and ran head-on into one another. Somehow Crow busted through the mess and ran eighty-one yards for a touchdown. He must have shook off fifteen tackles, the greatest single run I ever saw.

"And when he came back to the bench he patted everybody on the back: 'Great blocking, boys. Great blocking.' Ain't nobody blocked anybody, but he was giving them the credit. I knew then we were on our way."

The Aggies did not lose again until their last one, against Texas. They tied Arkansas, the defending conference champions. The game was played at Fayetteville, in the hills, and the Aggies were lucky to get a tie, although you would not have convinced Bryant.

Just the physical fact of playing at Arkansas was good for a thrill. There were no hotel rooms available in Fayetteville, and visiting teams usually spent the night in Fort Smith and traveled an hour by bus through narrow, winding mountain roads. The players began picking out signs on sheds and barns that dated back to the Depression, and soon they were joking about the size of their hometowns and trading putdowns.

The players may have thought that just the general din and humor was what set off Bryant, but it might have been the references to what the signs and the sheds stood for, an age and a way of life unknown to most of them.

Suddenly he was out of his seat and standing in the middle of the aisle, swaying, ordering the driver to pull the bus off the road. A mighty quick calm settled over the bus. "All right," he said, "nobody is interested in playing Arkansas so let's all get out, go sit under a big shade tree and have a picnic. I'll send the driver into town for hot dogs, Cokes and marshmallows. Then we'll cancel the game and spend the day telling stories."

He stood there and waited. Then, quietly, he said, "Okay, let's go on and play the game." For the rest of the trip, the players had nothing to do but concentrate on their assignments. Then the bus reached the stadium, and a beefy, red-faced fan waving an Arkansas banner signaled the bus to stop. The driver opened the door for him and he looked inside and asked, "Which one of you is the Bear?"

Jerry Claiborne pointed to Coach Bryant. It was clear now that the man was drunk. Bryant's disposition did not improve when the intruder claimed to be a cousin from Fordyce, adding, "Course, I'm pulling for Arkansas." With that, the Bear put a hand against his shoulder and shoved him out of the doorway. As the bus moved on, he muttered, "Ain't nobody who roots for Arkansas getting on this bus."

At halftime the game was scoreless and Bear was in a rage. "I'll never forget it," said Dennis Goehring. "He went from one player to the next—we were sort of cowering on our little stools—telling them they were playing like dogs. Well, he came to a little player named Henry Clark, and he grabbed Henry by the shoulder pads, lifted him up, shook him, put him back down and said, 'Henry, you ain't playin' worth a damn.' And Henry, poor Henry, looked up and said, 'Hell, coach, I ain't even been in the game yet.' "

The leaders on that team were the juniors, the last of the Junction Boys, Pardee, Stallings, Goehring, Don Watson, Bobby Drake Keith. Watson was a wispy 160-pounder who scored the last touchdown of the epic rally against Rice. On Monday morning, as the players flopped into their seats in the meeting room to watch the film, Watson assured them, as Rice went two touchdowns ahead: "All right, guys, don't anybody go away. We're gonna beat the hell out them in a minute."

On Thanksgiving Day, Texas rolled into College Station, cranked up a passing game and handed the Aggies their second loss, 21–6. Bryant was still having a problem beating teams that wore the despised orange jerseys.

It was a sad ending to a season that had taken a joyful turn, and to compound matters the Aggies were stuck at home, serving their probation for recruiting fouls. There would be no redemption.

"We knew all along that we couldn't go anywhere," said Gene Stallings, "and we didn't think about it. But toward the end of the 1955 season, Coach Bryant promised us a trip of some kind. I don't know if he meant to Caldwell or Hearne or Dallas or Hawaii, but he did say that if we won over Texas we were going to take a little trip. But we didn't win."

Bryant would confirm that he had arranged with the coach of the University of Hawaii to stage a so-called "exhibition" game with the Aggies. It would have been their Probation Bowl. "I had it all set up," said Bear. "We could have done it, then, because no one ever thought of it before and there was no rule against it."

"All I know," said Stallings, "is that we got beat bad by Texas, and it never came up again."

September 1956

The Aggies were about to end 12 years of frustration. They would do it against the odds, with victories that were seldom by comfortable margins, the outcome of most decided in the closing minutes.

It was like the story of the ship captain who brought a cargo of bananas from South America to San Francisco. When they docked, they were met by the merchant who had bought the bananas. And the captain began to explain what they had gone through: how stormy seas had threatened to capsize the ship; how they had to fight off pirates and survived a typhoon and all the crew had gotten scurvy . . .

And the merchant replied, "Just sell me the bananas."

In football, nobody sold bananas like Bear Bryant. And in 1956 the Aggies came within a tie of a perfect season, in the process overcoming at least one hurricane.

I will always believe that Bryant saved the second game that year, a 9–6 win over LSU, by not allowing an official to give in to the crowd. Tiger Stadium, in Baton Rouge, was a madhouse, as it usually is. Opposing teams call it the Pit. LSU was moving toward what would have been the winning touchdown with time running out. An LSU receiver caught a pass, right at the sideline, that would have kept the drive going. About the time the receiver's feet hit the ground, Bryant was there, having sprinted from his spot in front of the Aggie bench. He waved a finger in the official's face and (I learned later) yelled at him over the roar of the crowd: "If you got a gut in your body, you'll call it out of bounds."

The official signaled the pass was incomplete. A&M held on to win.

The Aggies were 3-and-0 when they made the short trip down the Hempstead Highway to meet the University of Houston Cougars. It was a physically bruising game that saw the Aggies lose a starting end, Bobby Drake Keith, with a broken jaw. The score was 14-all when the Aggies put the ball in play at their own five-yard line, with four minutes left. They raced the clock to the Houston one-yard line, with time for one last play.

Bryant started to let Loyd Taylor attempt the field goal, then had a baffling change of mind. "I figured that with Pardee and Crow in there," he said later, "we ought to get a yard." But Osborne kept the ball and rolled out, someone missed a block, and the Aggies were thrown for a loss.

The tie haunted them the rest of the year, if not longer. The call can only be understood by considering two factors: A field goal was still a kind of sissy weapon in the 1950s, certainly in the Bryant scheme of things. Nor was a kick from any distance, even an extra point, considered a sure thing. But most of all, the thought, the mere hint of being unable to gain one yard went against his grain. He would have seen it then as a form of surrender. The term was not in popular use at the time, but we are talking *macho* here.

All of this was a preamble to the clash with Texas Christian, ranked fourth in the nation and a convincing winner over Kansas, Arkansas and Alabama. The Horned Frogs had jumped to an 8-point favorite in the betting line after the Aggies were held to a draw by Houston.

In the four years that Bryant coached at A&M, the rivalry with TCU became special, as it had not been since the 1930s and would not be again. The feeling grew in part out of the respect between the coaches: the folksy, secure Abe Martin was one of the few in the conference who did not seem to resent Bryant. But the main attraction was the matchup of great teams, with talent quite similar. Each had a super back, John David Crow against Jim Swink, and an all-American tackle, Charlie Krueger versus Bob Lilly.

Swink, a senior, was a game-breaker whose touchdown runs were so spectacular that rival coaches requested TCU's films for their clinics. The week before Rice faced TCU, Coach Jess Neely showed his booster club the film of Swink scoring four times against Texas. On one run, he was all alone the last 40 yards, not a Texas player in the frame. "Our job," summed up Neely, "is to get someone in the picture with Swink." (Rice kept it close, but lost.)

The rivalries within the Southwest Conference require some explaining. Think of Lebanon and the several factions within the Muslim faith. Every game is a grudge match. A&M and Texas have been slugging it out since 1894, with the kind of hate that lasts a lifetime. TCU and SMU are geographic enemies (Fort Worth and Dallas), and join Baylor in the war of the church schools. Everyone has an axe out for Texas, but especially Arkansas, across the state line.

Texas high schools supply mostly homegrown talent for all the colleges. The recruiting is therefore more cutthroat than normal, and the players grow up knowing about each other.

These tensions and a few more had been dropped in the blender on October 20, 1956, when the Frogs and the Aggies, the preseason favorites, kicked off at old Kyle Field. The game was a sellout, with 42,000 plus taking their seats under hazy skies, with gusty winds offering only a suggestion of what was to come.

The scene that day was almost biblical in its fury and darkness. The Aggies drove to the TCU 25 in the first quarter, and were not to threaten again until the final period, fighting off frequent TCU raids and a roaring storm that reached hurricane proportions. The weather bureau measured the wind at gusts up to 110 miles an hour.

Chuck Curtis had completed his first six passes for the Frogs when a torrential rain came, lightning stabbed at the sky and the Kyle Field light towers swayed in the wind. Most of the spectators were driven to cover under the stands, but few left the stadium. Few would have dared the walk to the parking lot. The cadet corps held firm, wildly cheering each Aggie goal line stand.

The wind whipped umbrellas out of the hands of the few who thought to bring them, or turned the spokes and canvas inside out. After the game, the cleanup crew counted nearly 5,000 women's hats floating in the water under the stands, a sad reminder of fashion undone.

At Easterwood Airport, ten private planes were destroyed and nearly a hundred suffered damage. Plate glass windows were blown out on stores all over town, and the "Welcome to Bryan" sign on Texas Avenue was flattened.

The skies turned dark as night in the second quarter and from the press box, for several minutes, it was impossible to see the field. The wind kept blowing the ball off the line of scrimmage, and once the referee stopped the game and called both teams to midfield. No one could hear him, a fact that may have escaped the official, who waved them back into action.

In the eerie afternoon darkness, TCU had drives stopped at the Aggie 2, and once six inches from the goal, and at the 16-, 23- and 13-yard lines. At one point the Frogs had a first down at the 2.

Swink dived into the end zone, but a teammate was offsides, and on fourth down the Frogs lost the ball on a fumble at the 5.

Whereupon the Aggies fumbled it right back. An A&M penalty gave the Frogs five tries, and they failed to score, Jack Pardee twice meeting Swink at the goal line.

It is hard to imagine a game played under worse conditions, the fans wet and miserable and driven from their seats. But the game continued, the players leaning into the wind, sometimes blinded by the rain, reacting as much by feel as by sight.

For all the turbulence, the first half was scoreless. With phone lines to the press box cut off, Bryant had improvised by asking Elmer Smith to climb a ladder and wrap himself around one of the poles supporting the scoreboard. From that vantage point, Elmer would look out over the field, see what he could of the TCU formations, and drop notes to a manager who delivered them to the bench. He could brace himself against the scoreboard, but when the wind blew away his ladder Elmer was left clinging to the pole. "*Help*! Get me down from here!" he shouted, over and over. He was still there when the teams went to the dressing room at halftime, his cries unheard, hanging on with both arms to a pole that seemed to him to be swaying wildly. He made a nervous-looking steeplejack. When his absence in the locker room was noticed, Bryant sent someone out to rescue him.

The weather began to improve in the third quarter. Near the end of the period, another Aggie fumble enabled the Frogs to travel just 30 yards to the game's first score. From the 7, Curtis passed to end O'Day Williams, who caught the ball as he was falling out of the end zone. TCU missed the extra point and led, 6–0.

The Frogs threatened again after blocking an Aggie punt. But Don Watson intercepted a first-down pass in the end zone, and the Aggies started their game-winning drive from the 20. "The sun came out about that time," said Bryant later, finding it unnecessary to draw any symbolic connections. "We had an ole option play that I borrowed from Bud Wilkinson . . . it's really a quick flip, run or pass, and we put it to good use."

So they had. John David Crow ripped off a 21-yard gain, and then Watson broke loose for 37, all the way to the TCU 20. Crow cleared to the 8, and from there the Aggies faced a third-and-goal.

They had not attempted a pass all day. Roddy Osborne took the snap and headed to his left, then pitched out to Watson, who passed to Crow at the goal line for the touchdown. Taylor kicked the point that gave A&M a 7–6 lead with nine minutes to play. TCU would make only one first down the rest of the way.

No unbeaten team had a less likely statistic than those '56 Aggies. In a 10-game schedule, they completed a total of just 38 passes, 9 for touchdowns.

After the game, Bryant's press reception was brief. "There has never been a team with more guts," he said. "Now I want to get home and get out of these wet clothes. I don't want to die if I can help it, although this would be a good time."

Years later, Bryant reflected: "My son, Paul, who was about eleven, and I walked across the campus and all the way home, which gave me time to soak it all in. It was *sooo* good. That year we had a truly great football team. In our conference games we scored the first time we had the ball in the second half in every game but one, and that's pretty convincing."

The Southwest Conference has rarely had three stronger teams in one season than it had that year. The third was Baylor, big and tough, with a terror of a guard in Bill Glass and a halfback, Del Shofner, who would be a star in the NFL.

Played at Waco, the game was what Bryant called "a blood-letting." The tackling was so fierce that bodies just went sailing; it looked like the Flying Wallendas had come to town.

The Aggies won, 19–13, with a touchdown by Crow deciding it. As Bryant saw it, the ending was out of the sports pulp fiction of another day: "On fourth down from the six, with all the marbles riding on it, Crow said, 'Give me that cock-eyed ball and I'll put it in there.' And they did."

Another conversation in the huddle produced an earlier touchdown. "Roddy Osborne hit Watson on a long pass," said Jones Ramsey, "after the players argued with him in the huddle that he couldn't throw the ball that far."

There was a sidelight to the game little noticed that day. It was to be the last time Kenneth Hall suited up for the Aggies. Jack Pardee had been favoring an injured shoulder; by the end of the season both would be hurt. Bryant had told Hall during the week that he would start, for the first time, against Baylor. Just before the kickoff, he changed his mind. Or, perhaps Pardee changed it for him. Jack kept glaring at him, according to Bear, until he put him back in the lineup.

Hall saw spot service. On one play, he took a handoff and bolted over the middle for a gain of 12 yards. But he fumbled as he was hit, Bryant yanked him from the game and he never returned. He made up his mind that night to leave the team.

Later, too late, the film showed that the run was a beauty, with two or three Baylor tacklers bouncing off Hall. The fumble was a fluke. Someone's knee hit the ball.

With A&M unbeaten after eight starts, the NCAA Council met on November 13, four days before the Rice game, to vote on whether to lift the team's probation. The Southwest Conference had already done so at its spring meeting.

In spite of a surprising display of support from some of their rivals, the Aggies were given no relief by the NCAA. Bryant had been openly critical of what he regarded as the selective enforcement of the rules by the organization and its executive head, Walter Byars. Privately, Bear felt the probation was continued because part of the original punishment had been without effect. The NCAA had released from their letters of intent all 95 freshmen recruited by the Aggies in 1955. Free to sign with any other school in the country, every prospect kept his commitment.

Ed Price, of Texas, spoke up: "Our feeling was expressed by our conference some time ago. A&M would have been a terrific attraction and a worthy opponent for any team in the United States." TCU's Abe Martin echoed the sentiment: "The ruling stymies a top bowl team."

Bryant was depressed that week, bitter that his team would not appear in a postseason game for the second year, fearful that the news would cause a letdown against a dangerous Rice team.

He was unable to sleep the night before the game. At around three o'clock, he slipped out of bed, careful not to wake Mary Harmon, dressed and drove aimlessly for an hour or so before he finally swung into his parking spot at Kyle Field. Elmer Smith noticed the light on when he entered his own office a little after 5:00 A.M.

*   *   *

After a while, Bryant poked his head in the doorway and asked if Smith would mind taking a ride with him. Elmer described what happened next:

"We drove through the back streets of College Station just as dawn was breaking. Coach Bryant never said a word. Finally, we stopped at an old frame house, a mile or so from the campus. A small boy, about ten years old, was on the porch crying. His mother was trying to console him. Coach Bryant got out of the car, went up to the boy and put his arm around him. You could see him talking to the mother. After a few minutes he returned to the car.

"I didn't know what in the world was going on. He didn't say anything on the way back to the office. When we got there the other coaches had started to arrive and it was time to think about the game. He was worried about the team not being ready for Rice, but we won [21–7]."

The coaches offices were next to the players' locker rooms. There was nothing fancy or modern about any of it. The whole area was uncarpeted, dark and sometimes damp.

"Nearly everybody had cleared out," he went on, "and Coach came over and said, 'Elmer, if you're wondering what that was all about this morning, I ran over a little dog on the way to work. It was too early to go around waking people. But before I could think about the game, I had to go back and find the right house. When you saw me talking to that little boy, I was just telling him there would be a new puppy at his door this afternoon."

And there was.

I no longer recall how long I waited before I wrote that story for my newspaper, or if I wrote it the way Elmer Smith had told it. The story was too private, too tender, almost too cornball to print, and I suspected that some people would not believe Coach Bryant capable of it.

Now with Texas coming up, the Aggies were closing in on an unbeaten season. Bryant took an approach to the game that had to startle anyone familiar with his history. On his weekly television show, which aired the Sunday before the game, Bear said flatly that the Aggies were the better team and if they played up to their ability Texas had no chance to win.

His co-host was Lloyd Gregory, a former Houston sports editor and a Texas ex. Lloyd had brought along one of those bobble-head football dolls they sell at the stadiums, this one in Longhorn colors, and he parked it on the desk in front of them. The forcefulness of Bryant's prediction surprised Gregory, too. He asked Bear why the Aggies seemed to have so much trouble beating Texas. "I don't know," he said. "They just seem to hate us more than we hate them." And then he took a swipe at the doll, whose head bobbed furiously for the next several seconds. Bear liked the effect and, for the rest of the show, whenever his co-host mentioned Texas, he swatted the doll.

The game had taken on a meaning for him that went beyond a conference title and an undefeated season, and apart from the fact that they had nowhere to go. Beating Texas, healing all the old Aggie wounds, was what he had been hired to do.

He would not allow anything to go wrong. Crow and Taylor were in the lineup, even though each of them had a broken bone in his foot. Bryant refused to bring his team out of the locker room until after the Longhorns had played their song, "The Eyes of Texas." He was not going to have his players blasted with it as they hit the field, and the crowd roaring, a musical reminder that this was Memorial Stadium. Even when one of the officials told him Texas was on the field, waiting, he shook his head and said: "I haven't heard that song yet." The kickoff was delayed five minutes, until the Texas band struck up "The Eyes," after which the Aggie team appeared.

The Aggies jumped out to a 14–0 lead and controlled the tempo, but Texas scored just before the half. Then Jack Pardee returned the kickoff 85 yards for a touchdown to open the third quarter. He ran back another one 54 yards and intercepted a pass as the Aggies won it, 34–21, to smash forever the Memorial Stadium jinx.

"We were about five touchdowns better than Texas," Bryant would remember. "But as late as the fourth quarter, we were leading by only a touchdown."

Added Jones Ramsey: "I was impressed with how much the Longhorns played over their heads. A&M was never really in any danger of losing. But the Aggies respected that tradition, and they lived in fear until the end."

Bryant had told the players before the game they would not spend the night in Austin. One of his theories was that after living the monastic life in College Station, they tended to get a little crazy at the thought of all those Texas coeds. After the game, his players threw him into the shower to celebrate the win and the conference title. When he emerged, he said, "My limited vocabulary won't permit me to tell you how proud I am of you. I didn't mean it about not staying over. Act like a champion. Have a good time. And I'll see you next week."

The championship was their first since 1941. The Aggies had not gone unbeaten since 1939.

Meanwhile, the loss assured Texas of a coaching change. Ed Price was out. A young contender for the job was Darrell Royal, the onetime Oklahoma quarterback, then coaching at Washington. Royal had asked Bud Wilkinson to recommend him, and his former coach said he would. He called Bryant for an endorsement and Bear told him, "Hell, no, Darrell. I don't want you coming in here and whipping our ass."

Texas hired Royal. Later, D. X. Bible would remember Royal asking how much Wilkinson's support had helped him get the job. "What do you mean?" said Bible. "Bud didn't call."

Royal did a double-take. "Then, who did recommend me?"

Bible was surprised he didn't know. "Paul Bryant," he said.

Bryant thought the '57 team would be his best. But in his home one night, as he reviewed the season just past, he had amends to make. "What some people didn't appreciate," he said, including himself, "was that boy backing up the line all year with two bad shoulders."

He meant Pardee, who had a storybook career—is still having one—but was at times overshadowed by Crow. Bryant may have made up for his earlier slights by crediting Jack, in his autobiography, with catching the pass that gave the Aggies their only victory in 1954. Years later, when this distinction was remarked upon, Pardee said, "That's not right. Gene Stallings and I were the starting ends in that game and I think Gene caught the pass for the touchdown. I caught a short one to set it up."

Unused to hearing Bryant contradicted by his former players, I asked Pardee if this were the sort of detail he remembered clearly. Could his memory be trusted? "I believe so," he said. "I also remember that we were driving for a score, and I let a defensive man shoot the gap, throw us for a loss and kill the drive. That was when Coach Bryant decided to move me from end to fullback."

In the class of high school ball that spawned Jack Pardee, careful records were not kept, but he may have been the greatest scorer in six-man football the state of Texas ever knew. His senior year he scored 57 touchdowns.

High school was at Christoval, in West Texas, with a student body of less than 100, the sons and daughters of farmers and oilfield workers.

One reason we can be sure that religion is important in Texas is because people keep comparing it to high school football. Pardee would laugh out loud when he remembered his high school career. Not because it was funny, but because it made him feel good all over. It was like looking at your baby pictures.

In the six-man lineup, Pardee was one of two halfbacks. The other positions were, and are, the quarterback, center and two ends. The game was still being played in the 1980s, in West Texas and other rural areas of the country. "Where you don't have consolidated schools," said Pardee, "and maybe ten boys are big enough or good enough or have the time to play, you don't have much choice.

"It's an exciting game. The ball has to be in the air on every play—a lateral or a pass. It's against the rules to run a quarterback keeper. The defense is too spread out. What you end up with is no offensive linemen, just skill people."

If certain economic trends continue, you reflect that six-man football could be the basis for a new professional league.

Pardee went into coaching, produced winning teams with the Bears and Redskins and won championships in the two expansion leagues, the WFL and the USFL. Coaches have come out of un-expected backgrounds, including the Ivy League. But Jack is the only one we ever heard of who was a product of six-man football.

Replacing Pardee at fullback would be the undoing of the '57 Aggies. And Bryant may have suspected as much when he praised him that night in his home. But he was in general very upbeat, and Ramsey and I sat there with him in his den, talking football, long after the other writers and the last guests had left and Mrs. Bryant had gone to bed.

The den was long and narrow with a parquet floor and big, comfortable chairs. It was where Bryant watched football games on television, or listened to them on the radio. It was pleasant that night, drinking and talking, although the coach and Ramsey did more of the former and I led in the latter category.

At one point, I said something that caused Bryant to sit up and ask, "Does it matter to you what people think?"

I said it did.

He looked at me closely. "Why?"

I said, "I guess I want to be liked."

He sat back in his chair with a kind of thump. "I'd rather be right," he said. "As long as I know I'm right, I don't give a damn about the rest."

Bryant did not laugh at anyone's weaknesses. Over the decades he had a few of his own. But he thought you had to be honest about them, or you wouldn't win.

That night in his home, he noticed I was not taking notes. "I don't see you writing anything down," he said, suspiciously. (I admired Tex Maule, who rarely took notes, and had told me, "If they say anything interesting I'll remember it." Of course, I did not know then how often Tex made up quotes.) I told Coach Bryant that this was an experiment. He said, almost too eagerly, "Okay, let's have a little quiz."

He asked me to repeat certain things he had said about his players. I blew the first four or five questions and he commanded, "Okay, get out your pad and pencil and we'll start over."

Of course, miniature tape recorders were not yet in fashion. His point was that his players were going to read what he was quoted as saying, and he wanted it to be right.

The next morning, a Sunday, the phone in my motel room rang eagerly. As I fumbled for it, I glanced at my watch—it was 6:30. Coach Bryant was on the line. He asked if I was awake and I said, sure, of course. He said, "Good. Do you have your notes from last night?"

Puzzled, I said yes.

"Do me a favor," he mumbled. "I had a little too much to drink and may have said some things I don't want in the paper. Read your notes back to me."

I had him then. It was all I could do to keep from laughing. I said, "Okay, Coach. Let's have a little quiz."

After only three years, I had reached a point where I could second-guess him. That fall of 1957, on my weekly trips to A&M, Bryant began saving a seat for me when he had lunch with his coaches in the cafeteria. We would sit there without trays, eating the good food, rich in carbohydrates, that Bryant had ordered for his players. And the other coaches accepted me, and assumed that because I was with Coach Bryant I understood what they were talking about when he brought up a change he wanted to make, or discussed some new technique they had tried.

He had a talented staff, and always did, wherever he went. Bum Phillips, who would earn a national reputation of his own, had joined the Aggies that spring out of high school jobs in towns named Port Neches and Nederland. Phil Cutchin and J. T. King would go on to head coaching jobs. And Willie Zapalac should have had one. He later worked for Darrell Royal, and in 1985 Willie was with Bum, in New Orleans, where both ended their long careers.

One day Bryant looked up from his lunch and said, "I guarantee you, Richard Gay would be an all-American if we moved him from fullback to center."

I thought that was a pretty strong statement. When no one commented, I said, "Then why don't you move him to center, Coach?"

And Bryant turned in his seat and said to me, "Well, Coach, if I did that who the hell would play fullback?"

Gay was a head-hunter out of Louisiana who may have been as fine a one-on-one tackler as A&M ever had. He was mean enough to play in the line. I thought I knew who Bear could move to fullback, but the other coaches had enjoyed his retort so much that I kept my mouth shut.

And Bryant second-guessed himself the rest of that year, and for many more to come. Long after he was a legend at Alabama, he said, "I did a lousy job not making some changes that summer. I should have put Crow at fullback so we could have run the option both ways. Then I could have put Gay at center, with Roddy Osborne or Bobby Joe Conrad at left half. We had Jimmy Wright and Charley Milstead for quarterback. I thought about it right up to fall practice, but got talked out of it. We would have won the national title if I had made those changes. I don't think it would have been close."

In hindsight, the change appealed to me because I thought Jimmy Wright deserved a crack at quarterback. Out of Edinburg, Wright had an NFL arm and a happy disposition. Smokey Harper, who had an uncanny ability to judge what was inside a player, loved him. In four years, Jimmy never spent a minute in the whirlpool. At practice, he always hit the field first and left it last. He did not pose a big threat at running the option, but that wasn't the reason he never became the Aggie starter.

"We would have won the national title with Jimmy," said Bobby Marks, the all-conference end, who later coached under Bryant at Alabama. "But Jimmy was kind of independent. Of all the kids Coach Bryant recruited that first year, he was the only one who wouldn't go to him and say, 'Coach, here's my body. Mold me.' "

As did so many of the others, Wright went into coaching and had a turn as a head coach, at Wichita State.

The Aggies opened the 1957 season in Dallas, with a 21–13 victory over a good Maryland team. More interesting to me than the game was the press gathering later in one of the small banquet rooms at the old Adolphus Hotel. Dr. Curly Byrd was there, still the president of Maryland, now beaming on the Bear and enjoying the success of this wayward child. It was a kick to hear them tease each other, Bryant and the man who had launched his career, then chased him away.

Dr. Byrd was in the back of the room, standing, taking it all in, when Harold Ratliff, with the Associated Press, known in the trade as the Needle, kept egging Bryant on about being a genius. He kept asking Bryant if he thought he was one. When Bear tried to change the subject, and talk about how slow or small or thin his Aggies were, Harold would dig him some more: "That doesn't matter, Bear, 'cause you're a genius. Admit it."

Finally, one of the Aggie assistants, Pat James, could stand it no longer. "Harold," he spoke up, "there are no geniuses in coaching."

Then Bryant's deep voice rumbled across the room. "Pat," he said, quickly, "do you want to keep your job?"

The Aggies thundered on, and after six games were ranked first in the nation, followed by Oklahoma, Auburn and Michigan State. Their string of games without a loss had reached 18, and if Bear needed anything to keep him humble there was a trip coming to Fayetteville. The hills were alive with the sound of the Arkansas fans calling the pigs, with their famous cry of "Sooey," repeated over and over, followed by sharp, ear-piercing whistles. It was not exactly a sound confused with violins.

A crowd of 60,000 packed the stadium to see the Aggies fight off an upset bid by the Razorbacks, another Top Ten team. With a minute and 20 seconds left, the Aggies led, 7–6, and had the ball at the Arkansas 12-yard line. Bryant sent in a sub to tell Roddy Osborne to keep the ball on the ground and *use up the clock*. It was Osborne's intention to do so when he called an option, with Crow as the flanker. He planned to run the ball wide, but when he made his fake he looked up and saw two things: an Arkansas tackle on top of him and John David wide open at the goal line. The next thing he knew, the ball was in the air.

An Arkansas halfback named Donny Horton, a track sprinter, anticipated the play. He cut in front of Crow, intercepted the pass and at full gallop set sail for the Aggie end zone, and victory, 91 yards away.

Only Osborne had a chance to get him. Bryant always called Roddy the slowest back on the team, but he not only matched Horton step for step, he fought off a blocker and made the tackle just inside the 30, keeping the play in bounds and the clock running. While Horton was dashing down the sideline, past Bryant and the Aggie bench, ecstatic Arkansas fans began to pour out of the stands.

The Hogs completed a pass to the 19, where Crow made a touchdown-saving tackle. A run picked up just two more, and on the next play George Walker threw for the end zone, where Crow made the interception to save the win. Bryant called them two of the greatest defensive plays he ever saw.

On Monday, Bryant made his usual phone calls to coaches around the country. He described the Arkansas finish to Bobby Dodd of Georgia Tech, who said: "Bear, there's one thing I don't understand. If Osborne is as slow as you say, and the Arkansas boy is as fast as you claim, how did your boy make the tackle?"

Bryant replied, with conviction: "Oh, Bobby, that's easy. The Arkansas boy was just running for a touchdown. Osborne was running for his *life*."

With a win over SMU the next week, the Aggie streak had reached 19 games without a loss. But they had run out of great escapes. The heartbreak they almost discovered in the Ozarks was waiting for them now in Houston.

Returning to the scene of their unforgettable rally in '55, the Aggies blew the whole package: their unbeaten string, their number

1 rank in the land and another conference title. The Aggies fumbled six times and had three drives stopped inside the 20. The Owls won, 7–6.

Rice quarterback King Hill made the all-America team that day, scoring his team's touchdown on a sneak from the 1, kicking the extra point, intercepting two passes and punting out of bounds at the 1 in the final four minutes.

The Aggies had needed four downs to score from the 2, Osborne carrying on each play and finally slicing over left tackle, starting the fourth quarter. But Loyd Taylor's kick for the tying point was wide.

The Aggies got the ball for the last time after Hill's magnificent punt nailed them to their own goal. Still, they made a valiant effort to pull it out, driving 75 yards against the clock to the Rice 24. Crow broke loose for 21 and seemed to have a clear field in front of him, but he stumbled and King Hill made the tackle.

The Aggies just missed breaking the play they needed as time ran out. It was a trick play called the Bumarooski, in honor of the coach who designed it, Bum Phillips. The play involved a direct snap to a halfback, who placed the ball on the *ground*, behind the legs of a halfback in front of him. Then the back who took the snap wheeled and faked to the fullback coming around the right side. As the defense pulled toward the fake, the halfback (Taylor) picked up the ball and broke up the middle.

The play had been crafted for Bobby Joe Conrad, who was not in the game. It required a five-second delay, but Taylor, a little overanxious, beat the count. They gained nine yards, to the 24, but the Aggies needed a touchdown, and the clock ran out before they could get off a final pass.

Before the kickoff, Bryant had asked me to stop by his room at the Shamrock Hilton after the game. I wasn't certain the invitation still held, but I went. He was alone with Mary Harmon and two friends, Bob and Kate Bernath, from College Station. Bob sponsored his TV show. Bear was in a sullen and almost silent mood, but finally was persuaded to go downstairs to the Cork Club for dinner.

A story had appeared in the papers that morning reviving the rumor of Bryant accepting the Alabama job. I think he may have wanted to talk about the story, but changed his mind. He was in no mood now to talk about anything. He was nursing a Scotch when a man approached the table, introduced himself as an Aggie, said that no matter what happened that day they were behind him, and offered his hand. Bryant ignored it, lifted his glass and took a long, slow drink.

The embarrassed stranger withdrew his hand, wished him luck against Texas and fled. Bryant never looked up.

Kate Bernath could not contain herself. "Paul," she said, "I believe that was the rudest thing I have ever seen. You made that man feel like a fool."

"Good!" said Bear, slapping his glass down. "That's exactly how I wanted him to feel."

His team had suffered a defeat as big as any in his career, and he was mad and miserable and he did not want a partner. The scene is not one Bryant would have remembered proudly. Chances are he would not have remembered it at all. In his early and middle years, the Bear, as the saying goes, did not suffer fools gladly. He did not suffer losing gladly. He did not suffer suffering gladly.

Chapter 7

Mama Called

November 28, 1957

Bryant always said that to be successful a coach needed two things: a five-year contract and an understanding wife. Mary Harmon went through the entire cycle: she cried when she first saw College Station, and she cried the day they left. But in no time, she was so pleased to be back in Alabama that Bear wished he had made the move years earlier.

Leaving A&M may have been the hardest move of all. To begin with, it was the first time he quit a job simply because of another offer. He felt his hand had been forced at Maryland, where Dr. Curly Byrd meddled in his team, and at Kentucky, where he resented the large shadow of Adolph Rupp.

It was clear to anyone around him, as well as to those who supported either A&M or Alabama, that Bryant had postponed the decision as long as he could. His name cropped up whenever the Tide had a coaching vacancy, or seemed likely to have one. But as late as the second week in November, Bryant turned them down. He had recommended his friend, Jim Tatum, his successor at Maryland, then the coach at North Carolina.

But Dr. Frank Rose kept insisting that Alabama planned to hire a coach "with a remarkable record in his profession . . . a good recruiter, who knows the South—a nationally recognized man."

The description sounded familiar. But the rumors had been in print since October. Even George Preston Marshall, owner of the Redskins, got into the act. Marshall had tried to hire Bryant away from Kentucky back in '49. "I asked Paul about the rumors and he said they were absolutely untrue. He has a long-term contract at A&M, he is happy there and intends to honor that contract." Marshall added that Bryant had suggested the names of two other coaches, besides Tatum: Frank Moseley of Virginia Poly, and Harry Gilmer, the old Alabama passing great.

After the Rice game, the Birmingham papers began quoting unidentified friends as saying that the Bear was coming. "Aw, that's the same old stuff," he said. "I can't get any work done for the telephone ringing. I'm trying to get ready for the Texas game and that's the only thing I want to talk about."

I asked him one day if it might not dispose of all the speculation if he said, flatly, that he would not return to Alabama. "No, I wouldn't want to say that," he said, "because I might do it."

I believe I knew right then that A&M had lost him. But it only meant, I told myself, that his mind was still open.

Texas gave the knife another twist by beating them, 9–7, for the third time in the Bear's four years. The Longhorns scored in the first six minutes, after a 62-yard quick kick by Walter Fondren rolled dead at the Aggie 4. The winning points came on a 38-yard field goal in the third period by Bobby Lackey, the Texas quarterback, who ran and passed for a total of 36 yards, in a game dominated by the defenses.

A&M was scoreless until the fourth quarter. In defeat, Crow was magnificent. He carried the ball 21 times for 64 hard yards. He completed a pass, and caught one from Osborne for 57 yards, running past one defender and right through another. He was tackled at the 10, and three plays later scored from the 1. He was all over the field, knocking down passes and making tackles. And after his catch and long run, he was slow to get up, like a fighter trying to clear the cobwebs. He was the picture of an athlete completely spent, who would take to the locker room nothing but his bones and a uniform soaked and soiled.

The Aggies had lost two games and the conference title by three points, and fallen from number 1 in the nation to number 10. Rice became the host team in the Cotton Bowl. Texas went to the Sugar Bowl with a 5-4-1 record. The Aggies would have to settle for the Gator Bowl, in Jacksonville, against Tennessee.

After the Texas game, Bryant was still unprepared to confirm that he was bound for Alabama. But he was, and he had stretched the language as far as he could to keep from denying it. I felt the same as the players: I wasn't going to believe it until I heard him say the words.

The writers elbowed their way into his tiny office, jammed so tightly they could identify the brand of deodorant the next guy was wearing, if any. Bear began to talk. And I knew he was gone.

He said that the loss to Texas had no influence either way on his decision. "I'd like to think I haven't considered it yet," he said. "I'd like to think I have been preparing for Texas.

"There is one and only one reason that I would consider [the Alabama job]." The furrows in his forehead deepened, and his words came slowly. I had the distinct feeling that he was speaking now to the people who had supported him at A&M and the players he would be leaving behind.

"When you were out playing as a kid, say you heard your mother call you. If you thought she just wanted you to do some chores, or come in for supper, you might not answer her. But if you thought she *needed* you, you'd be there in a hurry."

This became known as the "Mama Called" speech. No one had done so much for motherhood since Al Jolson. Still, to the people who knew him best, that sentiment said it all.

The answer was not quite a yes but considerably more than a maybe. The delay was not hard to understand. The Aggie season had ended in ashes. Bryant felt he owed it to the team to stay through the bowl trip, after they were banned in 1955 and 1956, the probation years.

It is not clear, even now, when the Bear ever directly told the Aggies that he was leaving to return to Alabama. I know he tried. Twice, three times, he started to tell them why he had to go back to Alabama. He never finished. He finally left the room, and I think Carney Laslie and Phil Cutchin answered the players' questions as best they could.

He had not signed a contract yet. It is possible he had not even agreed on all the terms. The night of the Texas game, a few of us had dropped by his home, and I was standing at his elbow when he took a phone call from an old Alabama classmate. I could not hear the exact words, but there was no problem guessing the question: "Look, Paul, I won't tell anybody if you ask me not to, but everybody is going crazy over here wanting to know if it's true. Are you coming back?"

This was an old friend Bryant had known nearly 30 years. He said, "It's sonsabitches like you who cost me the national championship," and he slammed the receiver.

He was going back to where he belonged, to the one job he always knew one day he would want, and now he felt guilty about it. And he was mad at himself for feeling guilty.

I could indulge in no more wishful thinking of my own. I felt a lot of what the players felt, and more. Win or lose, like him or not, they were going to leave every four years. For all I knew, I might still be writing about college football the rest of my life, and I could not imagine covering the Aggies without Bear Bryant. It would be like interviewing the furniture. I was prepared to do some serious sulking.

But there was no reason to hold back the story. In the December 1 edition of the *Post*, I wrote that the decision was final, that Bryant had accepted the jobs of head coach and athletic director at Alabama, responding to his old school's SOS.

Two days later, I filed a follow-up story:

College Station — Texas A&M, a familiar name in coaching traffic, Monday granted with regret Paul Bryant's request for a release from his contract and immediately set in motion the machinery to hire its fifth head coach in 10 years.

Bryant informed Dr. Chris Groneman, chairman of the

athletic council, that he would continue to coach the team through its Gator Bowl assignment December 28 at Jackson-ville, Florida.

The story said that Carney Laslie would leave for Tuscaloosa to organize the recruiting effort for the new Alabama staff. Phil Cutch-in's name was mentioned as a possible candidate for the A&M job, although the players were known to favor one of the lesser known assistants, Bum Phillips. The Aggies were gracious to Bryant in their public statements.

"It would be wonderful to get a coach of national reputation," Dr. Groneman observed, "who could continue what Paul has started. He did a magnificent job and just about the impossible. A&M is better off for his having been here. We certainly wish him well."

A certain amount of editorial bias crept into the copy:

> The Aggies are not back where they started four years ago, when Bryant left Kentucky to perform the most rapid and complete transformation in college football.
>
> He took the challenge out of the Aggie job. He restored their winning tradition, reopened the recruiting channels and for three giddy weeks in 1957 had them atop the national standings.

There is no point now in trying to debate the morality of coaches breaking long-term contracts, or the hurts suffered by the players who came to a school, believing in the man who recruited them.

Bryant had been steadfast in this respect at A&M, refusing to give any prospect his word that he would not leave. He had made and not kept such a promise at Kentucky and vowed not to repeat that error. He would not commit himself again to a recruiting class for four years until 1979, at Alabama, and he felt free to give that assurance because he had a record to break, and he planned to coach until the record fell.

That December of 1957 was a strange and listless and bittersweet month at Aggieland. Bryant worked hard on the game plan and was attentive to the players. He did not act like a fellow who had a date to be somewhere else.

Crow received the Heisman Trophy that month, and Bryant sent

Elmer Smith, the man who recruited him, to accompany John David to New York. Crow was the third Southwest Conference player to win the award, joining Davey O'Brien of TCU (1938) and Doak Walker of SMU (1949). He was Bryant's only Heisman winner.

Crow won under difficult conditions. He was a two-way player, whose contribution on defense went unmeasured. He rarely carried the ball more than 10 or 12 times a game. One night he carried 7, and reporters asked his coach if anything was wrong with him. "There is nothing wrong with John David," snapped Bryant, "that giving him the ball wouldn't cure."

The Heisman voting had not yet become a kind of Star Wars on Madison Avenue, fought with four-color advertising fliers and a blizzard of numbers. Crow's stats were never that impressive. He did not lead the country, or even the conference, in rushing or scoring his senior year. In fact, he gained a little over 500 yards. But Bryant had an answer. He told Jones Ramsey to go through the play-by-play charts of the season, and he would find that Crow led the nation in a category called, "Players Run Over."

(Ramsey used the same stat 20 years later to help the case of Earl Campbell, of Texas.)

The campaign to snare the Heisman Trophy for Crow consisted, really, of one sentence, but it was mighty effective. The line was Bryant's: "If John David doesn't win the Heisman, they ought to stop giving it." To this day, Crow believes those words won it for him.

But Crow was no invention. He ran inside and he ran wide, he caught passes and on occasion he threw them. He returned kicks, played safety and never missed a tackle in three years. He was a picture player, 6'2" and 220, with power and speed, and he loved to hit, gloried in the roughness of the game.

Crow was the first player picked in the NFL draft that year, and played 11 seasons with the Cardinals and 49ers. In his first pro game, he ran 83 yards for a touchdown. Always an unselfish player, he volunteered to play tight end in his final season with the 49ers, even though he needed only 41 yards to join an elite group of backs who had gained 5,000 yards on the ground, in the days of the 12-game schedule.

The trip to New York may have been more exciting for Smith than for Crow. The season had been a rigorous and emotional one for the coaches, and Elmer was impressed with the hospitality of the Downtown Athletic Club. There was always another cocktail party, with waiters weaving past carrying trays of glasses that were always filled. Elmer had been home a week when the chancellor, Dr. Tom Harrington, stopped by his office to personally deliver a copy of a group photograph taken in a New York night club.

"Elmer, you told me in New York you wanted this," the chancellor said.

"To tell you the truth, Dr. Harrington," said Elmer, "I didn't even know they took a picture."

I had followed Bryant and Crow, the Junction Boys and the Team of Tomorrow, for four years and now it was ending. I felt a confusion far out of whack with what my obligations as a reporter required. I had collected a variety of wild and original memories, gained some exposure as a writer, and made friendships I hoped would last.

But there was a fear that related in some way to any kind of graduation night. It is the feeling you get that you will never be this young again, or have so much fun, or share such different times. You just know that a part of you is gone. You sign the yearbooks and swear to stay in touch, and 10 or 20 years later you attend a reunion and stare across the room at faces you can't quite identify.

Three of us from the *Post*, Clark Nealon, John Hollis and myself, flew to Jacksonville to cover Bryant's farewell as the Aggie coach. One night, Clark, who had given both John and me our starts, turned in early and told the two of us to check out the town. A cab driver wound up taking us to a joint on the outskirts of town, where I got into a crooked dice game and lost most of my expense money.

No one did very well that week concentrating on the game, including the A&M players. When Bryant complained one day to the coaches about how distracted the team seemed, someone finally got up the nerve to tell him it was because they had been unable to sell their game tickets. Bear told one of the coaches to gather them all up and he'd buy the damned things himself, and he did. They probably took 50 players to Florida, and each received two complimentary tickets. Under the circumstances, they were probably glad to get $10 apiece for them. It must have cost Coach Bryant a thousand dollars just to begin getting their minds on the game.

He knew how unsettled most of them were and what little heart they had for the game. But he was determined not to let them be embarrassed. Before practice one day, at the team meeting, Bryant paced the floor until everyone in the room began to fidget. Then he began to turn and single out different players and just zap them:

"You know what they're saying about you, Crow? They're saying you don't care anything about this game. You just want to make sure you don't get hurt so you can sign a big pro contract.

"Krueger. You know what they're saying about you? They say you don't give a damn, either. All you're worrying about is which all-star game you're gonna play in and how much it pays."

Crow and Krueger had literally jumped in their seats and now all the players were up straight, waiting, every eye in the room on Coach Bryant. He would walk around and then stop and point:

"Osborne. You're not thinking about this game. You're thinking about some banquet you're going to speak at.

"And Richard Gay. Your mind isn't on football. Football can't do anything for you. You're thinking about getting married and falling into a $50,000-a-year job."

He kept moving. "John Tracy. You know what they're saying about you? They're saying you won't even go on the field. You've been hurt all year and you're petting yourself and feeling sorry for yourself and you probably won't even suit up."

The thing is, Bear had struck some nerves. It was money time for Crow and Krueger. Gay was engaged to a girl whose father was very big in Coca-Cola stock. And Tracy had not played back to his sophomore form.

Then Bryant stood in the center of the room and did a slow turn. "Do you know what they're saying about the rest of you? Nothing. Not a damned thing. They don't think you'll play good enough to mention."

He let that sink in. Then he raised his voice just a tad. "And do you know who *they* are?" He crooked his thumb at his own chest. "Me. I'm the one saying all those things."

Then he walked out the door and headed toward the practice field for the only good workout the Aggies would have that week. They played a gutsy game against a good Tennessee team, and lost, 3–0. They had a chance to win it late, maybe two chances. But the only thing I really remember about the game is John David Crow tackling Bobby Gordon, the Tennessee tailback, in the open field, colliding head-on like two freight trains, and for an instant both of them appearing to be knocked out.

That was how the season and the Bear Bryant era ended at Texas A&M, with losses by one, two and three points.

Three Aggies were voted to the College All-Stars, who upset the NFL champion Detroit Lions in Chicago, 35–19, in the summer of 1958. Krueger started at tackle. Crow was recovering from a knee injury and did not suit out, and the unlikely hero of the game, and most valuable player, turned out to be his understudy, Bobby Joe ,Conrad.

Conrad came off the bench to kick four field goals, a feat that led to a funny exchange in the locker room of the All-Stars. Reporters asked Conrad how many field goals he kicked in college.

"None," he replied.

How many did you attempt?

"None."

Conrad explained that Loyd Taylor was the Aggie place kicker during his varsity years at A&M. Bryant started the player who performed best in practice, and during the week Taylor out-kicked him.

Then Bobby Joe revealed that the closest he came to kicking a field goal was against SMU in 1957. The Aggies led in the fourth quarter, 12–7, and faced a fourth-and-five situation at about the 20. Taylor was on the bench, ineligible to return under the complicated substitution rules of that period. The kick was within Conrad's range and they clearly needed more points, with SMU's sophomore passer, Don Meredith, playing bombs away.

Coaching from the sidelines was then a 15-yard penalty, so while the Aggies talked it over in the huddle, Bryant tossed out the kicking tee. Eagerly, sensing his big opportunity at last, Conrad picked it up. A piece of adhesive had been taped to the bottom of the tee with instructions to run Crow off tackle. John David picked up the first down and the Aggies went on to score.

A brief argument developed over who should attempt the extra point. Crow did, taking the position that it was his touchdown, his kick. The point was good. The Aggies won, 19–7.

Conrad had a long and productive career in the pros as a wide receiver, and doubled as a kicker until the specialists took over.

*   *   *

You can measure the status Bryant had achieved by the difficulty the Aggies had in replacing him. They staged a coaching hunt that reached such comic heights that *Life* magazine ran a major feature story on it, with a double-page photograph of the house the Aggies had given Bear, and then bought back from him for $27,500, a handsome price in the 1950s. It was a rambling, one-story, all-brick contemporary home, in a nice neighborhood.

The headline on the *Life* story read: A $27,500 HOUSE GOES BEGGING AT TEXAS A&M. While the athletic council was conducting the official search for Bryant's replacement, certain well-to-do Aggie exes were holding interviews on their own.

Among the early contenders were Red Sanders and Jim Tatum. I was at Bryant's home the night Sanders and his wife came calling. I thought I had stumbled across some inside information when I overheard Mary Harmon tell Mrs. Sanders that the commode in the master bathroom needed fixing. The next day I wrote the story that Sanders had the job. It was the first of many wrong guesses by many writers.

At various times the Aggies seemed to have everyone lined up but Amos Alonzo Stagg. Duffy Daugherty said no, but recommended Dan Devine, who was not well enough known for the Aggie exes. Then Frank Leahy, of Notre Dame fame, was announced as the new athletic director and head coach, in what appeared to be a real coup for A&M.

The next day, Leahy qualified it by saying he was "ninety-nine percent sure" he would accept the jobs. At the time, he was in a hospital, where doctors soon announced his health would not permit him to return to football.

All the while, stories from "reliable sources" kept popping up, one day's reports at odds with the previous day's exclusive. In January, one paper reported that Jim Myers of Iowa State would be the new coach. While Myers and his wife were on the campus, the ex-students flew in Eddie Erdelatz and his staff from Navy.

Myers withdrew, before learning that Erdelatz had said no. Caroline Myers was quoted in papers across the country saying, "I'm glad we didn't go into a situation where the alumni seem to have that much control."

A week later, the Aggies introduced their new coach: Jim Myers.

In Tuscaloosa, Paul Bryant followed the developments with a

bemused interest. When a friend tried to tell him on the phone how bizarre the hunt had gotten, he laughed and said, "Yeah, I saw the picture of my house in *Life* magazine."

In the last three seasons, the Crimson Tide had won four games under J. B. (Ears) Whitworth, had scored once against Auburn and not at all on Tennessee. This was the kind of record Bryant had inherited at each of his stops. Of course, there would be no more stops. The return of Paul William Bryant was viewed in Alabama not simply as another coaching change.

It was a Restoration.

At his first press conference, Bear frowned as Benny Marshall, of the *Birmingham News*, said, "Coach, the alumni are expecting your team to go undefeated next season."

"The hell you say," said Bryant. "I'm an alumni, and I don't expect us to go undefeated."

Bryant wanted to clamp a lid on that kind of talk right off. Yet the runaway optimism of the Alabama faithful was not entirely unwelcome. Bear no longer had a pressing need to be the eternal, raggedy-assed underdog. His team would win the national title in his fourth season, giving new meaning to the phrase *five-year plan*.

If he was on the verge of growing rich in Texas, where friendly Aggies were cutting him in on oil and apartment deals and a car dealership, it would happen bigger and faster in 'Bama. Sponsors flocked to him. In keeping with the campaign to beautify America, highways across the state were decorated with billboards featuring the likeness of Bryant. In one hand he clutched a Coke, in the other a bag of potato chips, and the advertising message read: A GREAT PAIR, SAYS THE BEAR.

Now he was at the crest of a career that had been filled with storm and thunder and continuing success. He could well afford to let the chips fall as they may. He knew he would not again need a moving van. He knew that he could rally an entire state behind him, even the press, and he would never have to turn his head or wink at a rich ex to recruit the best of the schoolboy talent.

This was to be his last rebuilding job, and he attacked it with the same formula that had worked at Maryland, Kentucky and Texas A&M. That alone accounted for a major change in the Bear's coaching philosophy. For the last time, he would drive off players by the carload, which is easier to do when the material was recruited by someone else. He established the same unforgiving work ethic and kept his own lunatic hours.

He was in his office at 5:30 A.M. on New Year's Day.

Meanwhile, Jerry Claiborne, who had been rehired off Frank Broyles's staff at Missouri, Laslie and Hank Crisp had carried the Bryant flag across the state and hauled in what may have been Alabama's best freshman class ever. They would come of age as seniors in 1961 on a national championship team: Pat Trammel, Billy Neighbors, Tommy Brooker, Bill Oliver, Mal Moore, that crowd.

If anything, he felt pursued by fewer demons than in the past. He was home. Hank Crisp had recruited him, and brought him back when he tried to quit, and now stepped aside so Bear could have the athletic director's job. On the first day of spring practice, he opened the gate and walked onto Denny Field and said, "There's not a spot of ground out there that doesn't have a little of my blood on it."

Even after he weeded them out, the varsity had enough left to finish with five wins (including a 17–8 upset of Georgia Tech), four losses and a tie. The Crimson Tide stayed home that year and Bryant would always regret it. They went to a bowl game after every season the rest of his career, 24 in a row. It might have been 25. It reached a point where Bear would say, "We could wallow around and win three games and some bowl, somewhere, would invite us to play."

He thought bowl games were important, not for the money or the exposure, but for the extra month's practice. It meant a head start for next year's team.

Alabama improved each week in 1959, after an opening loss to a Georgia team starring Fran Tarkenton, 17–3. The rest of the way the Tide won seven, tied Vanderbilt and Tennessee and gave up a total of 35 points. They finished the regular season with a 10–0 conquest of Auburn, their first in six years. For that game, Bryant shifted Scooter Dyess, a 150-pound halfback, to split end, and he caught a 50-yard pass for the only touchdown.

That win, among so many others, illustrated perfectly Bryant's theory that all games are decided by five or six plays. The key is to have the right people on the field, in the right places, when those plays occur.

Then Penn State beat them in the first Liberty Bowl, 7–0, a game historic not for the outcome or the matchup, but because Alabama played against a black football player—tackle Charlie Janrette—for the first time in 67 years.

The times they were a-changing. Slowly. But changing, nonetheless.

By his junior year, Pat Trammell was being described by Bryant as the best leader he had ever coached. He had grown to 6'2" and 200 pounds, average as a passer, average as a runner, but exceptional at doing whatever it took to win. Trammell was bigger than most of the linemen. It was a small Tide in 1960, but the team won with quickness and intelligence.

Trammell was a doctor's son from Scottsboro. A teammate, Bill Oliver, tells how Pat intimidated some of his rivals as a freshman. He barged into a room where they were sitting around a table. He flipped a switchblade knife into the tabletop and as it quivered he asked if any of them were quarterbacks. No one answered. "Right then," said Oliver, "they all became halfbacks."

The incident may have been a put-on. But from then on, the Class of '61 took its cue from Pat Trammell.

The defense was better than ever in 1960, allowing just 56 points, 20 of them in a loss to Tennessee. In one of the school's sweetest wins, they came from 15 points behind to beat Georgia Tech, 16–15. They had lost their quarterback (Trammell) and their kicker (Brooker) to injuries. They won it with time running out, on a field goal by an end named Richard O'Dell, who had never before attempted one.

A field goal by Brooker produced the only points in a win over Auburn, and the Tide accepted a bid from the Bluebonnet Bowl in Houston to meet the Texas Longhorns.

The game paired good friends, Bryant and Royal, and teams strikingly alike. Both gave up size for quickness, won with their defense and distrusted the forward pass. Royal had said, "Three things can happen when you throw the ball, and two of them are bad."

Bryant always told his quarterbacks that if they had five yards of running room, take it, even if a receiver was open downfield. "Someone in the stands with a rifle might shoot the receiver," he said.

His former players from A&M turned out in force, and even many of the exes who felt they would never forgive him for leaving. The game turned into a reunion, but the outcome was not hard to predict.

After each team had kicked a field goal in the first half, I looked around the press box and said, "Men, I think we've seen all the scoring we're going to see." And so the game ended, 3–3.

The next year Alabama struck the mother lode: 11 straight wins, a conference and national championship. Six of the games were shutouts, including the last five. Only one team scored as many as seven points against them. The Tide outscored its opposition, 297 points to 25. The heart of the defense was Lee Roy Jordan, who made the all-America team at linebacker as a junior.

Now a Bryant-coached team returned to the Sugar Bowl for the first time since Kentucky's upset of Oklahoma on New Year's Day, 1951. The opponent this time was Arkansas, coached by Frank Broyles.

In his debut as a head coach, Broyles had sent his Missouri team against Bryant's '57 Aggies. Frank recalled how Bear had walked over before the game, draped an arm around him and said, "I've been looking over your squad . . ." Frank preened, expecting a compliment—"and I don't believe you have a single athlete."

Concluded Broyles: "I thought it was kind of unusual for your opponent to tell you before the game that you don't have a chance of winning."

Bryant had reason to remember that encounter, too. Jerry Claiborne had left his staff to coach the offense at Missouri. During a team meeting the week of the game, Bryant turned to Charley Krueger and asked, "Charlie, how does Coach Claiborne like to start a game?"

"By running at the other team's strength," came the answer.

"Then where will the first play come?"

"Right at me."

It was simply a direct answer to a direct question, no boast intended or imagined. The next day Missouri's first play sent a halfback on the power smash off tackle. Krueger played off two blockers and tossed the runner for a loss. The Aggies went on to win, 28–0.

I had my own reason to remember the game, as well. On one

of Alabama's trips to Houston in the early '60s—I no longer remember which one—I wrote something that Bryant took as criticism. I had saved a few Aggie anecdotes and cranked out a story thick with nostalgia.

One of the stories was told me by Charles Milstead, a sophomore in 1957, and the player Bear most regretted leaving. Charley was tall and blond and talented. He was the perfect T quarterback, but Jim Myers, an old Tennessee guard, had brought the single wing to A&M and Milstead was his tailback. He led the nation one year in total offense and punting, but the change may have cost him a career in the pros.

Milstead started that day against Missouri, with John David Crow injured and Osborne moved to halfback to replace him. The first time they got the ball, Milstead moved them the length of the field, hitting seven or eight passes in a row, the last one for the score.

He was walking back to the huddle for the extra point when Jimmy Wright checked in to replace him. As Charley crossed the sideline, Bryant reached out, grabbed him by the shoulder pads and shook him. "Don't ever do that again," he complained. "You'll get them used to scoring easy touchdowns."

Milstead never left the bench the rest of the day. After the game he was sitting in front of his locker, staring at the floor, when he suddenly found himself looking at a pair of dusty, scuffed brown shoes. He raised his eyes and waited for Coach Bryant to speak.

"You might at least have the guts to ask me what you did wrong," said Bear.

Milstead could hardly keep his voice from cracking: "What did I do wrong, Coach?"

"I can't think of a damned thing you did right," snapped Bryant.

It was just another insight, I thought, into how he set his standards, and how he thought, his conviction that passing teams tended to go soft. There was nothing in the game plan to prevent the quarterback from throwing the ball, but the plan was drawn for Osborne, who hardly ever did. Bear's reaction was funny because he had special hopes for Milstead, and you could see his psychology at work. He was more likely to jump on a player after a win for misdeeds, real or imagined. If a play had gone wrong or the game been lost, he would pet an offender and take the blame himself.

At practice, the day my story appeared, Bryant spotted me on the sideline and headed in my direction. The smile on my face froze when he said: "Mickey, I expected that shit from the other writers, but not from you."

I stood there speechless as he walked away. I avoided him for the next day or two, but in the locker room after the game he saw me hanging on the edge of a crowd of reporters, and he called out over their heads: "I owe you an apology. I saw Charley, and he said that really happened."

It was classic Bryant: to worry that Milstead's passes would make his team lazy, to get angry with me for printing the story and then to make his apology in public. I was not aware how persistent were the charges that his brand of coaching was abusive and brutal, or how sensitive he had grown to them, and with good reasons. Those charges, and worse, were soon to be circulated across the country.

Man of Moods: A fortyish
Bryant reacts to press questions

Those Fighting Fordyce Redbugs, Arkansas state champs in 1930; Ike Murry is at center, Bryant second from right

In a symbolic pose, Bear peeks over shoulder of the Baron, Adolph Rupp; Kentucky couldn't hold both

1951 Kentucky football staff: from left, sitting, Ermal Allen, Bryant, Carney Laslie; top, Vic Bradford, Charles McClendon, Paul Dietzel, Jim Owens, Buck-shot Underwood

Bear gave Kentucky its first winner in 12 years

Bryant briefs Red Grange (left) and Lindsey Nelson before national telecast

Heisman Trophy winner John David Crow has answers for young *Houston Post* reporter

The Bryants return to Alabama: with Mary Harmon and Paul, Jr. (1958)

Bryant seems perplexed by 3-3 tie in Bluebonnet Bowl with Darrell Royal's Texas team

Agent at far left is guarding either Coach Bryant or President Kennedy; Pat Trammell is next to Bear, Mel Allen looks over JFK's shoulder

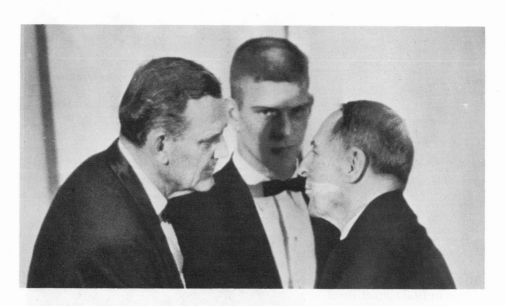

General Douglas MacArthur congratulates the coach and his QB, Trammell, after 'Bama received MacArthur Cup as '61 national champions

With attorney Winston McCall, Bryant walks to court for libel trial against *Saturday Evening Post*; behind them, Charlie Pell and Jim Sharpe

Oklahoma's Bud Wilkinson gets a New Year's Eve laugh, but Tide won 1962 Orange Bowl

Joe Namath, "the best pure passer" he ever coached, tested Bear's discipline

So long ago, hair may have been Howard Cosell's own

Celebrating college football's 100th birthday: Paul Dietzel, Don Hutson and his "other end" (1969)

Preparing Ken Stabler (12) and tailback Tommy Wade (38) for Cotton Bowl date against his old Aggie team

Bryant signs a boyish Richard Todd for Alabama; assistant coach John Crow looks on

Notre Dame's Ara Parseghian helps stir Café Brulôt in ritual at Antoine's before 1973 national title game

Alabamans all: Bear, Governor George Wallace, Auburn's Shug Jordan

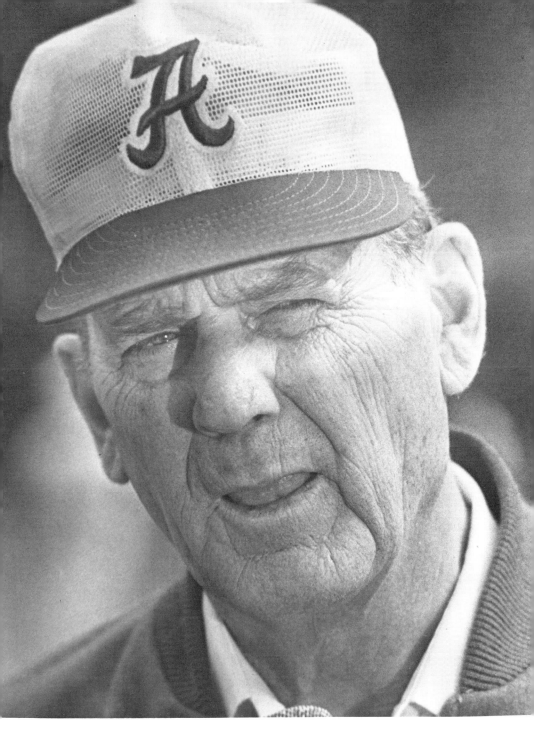

Blanda once said: "This is what God must look like"

A victory ride after Tide held off Penn State in 42nd Sugar Bowl

His college and first pro coach, Weeb Ewbank, holds a reunion with Joe Willie Namath

A lifelong baseball fan, Bryant visits with Yankee star Reggie Jackson in spring, 1978

President Gerald Ford and Alabama's Dr. David Mathews climbed the tower for coaches'-eye view

With Penn State's scholarly Joe Paterno before Sugar Bowl rematch, New Year's Day, 1979; Alabama won again

Headline tells the story, January 26, 1983: Alabamans mourn

A veiled Mary Harmon Bryant, with son Paul, at graveside service in Birmingham; she followed Bear in death a year later

Mickey gets a lift from Bear, TV host Lloyd Gregory

Chapter 8

The Trial

The phone call, from a friend, was a troubling one. Dan Jenkins, now with *Sports Illustrated*, was on the line in late January 1963 asking if I had talked recently with Coach Bryant. Not since the bowl games, I said.

Dan wondered if I would check out a rumor. The magazine had heard that the *Saturday Evening Post* was about to publish a sensational story accusing Bryant and Wally Butts, the former Georgia coach, of having conspired to fix the previous year's game between their teams.

The information was so staggering, I did not understand what I was expected to ask. "Just find out if Coach Bryant knows about the article," Dan said, "and how strong his denial is."

I said, "Dan, I'm not going to ask him to deny it. I know the story can't be true."

"Then just let us know what his reaction is when you call. We may want to run something, if the *Post* is going ahead with it."

My call to Coach Bryant went right through. This was not one of those times when I could clear my throat and tap dance around whatever question I had to ask. So I just laid it out. I told him about

129

the call from Jenkins, the tip that *Sports Illustrated* had, the accusation that the *Saturday Evening Post* was supposed to be making. I said I was calling because, even if he was aware of the story, I thought he should know that it was starting to circulate.

There was a deadness in his voice and he didn't waste any words. "Yeah, I've heard about it. I appreciate the call. But there isn't anything I plan on saying about it just yet. My lawyers are looking into it."

I called Dan back and repeated the conversation. In its next issue, *Sports Illustrated* ran a small item, known in the trade as a teaser, that the *Post* was about to break a story containing disclosures that would shake the Southeastern Conference.

The article appeared in the issue of March 23, 1963, under the headline, THE STORY OF A COLLEGE FOOTBALL FIX. The story, written by Frank Graham, with a contribution by Atlanta sports editor Furman Bisher, alleged that Bryant had received secret information from Butts in a phone conversation on September 13, nine days before Alabama and Georgia would play at Legion Field. An Atlanta insurance man, George Burnett, claimed to have been plugged into the call through a crossed wire. He took the notes that became the basis for the *Post* story and accusations.

The episode developed a history of its own, how and why the words got into print, where it led and what the results were. It was a complicated piece of business, and it had a lot to do with the reputation Bryant brought with him to Tuscaloosa.

The chain of events that brought Bear Bryant into an Atlanta courtroom actually started on the afternoon of November 18, 1961. Alabama was winning easily over Georgia Tech, and late in the game Tech punted, and when a halfback named Chick Graning ran downfield to cover it, he was blocked by Darwin Holt, an Alabama linebacker. Holt applied what coaches call a forearm shiver as they went out of bounds. Graning suffered a broken jaw. To compound matters, the officials missed the play and no penalty was called.

The incident was loaded with irony. Holt had been recruited by Bryant at Texas A&M, flunked out, attended a junior college, and then followed his old coach to Alabama. He was not a great player nor a dirty one. He stood about 5'9" and weighed at his peak 170, but had a 19-inch neck. With the exception of the other linebacker, Lee Roy Jordan, he was the hardest hitter on the team.

Bryant and Bobby Dodd, the popular Tech coach, had been the best of friends. But the Atlanta papers played the story big, and long, as a deliberate hit, and Dodd did nothing to cool it down. The friendship was ruptured. Tech would shortly drop Alabama from its schedule and withdraw from the Southeastern Conference.

A few months later, an article appeared in the *Saturday Evening Post* entitled "College Football Is Going Berserk." The Holt-Graning incident was at the center of the story, and Bryant was described as not only condoning but teaching a style of football described as brutal and cruel.

The controversy had been refueled as Alabama opened the 1962 season by trouncing Georgia, 35–0, at Legion Field. In January, Bryant's attorneys had filed a $500,000 libel suit against the magazine and the author, Furman Bisher. That suit was still pending when the *Post* dropped its bombshell, accusing Bryant and Butts of conspiring to rig the game.

Bryant filed his second of three suits, this one for $5 million. Butts sued for $10 million, and it was his case that would be heard first, starting in August 1963, in Atlanta. It was shaping up as the most dramatic trial involving sports since the Black Sox scandal of 1919. These were not uneducated, underpaid baseball players seduced by gamblers, nor naive college basketball players shaving points for easy money. These were coaches, among the most famous in the land, so-called molders of character.

The personalities and private lives of the two men were part of the issues. Bryant had not invented hard-nosed football, but he had become the leading apostle of it. This was in an era when the practice of spearing—driving your helmet into an opponent's chest or head—was legal. Bryant often used the phrase "butting heads," and his teams played that game to the hilt.

It was a short leap from there to the accusation that his brand of football was devoid of values, that fair play and sportsmanship were signs of weakness, that what he coached was win-at-any-cost football. Was it hard to imagine such a man receiving, and using, information that came from an embittered ex-coach? For a surprising number of writers and fans, initially, it was not at all hard.

Butts was vulnerable. A rotund man, who almost resembled Edmund Gwenn, he had been the subject of considerable gossip over the years on the Georgia campus. There had been a long relationship with a woman not his wife, years of hard drinking, poor investments that had left him nearly penniless. He had resigned as the Georgia coach in January 1961 under pressure from the athletic council. Testimony in the trial would confirm that he had been warned that if he did not step down, his "night life" would be made public.

Butts had coached for 35 years, 20 of them at Georgia. Curiously, in view of the feeling that he was unfit to coach, the school allowed him to stay on as athletic director. His successor as coach was Johnny Griffith, who had been given his first coaching job by the man now accused of betraying him and his team.

In the last week of February, two meetings were held in Atlanta with the commissioner of the Southeastern Conference, Bernie Moore. In one, Moore heard the story told by the insurance man, George Burnett. A few days later, Moore met with the presidents of the two universities, Dr. Frank Rose of Alabama and Dr. A. C. Aderhold of Georgia. He described the complaints being made against the two coaches.

On March 15, a week before the magazine was to appear on the newsstands, Bryant and Butts held separate press conferences to deny the charges. Their attorneys had warned the *Post* that the information was false and they would be at risk to publish it. The *Post* had gone to press.

The Sunday after the article appeared, Bryant went on state-wide television to again declare his innocence. The board of trustees, his friends and players rallied around him. Butts took and passed a lie detector test. The attorney generals of Alabama and Georgia announced they would begin investigations into the charges.

There was no great movement to close ranks behind Wally Butts. The Georgia administration and coaching staff supported the position of Johnny Griffith, whose quotes in the story made it appear that he suspected Alabama of having his team's plays.

There were fresh rumors that the *Post* had more damaging material yet to come. Instead, in the issue of April 27, an editorial asserted that the magazine stood behind its charges, and believed them to be true. Bryant's attorneys, William S. Pritchard and Winston B. McCall, responded by filing yet a third suit for another $5 million, bringing the total to $10.5 million.

Meanwhile, months earlier, Bryant had taken an interesting and confidential step. For reasons of his own, he never made a public disclosure of it and the details are told here for the first time. When the first blind item ran in *Sports Illustrated*, and was picked up by newspapers across the country, he flew to Washington and arranged through a friend to meet secretly with Robert Kennedy, the attorney general of the United States and the brother of the president.

It was a disturbed Paul Bryant who was ushered into the solemn offices of the Justice Department. The story had not yet broken fully into print, but the first hints had appeared that a scandal in college football was brewing. Two Southern coaches were said to have rigged a game. After a few minutes of small talk, Bryant asked Robert Kennedy if he had seen the morning papers. He said that he had.

"I was one of the people," said Bryant, the words coming hard, "they were accusing."

The attorney general had his coat off, his shirt sleeves rolled up, his tie loosened at the knot. He looked him in the eye. "Why don't you tell me about it," he said. And Bryant did.

When he finished, Kennedy leaned across his desk and said that his department had already run a check on the rumors. He was satisfied that Coach Bryant, and Wally Butts, were not guilty of the charges.

Bryant said, "I know that. I just wanted to be damned sure you knew it."

Robert Kennedy offered his help, if and when it was needed. Bryant didn't call on him again. He had the assurance he had gone there to get.

(The details of this encounter were slow to appear in print. Kennedy had no reason to mention it and, for quite a time, maybe still, there was no benefit to mentioning in Alabama that you had gone to Washington for help. Bryant told me this story on the phone, on June 7, 1968, the day after the second Kennedy brother was killed by an assassin's bullet. Bryant planned to support Bobby

Kennedy, at least privately, in that year's presidential campaign. Given the fact that football coaching is sometimes considered the last true monarchy in America, it may surprise people to learn that Bryant's politics were not predictable. He disliked Richard Nixon, noting that when Nixon shook hands, "his palms were sweaty.")

As the summer passed, the story grew, the press and fans chose up sides, and the temperature rose. The attorney generals of Alabama and Georgia announced they were investigating the case. The matter reached the U.S. Senate, where the McClellan Committee on racketeering declared that it would look into the gambling aspects.

The $10 million libel action brought by Butts went to court first, in Atlanta, the first week of August 1963. The presiding judge, Lewis R. Morgan, and most of the attorneys on both sides, had either graduated from or attended the University of Georgia. Butts was represented by Bill Schroder, who once coached the Georgia freshman team. Welborn Cody, heading the legal staff defending the Curtis Publishing Company, was a former Georgia first baseman.

Although not related by old school ties, another of the plaintiff's lawyers, Allen Lockerman, brought a colorful distinction to the case. A former FBI agent, he was one of the six who killed John Dillinger. He had been stationed in front of the Biograph Theatre, next to Melvin Purvis.

Butts, fighting to clear his name, was accompanied to court by his wife Winnie and his three married daughters. Many Atlantans doubted the case would ever come to trial, believing that Butts would be reluctant to risk a possible exploration into his private life.

A pretrial hearing had established some interesting, even puzzling twists. The case for Curtis was to be based on the scratch-pad notes taken by Burnett during the phone conversation he claimed to have overheard. As far as anyone knew, the conversation was not taped or recorded.

The two coaches never denied having talked the week before the game. They did deny, with vigor, having discussed anything remotely resembling Georgia football secrets.

From the outset, Bill Schroder drew the lines on which the case would be argued. In his opening statement, Schroder told the jury that the films of the game "will prove that what is charged cannot be true." He added: "I expect to show by a member of the Georgia coaching staff who is there now that no secret of any kind was divulged."

Thus a head-on clash was set up between the Georgia coaches themselves. It was believed that John Gregory, the line coach, had volunteered to appear on behalf of Butts, going against head coach Johnny Griffith and his chief assistant, LeRoy Pearce.

Burnett was the first witness called to the stand. Under cross-examination by Schroder, he testified that the *Post* paid him $5,000 for his information . . . even though no one from the magazine ever actually saw the notes he made.

On the stand, the heavyset, black-haired Burnett spoke slowly and clearly, his eyes seldom leaving Schroder's face. He said he talked from memory of the conversation to Frank Graham, Jr., under whose name as author the story appeared.

Burnett also testified that the very first line of the story, which stated that the conversation took place on September 14, was incorrect. It was one day earlier, he said. Burnett also flatly denied one of the quotations directly attributed to him in the article: "Butts also said to Bryant that Rakestraw [the Georgia quarterback] tipped off what he was going to do by the way he held his feet. If one foot was behind the other it meant he would drop back to pass. If they were together it meant he was setting himself to spin and hand off."

Under oath, Burnett said he never made the statement. Where Graham obtained this information was uncertain, along with the question of whether Graham would testify. (The reference, it later became apparent, was out of a time warp. Bryant had reminded Butts of an incident that had taken place eight years earlier, involving another Georgia quarterback in a game against the Texas Aggies. He had not mentioned the quarterback by name. Someone, in handling the notes, assumed he meant Rakestraw.)

Schroder also eased out of Burnett the admission that he had lied in a meeting with University of Georgia officials, when asked if he did not have a cloudy record (for giving hot checks).

The jury was all-male, a cross section of middle-class citizens from the Atlanta area. There were a feed-mill operator, a mechanic, a finance-company clerk, a sales manager, an architect, a real-estate agent, a supermarket clerk . . . ranging in age from about 42 to 60.

Judge Morgan, about 50, wearing shell-rim glasses, was alert and forceful and precise.

The gallery each day included George Poschner, a great Georgia end who came home from World War II a quadruple amputee, and who was there to support Wally Butts. The Southeastern Conference sent a Vanderbilt law professor, James C. Kirby, Jr., as an observer.

In a fascinating piece of stagecraft, the attorneys for Wally Butts were able to show the jury huge enlargements of the *Saturday Evening Post* article, using cardboard sheets six feet high. Whenever a defense witness admitted on cross-examination that he had been misquoted in the article, Schroder would invite him to step down from the witness chair and initial in his own handwriting the error or inaccuracy.

The denial by Burnett of a statement credited to him was topped by the surprise testimony of Coach Griffith, who said that the secrets described by the *Post* as "significant" were not secret at all. Griffith stuck to the opinion that some of the information allegedly given Bryant might have been helpful to Bryant. He said Georgia had concentrated in closed practices on the two formations named by George Burnett in his notes.

Griffith testified that Georgia's "slot right" and "pro-set" formations of 1962 had been, in fact, used in past seasons, and were common among conference teams and nothing new to Alabama. Taking each so-called item of "secret information," Schroder drew from Griffith the admission that very little could have been helpful to Bryant, who would have known about it anyway.

Even more damaging was Griffith's citing of further errors. In the article, Georgia end Mickey Babb was quoted as saying the Alabama players taunted them during the 35–0 defeat by yelling: "You can't run 88-pop [a key Georgia play] on us."

Griffith revealed that Georgia had no such play.

Under cross-examination, Griffith acknowledged that Butts had given him his first job, loaned him money, endorsed bank notes for him, made payments when the notes were in arrears, and that he still owed Butts money (the amount, though not brought out in questioning, was $350).

The defendant, the Curtis Publishing Company, suddenly rested its case shortly before 3:00 P.M. on Wednesday, August 7, after the jury had spent more than two hours watching movies of the 1962 Georgia-Alabama game. It was undoubtedly the first time in the history of American jurisprudence that a football film was shown in a court of law.

LeRoy Pearce, the Georgia assistant, explained the action as it related to the notes taken by Burnett. Pearce testified that the information might be useful to an opposing coach. However, when questioned item by item, he said some of the notes meant nothing to him, some were inaccurate, and some not unusual or essentially new, and that Alabama could not have relied very much on any of it.

The dramatic highlight of the trial came the next day, in a strategy shift by the plaintiff: Bear Bryant was called to testify four days earlier than expected. He had flown into Atlanta quietly the night before, and kept under cover at the Dinkler Plaza Hotel, where Georgia exes gathered in the 1940s and 1950s to toast the coach who had developed their championship teams.

So Bryant took the stand as the day's first witness, with the game movies no doubt still fresh on the minds of the 12 jurors and two alternates.

Bryant's appearance figured to prop up Butts, who was showing the strain of the trial. He looked pale and nervous, dressed each day in a dark suit, white shirt, thin red and blue striped tie, often staring at the ceiling for long, uncomfortable minutes.

In contrast to Butts, Bryant seemed to relish the battle. He loomed as a commanding figure, thick-skinned, resourceful and expressing contempt for his accusers. To him the charges were preposterous. There was electricity in the courtroom now. One point had nagged at the staunchest defenders of the two coaches: Telephone records showed they had talked for an hour and six minutes six days before the game. Why? What did they talk about?

Bryant began his testimony. No one had ever heard him speak more clearly or distinctly. He was eager and aggressive and the words raced from his lips. This was not the mumbling, self-effacing Bryant of press conferences yet to come.

He was dressed in a gray seersucker coat, white slacks and brown alligator shoes. When asked to review the notes which George Burnett had taken while listening in on the phone conversation, Bryant said: "I don't have my specs. I left them on the plane."

He tried attorney Schroder's glasses, found they didn't fit, and borrowed a pair belonging to Butts. He made quick work of the notes. Once, in response to what he would do in a situation referred to by Burnett, Bryant said, "If I didn't know that, I oughta be bored for a hollow head."

Then Bryant went to a blackboard to show through diagrams how, in his opinion, none of the alleged information could have been used profitably by Alabama. What he was doing was holding a clinic for the benefit of the jury. The jurors seemed to love it.

Asked what he and Butts talked about on the phone, Bryant could not recall any specifics, but he rattled off a dozen football subjects and one or two business matters which could have been raised. He said he talked on a regular basis to many coaches, adding drily: "Bob Woodruff, when he was at Florida, was even longer-winded than Butts on the telephone."

The theatrical high point of the trial, to that moment, came when Schroder read slowly and solemnly the *Saturday Evening Post* indictment charging Bryant and Butts with fixing the game and branding them as "corrupt."

Bryant's face was livid with contained anger, and he seemed to hold back tears as he listened. But when the attorney asked him if this were true, his voice was vibrant and emphatic when he answered:

"Absolutely not. If we did it, we ought to go to jail. And if we didn't, anybody who had anything to do with this [story] ought to go to jail. Taking their money is not good enough."

As a practical matter, the case was probably decided right then. The cross-examination of Bryant started out in a manner that had him angry, answering heatedly and leaning forward in the witness chair. But attorney Welborn Cody's questioning became milder as it went along. Bryant was dismissed after less than 10 minutes.

But there were more fireworks to come, when John Gregory, the Georgia defensive coach, narrated the game film for the second time. So eager and intense was Gregory that at one point, he said: "Here's the play where our quarterback's pass was intercepted. The *Saturday Evening Post* story says our moves were analyzed like 'rats in a maze.' The truth is that Rakestraw wasn't rushed at all and should have run for a first down."

Judge Morgan banged his gavel and warned Gregory that if he made any more such remarks his testimony would be discontinued.

In his cross-examination, Cody brought out that Gregory had signed a statement given previously to the state attorney general, saying that Burnett's notes might have influenced the outcome of the game. Gregory explained quickly that he had been handed a prepared statement, which he signed in Dr. Aderhold's office, at the request of the head coach. He did so, he said, fearing his job would be in jeopardy.

The question that hung over the courtroom was: How could he possibly keep his job now? At least, if Griffith kept his.

Bryant had been followed to the stand by two of his seniors, guard Jimmy Sharpe and tackle Charlie Pell, typical Alabama linemen of that era at 182 and 189 pounds. Both testified that no changes whatever took place in Alabama's plans for the Georgia game during the September practice sessions. Pell said that if a team knew an opponent's plays, the knowledge would be of little value unless it knew exactly when a certain play would be run.

"Could a football game be rigged or fixed without the players knowing it," asked William Schroder, "without the players participating in it?"

"No, sir," Pell said.

Pell and Sharpe so demonstrated their football acumen in diagramming plays and explaining defenses that, at the end of their testimony, Judge Morgan asked if they were studying to be coaches. In time, both would become head coaches at major colleges.

One writer noted that in their articulate responses, their manners and appearance, "they were a wonderful advertisement for any university or any coach."

At the end of the trial's first week, it was clear that if Curtis had a bomb it would have to drop it soon. The jury would have to weigh the harm done to the *Post*'s case by two puzzling, even shocking disclosures: Frank Graham, who did not appear as a witness, revealed in a deposition that he wrote the article based on an affidavit from Burnett, without ever seeing his notes. Burnett had promised that the notes would be air-mailed to New York. They never were. They had been given to Cook Barwick, an attorney for the University of Georgia, who had been assured by Burnett he would not offer them for sale. The notes remained in his possession until the trial.

And, finally, a former business associate of Burnett's, John Carmichael, testified he had been in the office when the phone conversation took place, and that the notes Burnett had shown him then were not the ones introduced into evidence. Times, dates, phone numbers and other references did not appear on the scratch paper he had been shown then. And missing were "doodles" Burnett had drawn on the first page. The inference was that the notes had been cleaned up, or doctored.

It was tempting to speculate how the proceedings grew. Burnett took his notes to Barwick, who mentioned them to Roderick Beddow, Jr., a Birmingham lawyer hired by Curtis to defend them in the original Bryant suit. Beddow sent word of the new development to the *Post*'s editors, or lawyers, and Graham was assigned to the story. He in turn brought in Furman Bisher, who also knew of the Burnett notes, to assist with the research. Would the *Post* have shown any interest in whatever Burnett heard, if the man on the other end of the line had been anyone else but Bear Bryant?

Although witness after witness claimed to have been misquoted, neither Graham nor Bisher was called by the defense as a rebuttal witness.

When Wally Butts took the stand on his own behalf, he appeared fortified by Bryant's performance. He was relaxed and affable. The color had returned to his face. For days he had sat there, listening to testimony that he, the former coach and still the athletic director at Georgia, had given the team's secrets to Alabama. Had any coach in the history of athletics ever endured such misery?

From some inner resource, Butts, 58, a little bulldog of a man, answered the endless questions, explaining his phone calls, his business interests and activities, his resignation as athletic director. The questioning avoided his private life.

As he had done with Bryant, Bill Schroder read slowly the searing statement by the editors of the *Saturday Evening Post*. Loud and clear came the words "fixed game" and "corrupt men" and "teachers selling out their pupils."

Schroder asked: "Does this editorial contain any truth?"

"No," said Butts, "and I would like to explain that for a time I hid from people, but not any more. I'm looking them in the eye, because it's not true." Then he broke into sobs. He stumbled down from the witness chair to a seat at the table with his lawyers, choking. Judge Lewis Morgan called a five-minute recess.

Those who knew him well conceded that Butts was no angel, but he was utterly incapable of staging any act. The accumulated grief and hurt and pressure of the last six months had simply overflowed. The people in the crowded courtroom showed what they thought by their impressive silence during the recess. Normally at these periods there is movement and chatter. This time the spectators stayed in their seats, quietly, some crying, many misty-eyed.

Butts regained his composure and walked back to the witness chair for more cross-examination. He denied he had ever bet on a football game, or even discussed with anyone gambling on the outcome of a Georgia game.

He was quoted in the article as telling Bryant: "Don't worry about quick kicks. They don't have anyone who can do it." Witnesses testified that Georgia did have a quick-kicker, Jake Saye, and had used him.

Another secret he supposedly revealed: that Brigham Woodward, the Georgia safety, committed himself fast on pass defense. Testified Butts: "If I were an opposing coach and knew this, I would fake a running play and throw over Woodward for a touchdown. The movies show that Alabama didn't throw the ball in his defensive zone at any time during the game."

Other witnesses favorable to Butts were Charlie Trippi, rated by many as the greatest player Georgia ever produced, who resigned from Griffith's staff only weeks earlier to join the pro Saint Louis Cardinals; and Lee Roy Jordan, Alabama's all-American linebacker, a starter in the '62 Georgia game, and at the time of the trial with the Dallas Cowboys.

Those two testified that the information contained in Burnett's notes could not have helped Alabama. And four Georgia players—Woodward, Babb, Ray Clark and Wally Williamson—swore under oath that at no time had they seen anything that indicated Alabama knew Georgia's plays. Clark and Williamson added that the Bulldogs were not in good physical condition for the game. "I think a lot of the boys were worn down," said Williamson. "At least, I was."

As the trial was grinding to a conclusion, the side dramas were unavoidable. Whatever the outcome, Georgia was a staff and team divided. Two of his returning players, Babb and Woodward, had contradicted Coach Johnny Griffith. And old friendships were being ripped apart. When the school's president, Dr. Aderhold, was asked

about Butts's character, he hesitated several seconds before reply-
ing: "I would say bad."

From the standpoint of both lawyers and laymen, the case had
its share of mystifying moments. None of the writers or editors
connected with the case testified in person. But three of them, in
their depositions, insisted they did not accuse Butts and Bryant of
betting on the game. If you were able to ignore this implication,
you were left to wonder what was the motive to fix a game Alabama
was favored by three touchdowns to win? The lawyers for Curtis
had to convince the jury that Butts was bitter and wanted to hurt
the young Georgia coach, Johnny Griffith, whose career he had
launched and to whom he had given repeated financial assistance.

Butts's feelings toward his successor would be far harder to measure than the testimony of the Alabama and Georgia players; the
admitted errors and denied quotes; and the *Post*'s expression of its
own policy under new editor-in-chief Clay Blair, Jr., who wanted,
and got, an image of "sophisticated muckraking."

The burden of proof was on the magazine and its attorneys, who
had to prove that Wally Butts and Bear Bryant "fixed" or "rigged"
the game between Georgia and Alabama in September 1962; that
they were "corrupt men" and "teachers selling out their pupils."

Certainly, in no jury trial involving a sports theme or sports
figures, could there have occurred a more emotional closing argument than the one made by William Schroder, referring to his client:

"I have lived in agony with this man: I have seen him deteriorate.
One of these days Wally Butts will pass on. The *Saturday Evening
Post* can't get to him then. I see it as a coffin with a red lining and
black lid. And his epitaph will read: 'Glory, Glory to Old Georgia.' "

The words were the title of the Georgia football fight song.

The jury found in favor of Butts, assessing general damages of
$60,000 and punitive damages of $3 million. When Butts telephoned
Bryant with the news, the Bear's first words were: "That's fine, but
what happened to the rest of it?" Meaning that, on principle, he
felt Butts should have gotten the full $10 million.

The reality proved vindication enough. The damages in the Butts
case were reduced on appeal to $300,000. The Bryant suit never
reached court. Within a week, Curtis Publishing made an offer to
settle and Bryant, electing to spare his wife and children any additional strain, accepted. He received $360,000—and a retraction.

Chapter 9

From Bear to Broadway

In a matter of weeks after a settlement had been reached with Curtis Publishing, Coach Bryant interviewed Charley Thornton, formerly of Tulane, for the position of sports publicity director at Alabama. The job had been vacant, more or less, for three years, with students handling the assorted details of the office.

Undoubtedly, Alabama was the only major college in the country that did not provide a typewritten play-by-play account of the game in its press box. None of the student P.R. people knew how to type. They drafted a fellow out of an art class to print the action *in longhand*, illustrating the margins with appropriate symbols of a player passing or kicking the football.

It was all very artistic and colorful, but not very efficient. Most of all, the procedure reflected Bryant's total concentration up to this time on the technical, or ground-level, view of a football program.

So Thornton flew in from Kansas, where he was then employed by the NCAA and Bryant's former nemesis, Walter Byars. On the phone, the Bear asked him how much he made.

"I told him $9,000," Charley would recall later. "He said, 'Whoo,

143

we're not used to paying that kind of money for a publicity man. But come on down, anyway. We'll see if we can get you a raise."

The day Thornton flew into the tiny Tuscaloosa airport, he was met by Bryant and his top assistant, Sam Bailey. Bryant was behind the wheel. The drive from the airport to the campus lasted 15 minutes or so at a normal speed, but Bryant, distracted, as he often was, tooled along at 20 miles an hour. Thornton tried gamely to carry on a conversation, asking the two or three sensible questions that came easily to mind. The weather. How his family was. How many lettermen were due back.

Finally, he said, "Coach, I read where you settled that lawsuit. How do they go about paying you when you win something like that?"

The silence in the car, said Thornton, "seemed like an eternity of dead time. Then he reached over and patted his coat pocket and said, 'I got it right in here.' He kept on driving and again, I'm sure it wasn't more than ten or fifteen seconds, but with him you know how long that could seem. Finally, he fumbled around in his pocket and he pitched something out on the seat. I reached over and picked it up. It was a yellow envelope his lawyer had delivered to him that week. Inside was a certified check for what was left of the $360,000."

Bryant had carried the check around for a few days, just enjoying the feel of it, delighting in the chance to show it to people.

"Talk about timing," said Thornton. "Coach Bryant always said timing was everything. Well, I figured my prospects had just improved a whole lot. He was in a really good mood."

Bryant believed in public relations and many who observed him through the years thought he eventually became a master of the art. But, up to then, he was like a man who bought a sausage from a vendor. He didn't want to know how it got to the cart or what went into it.

Bryant went back to his office and sent Thornton upstairs to inspect the publicity department. Thornton was shocked by what he found. The filing cabinets were so old and rusty they wouldn't open. Everything was World War II vintage, or earlier, and there were no typewriters. When Charley rejoined him, Bryant asked, lightly, "Well, what do you think?"

Thornton shook his head and said, "Coach, it's terrible."

Bryant did a double take. "What do you mean?"

Charley told him how much equipment was lacking, and that what they did have was too old.

Bryant said, "Well, you can buy equipment, can't you?"

Thornton said, "Yes, sir," and his spirits perked up.

Charley signed on for $10,000 and would be Bryant's publicity man, and later his assistant athletic director, for the next 20 years. Thornton, a short, sandy-haired man with mild, pleasant features, had a quality Bryant prized. He did not yes him to death.

"It didn't take long after I went down to Alabama," he recalled, "to recognize that most of the people there were more afraid of Coach Bryant than I was. Maybe I didn't have real good sense and should have been. Don't get me wrong. I was as intimidated by him at times as anyone else. But I think he trusted me because when I didn't think something was right, in my area, at least, or if he asked a direct question, I told him what I thought. He kind of liked that."

I don't think Bryant would have wanted to admit it, but the *Saturday Evening Post* controversy, the charges and the trial, had changed him. Not the part about fixing games. He didn't see how anyone could take those seriously. But he was worried by the picture of a coach who encouraged his players to engage in dirty football, whose coaching style verged on the brutal, who thought winning was all that counted and how you won was simply part of the pact you made with the devil.

Well, he did believe that winning was what he was put on earth to do. But he thought he had not lost sight of those values that came under the general heading of sportsmanship.

After the libel suit had been settled, I think Bryant decided to take a long, hard look at Paul Bryant. It was a look that had intimidated many a lesser fellow.

On the field he was, in every sense of the word, a tyrant. He prided himself and his teams on their toughness. But was there a danger that toughness unchecked might edge into cruelty? His critics were unyielding. If his players seemed to worship Bryant, the critics countered that even Genghis Khan was a hero to his rickshaw boy. Bryant cared about people in the only way that this condition can be measured: He thought about them, was there for them when he no longer needed them. He was even there for some who, as players, made only minor contributions, if any.

So even if he rejected the accusations, he had to be stung by them. He had to wonder: How many saw him this way, as heartless, domineering, egotistical, sadistic? And he began to change in the way he dealt with people, with his players, with the press, with everyone except the old friends who had never questioned whatever it was he did. They were small changes and a lot of it had to do with showing how he felt, now, rather than letting those around him guess, or find out years later.

None of this was based on what was expedient or popular. But in what might have been a poetic touch, or just a case of interesting timing, the beginning of the changes coincided with the arrival at Alabama of Joe Namath.

He was not yet the artist in white shoes, the kid with the laser beam release. He was not yet a character or a folk hero or even Joe Willie. He was a slouchy, sleepy-eyed pool hustler from western Pennsylvania, who had to beat out someone named Jack Hurlbut for a starting job. But Bryant could see what he was going to be. Bear gave him the name and Joe created his own legend.

The idea smacked of an inside joke, calling this street-smart Yankee by two names, in the Southern style. But Bear had grown up in a world of Billy Clydes and Bobby Joes and it came naturally to him. He seemed to enjoy the sound of it, as when he referred to John David Crow, up to then the greatest player he had ever coached. By design, or otherwise, it may have been a way of putting Namath in the company of Crow.

You tend to doubt that he was Joe Willie Namath around Beaver Falls, Pennsylvania. He did not, you understand, grow up whistling Dixie. Joe's idea of a private swimming pool was the Beaver River, on the banks of which the town's coal-mining families did their summer entertaining.

For a change of pace, the town maintenance man would turn on the fire hydrants so the kids could play.

It was out of this background that Namath came to Bear Bryant. He has sharp memories of the first conversation he ever had with the Bear. Not of the conversation itself, mind you, but the images around it. The varsity had already started fall practice by the time Joe registered, a little late, as he often was. He was wearing sunglasses, a checkered sport coat and a snap-brim straw hat with a pearl in the band. A student manager led him to the practice field and Bryant waved for Namath to climb the ladder and join him on his famous coaching tower. Until that moment, no player had ever been extended such an invitation.

"We talked for fifteen minutes," said Joe, "and I didn't understand a word he said. He pointed down to the field and said something like, 'that ole stud.' He was trying to relate to a young kid. *Stud.* That was the only word I understood my first three weeks there."

One way or another they related, proof of which is that by the time Joe left Alabama, the kid from Beaver Falls, Pennsylvania, had an accent more Southern than the Bear's.

Bryant had no trouble getting his message across once Namath put on the uniform. He fumbled one night during a freshman scrimmage, and with his leg in the grip of a tackler he made no effort to go after the ball. By the time Joe got to his feet, Bryant was out of the tower and on the field.

"Namath," he roared, "it's not your job to just pitch the ball out and lay on the ground and not do anything. *You don't just lay there.*" He grumbled some more and when Joe thought he was through he turned and headed back to the huddle. Suddenly, Joe felt a hand grab his facemask and spin him around.

"Namath," said Bear, "when I'm talking to you, boy, you say, 'Yes, sir,' and look me in the eye."

Quickly, Joe said, "Yes, sir, yes, sir," repeating himself so as to leave no doubt in Bryant's mind that the message had been received.

Against Vanderbilt, in his sophomore year, Namath was playing poorly and Bryant yanked him from the game. As he came off the field, he hurled his helmet to the ground in anger, and watched nervously as it took one bounce and landed at Bear's feet.

"He looked at it calmly, without any expression, and then he came over and sat down next to me on the bench and draped an arm around my shoulder. There were about fifty thousand fans in the stands and it must have looked as though he was giving me some fatherly advice, or cheering me up. But what he was doing was squeezing the back of my neck with one of those big hands of his. He was saying, 'Boy, don't ever again let me see you coming out of a ball game like that. Don't ever do it again or you're gone.'

"I said, 'Dammit, coach, I wasn't mad at you, or anybody else.

I'm just mad at myself for playing so badly. I deserved to be taken out of the game.' He drew back a tiny bit and gave me a long look. He said, 'Okay, Joe. I understand.' "

Fear heightens the senses. As Walt Michaels, who was on the Jets' coaching staff when Namath was a rookie, put it: "Everyone feels fear. A man who has no fear belongs in a mental institution. Or on special teams."

If Bryant tossed off a line that was even vaguely funny, the size of the laugh would be wildly out of proportion to the quality of the humor. Namath was on the team when the *Saturday Evening Post* article appeared. The first thing Bryant did when he could get his hands on an advance copy was to read it to his players—the best way to confront the charges and to reassure the team. "He got to the part where the magazine tried to say that, because we were supposed to have their plays in advance, we were able to hold Georgia to only thirty-seven yards in rushing. Coach Bryant stopped in midsentence. He looked at us and shook his head. 'Hell,' he said, 'that's too many yards to give them regardless.' That broke up the whole room."

The line should be taken as an example more of Bear's confidence than of his wit.

Bryant had never coached a player quite like Namath. Parilli was just as exciting as a passer, and more obedient, the kind of player coaches describe as "one of those trained pigs who will jump in the slop for you." So was Crow. Bob Gain was a straight arrow who accepted the rules, but not the endless hours and the iron fist.

Now here was Namath, with all that talent and charm and an air of sweet irresponsibility, ready to test the Bear and his discipline.

You get an insight into Namath when you learn that he captained his high school basketball team, a 6'2" guard who could dunk the ball, and the only white in the starting lineup. When he quit the team in his senior year in a dispute with the coach, the four other starters quit, too.

In a Southern culture where rigid racial attitudes still flourished, Joe Willie did not blend easily into the scenery. "We used to get into debates," he said, "and one of my nicknames was 'Nigger.' But I came to understand that. They were raised a different way than I was, so I didn't try to tell them how to live."

Namath came close to dropping out after his freshman year, and accepting a $50,000 bonus offer to sign a baseball contract, as a pitcher, with the Baltimore Orioles. Bryant sent Bubba Church, a former big-league pitcher, to talk with Joe. Bubba helped convince him to stay: "Look, Joe, they'll give you fifty thousand and you'll blow that in two years. You know you will. Then suppose your arm goes bad. Then what have you got? No college. No degree. Nothing."

Namath began to fit in. By design or not, his voice developed a soft Southern edge that over the years confused his friends and fellow Easterners.

Alabama had lost Pat Trammell and the rest of the senior leadership from its first national championship team in 1961. Bryant often tended to get sentimental over players who had finished their eligibility. His judgment of Trammell may have been shaded by the affection he felt, and the fact that Pat would die young, of cancer. In time he would refer to him as "probably the best" of all his college quarterbacks, a distinction that covered a lot of turf. He sent seven to the pros.

"Pat would have played in the NFL if he hadn't decided to be a doctor," said Bear. "He couldn't pass and he couldn't run; all he could do was put points on the board and win games. He called plays better than the coaches could, and he instinctively knew what the defense was trying to do. He was a tremendous leader . . . the players followed him around like they were following their mamas."

But 1962 was not indexed as a rebuilding year. Joe Namath was moving up as a trumpeted sophomore, and the players around him were so motivated, so savvy, that six of them would later win distinction as head coaches: Bill Battle, Richard Williamson, Charlie Pell, Jimmy Sharpe and Mal Moore.

Bryant did not adjust his offense to accommodate Namath's arm, not that year. Joe Willie ran the split-T and he ran it well. The season opened with one-sided shutouts of Georgia and Tulane. In the two games, he completed 16 of 21 passes for five touchdowns and ran for another. Not since World War II, and the heyday of a jumper passer named Harry Gilmer, had a quarterback so excited the Alabama fandom.

After seven games the Tide was unbeaten and still number 1 in the nation. Then came Georgia Tech, and the Bear had to relearn an old lesson: do not overcoach. His team had not lost in its last 19 starts, but for Tech he decided to shelve his basic offense and get fancy. He switched Namath to halfback and installed Jack Hurlbut, a junior who had transferred from Baylor, at quarterback.

Joe was an early casualty, injuring a leg on a savage tackle. He had been in long enough to throw an interception that led to Tech's touchdown. And he was back at quarterback when the Tide scored in the fourth quarter, went for two points and missed, and trailed, 7–6.

They had one final chance to win, a drive that reached the Georgia Tech 14 with a minute left. Alabama called one more play, hoping to score or get the ball closer for the field goal. Instead, Namath threw his fourth interception and the clock ran out.

It was the only victory Bobby Dodd's team could achieve in seven tries against Bryant at Alabama.

The chance to repeat as national champions was gone, but Auburn went down—in a game that endeared Joe to his coach—and they stopped Oklahoma in the Orange Bowl, 17–0, with President John Kennedy flipping the coin before the kickoff.

In the Auburn game, Namath needed only a completion or two to break Gilmer's school record for total offense in a season. Instead, on third and 13, he called for a quick kick, knowing the Tide would not get the ball back. While it was not necessarily a time to be unselfish—they led, 38–0—the call was consistent with the pressure defense Bryant advocated.

In other areas, Joe was still a puzzle to his coach. "I had a goatee my junior year," he remembered. "When I walked into his office to say good-bye that summer, Coach Bryant said, 'What the hell you got there, boy?' I said, 'It's a goatee, Coach.' He said, 'What's it for?' And I told him, 'Because I like it.' He just said, 'Oh,' and stared at me. I had it off by the time I returned to school."

There was talk of a dynasty in Alabama in 1963; you could see it coming over the Piedmont, like the rising of the sun. The Bear switched to a pro-style offense to take better advantage of Namath's gifts. But they misfired twice, first to Florida, 10–6, in a game that would grow in meaning. No other team would lick Alabama in Tuscaloosa in Bryant's lifetime.

They crossed up Georgia Tech, with Joe throwing just three passes and running 13 times for 53 yards and a touchdown. A 27–11 win avenged the upset loss of the previous year.

Then Auburn ended a four-game losing streak with a 10–8 squeaker. There was more bad news to come, what passed, at the time, for heavy stuff.

Bryant had heard that Joe Willie had violated the training rules, had been seen drinking in a night spot or two away around town. He went looking for him. Didn't find him. Was having coffee in the dining room when Namath walked in and casually sat down with him.

"Joe, I've got something to talk about with you," he said. "Let's go to my room."

Bryant kept a guest room in the dormitory. He repeated what he had heard and said, "Joe, you know I'm going to get the truth and I don't think you'd lie to me."

Namath admitted that he had broken the rules. Bryant had already taken a poll of his coaches. All but one suggested penalties that fell short of dropping him from the team.

The hard-liner was Gene Stallings, who had played for him at A&M. "If it had been me," said Stallings, "you'd kick me off the team, wouldn't you?"

Bryant nodded.

"Then I think that's what ought to be done."

Now Bear spelled it out for Joe. "Every coach but one thinks I ought to punish you but not suspend you. But you broke the rules. If you were allowed to stay on this team then I would have to resign, because I'd be breaking my own rules."

"I don't want that," Joe said.

"That's good," said Bryant, "because I've made up my mind to suspend you."

"How many days?"

"Not days. For the year. Or forever. Or until you prove something to me."

Alabama had two games left, against Miami in the season finale, and against Ole Miss in the Sugar Bowl. He offered to help Namath transfer to another school, or into the Canadian Football League, if he decided not to stay.

In view of the grief athletes can get into today, Joe's misconduct seems about as severe as lifting a towel from one's hotel room. Not the player nor the coach would say for the record what the caper had been, but Bryant was under wide pressure to reinstate him. Six thousand fans in Alabama signed a telegram. The other players, and some of the coaches, dropped hints. And Joe's mother called, crying. Bryant learned that Joe was not alone on the nights he broke training, but he would not turn in his teammates.

Bryant still would not reconsider.

Years later, as a pro, Joe Willie would tell a writer: "I deserved that suspension. The coach was 100-percent right." His eyes followed the pencil as the words were inscribed on a pad. "Make that 110 percent," he said.

Jack Hurlbut, a tireless worker who looked like an all-American in practice, but seldom prospered in a game, inherited Joe's job. Steve Sloan, a sophomore, was released from Bryant's doghouse to back up Jack.

Sloan had been benched after missing a tackle that allowed Florida to score its winning touchdown. He was restored to the offense, for emergency situations only. (Sloan was yet another Bryant pupil who would become a successful head coach.)

Hurlbut was ineffective against Miami, but the defense and kicking game saved it for Bama, 17–12. Now the drumbeat increased as the writers across the state, leaping on the Tide's problems at quarterback, predicted Bryant would forgive Namath his transgressions before taking on Ole Miss in the Sugar Bowl. The Rebels of Johnny Vaught were favored by a touchdown.

Instead Bryant groomed Sloan for the starting job, even though Steve had yet to complete a pass as a college player. He gave him a simple game plan and simple instructions: "You don't have to win the game; just don't lose it."

Sloan completed a pass—one out of eight. The Alabama defense contained Ole Miss and Tim Davis kicked four field goals in a 12–7 win.

Sloan would have his day.

Of course, so would Namath, who watched in street clothes as his team struggled to win its final two games. A question of attitude had been raised. Would Joe Namath fulfill his great promise?

In time for spring practice in '64, Bryant was satisfied that Namath had repented and earned his way back on the team. (At one point, Mrs. Bryant, worried about Joe getting depressed, smuggled him into their home for a week, prepared sleeping quarters in the paneled cellar, and cooked his meals. Bear pretended not to know he was there.)

For as long as he would coach, Bryant would drive home his point: From the best player on the team to the least, the rules were there for all. And the punishment.

By the start of his senior season, the professional teams were spreading the word about Namath. John Breen, who had brought George Blanda out of retirement in 1960 and signed him for the Houston Oilers, said: "Namath comes closer than any quarterback in the country to being able to step in and play with the pros right now."

Joe had won the respect of the coaches and the loyalty of his teammates by never sulking or complaining during his layoff. He would have around him a cast that included Ray Perkins, at end; Paul Crane, at center; and Jackie Sherrill, at guard and later full-back.

Bryant loved to experiment, to move players into new positions. I was reminded of a journeyman outfielder named Leon Wagner, known as Daddy Wags, who explained why his manager in Cleveland, Joe Adcock, didn't play him every day. "Joe likes to work on a player's weakness," he said. "My problem is that I don't have a weakness, but I'm trying to develop one, so Adcock can work on it."

Alabama had a weakness. Runners were not plentiful that year, nor of high caliber. The attack was geared to Namath's precious arm. He was as quick with a retort as he was with his delivery of the ball. In the second game of the season, a Vanderbilt linemen needled him: "Hey, number twelve, what's your name?"

Said Namath, "You'll see it in the headlines tomorrow." And on the next play he threw a touchdown pass.

Under any conditions, his arm would have been enough for Alabama to continue winning. But Joe's knee buckled against North Carolina State, and there was a little-told story behind it. Because he ran with the ball frequently, he wore special lightweight shoes manufactured in West Germany. To give him more support, he wrapped them in white adhesive tape. The impression was that only Joe among the entire team wore flashy white shoes, and he was nitpicked, unfairly, by writers and fans.

He reacted by leaving off the tape against North Carolina State. There may have been no connection, but late in the first half he tried to make a cut and his right knee went out. He had to be helped off the field. Namath limped through the rest of the season, making critical spot appearances, but Steve Sloan carried the load as the Tide finished 10–0 and won a second national crown. The voting in those days ended after the regular season.

Alabama agreed to meet fifth-ranked Texas in the first Orange Bowl game ever to be played on New Year's Night, in Miami. Joe predicted he would play, although few gave him a chance. Later, of course, people would come to accept more readily predictions made by Joe Namath in Miami.

More than 20 years later, I can recall few moments more electric than watching Joe Namath come off the bench in the second quarter and trot across the field. Alabama trailed by two touchdowns, Texas having struck on a long run and a long pass. The crowd came alive. So did Alabama.

The knee of Namath was heavily bound and he wore soccer shoes so his cleats wouldn't catch. His injury had been diagnosed as a double cartilage tear.

The score was 21–17, Texas, late in the fourth quarter, after Namath had thrown touchdown passes to Wayne Trimble and Ray Perkins. Joe moved them to a first and goal at the Texas 6 with time running out. The winning touchdown beckoned. Three straight times the handoff went to fullback Steve Bowman, and on fourth down Alabama still needed a yard.

The Orange Bowl was undiluted bedlam. This time Joe Willie Namath kept the ball, the lines collided and the crowd waited. One official indicated a touchdown. But the referee signaled no score, and the ball went over to Texas, on the lip of the goal line. The Longhorns had won.

Namath trotted to the bench for the final seconds and took a seat for the first time all night. Someone handed him a cup of water and he squished it through his teeth and spat it out. Then a bowl official in an orange sport coat walked up and told him he had been voted the game's most valuable player. Joe said, "Yeah," not a statement, not a question, and then crumpled the paper cup in his hands and threw it to the ground.

Leaving the field, Joe tried to tell his coach that he *knew* he had scored. Bear whispered in his ear and Joe jogged ahead, into the locker room, where he had no further comment on the subject.

The next day I was in a small group of people sitting with Coach and Mrs. Bryant beside the pool at his hotel. I asked him what he had said to Namath. "I told him," Bear replied, "to get inside the dressing room. It didn't make any difference. If you can't jam it in from there without leaving any doubt, you don't deserve to win."

Earlier that day, Namath and Coach Bryant had met in a room in another hotel with Sonny Werblin, owner of the Jets, and Joe had signed the contract that made him the highest-priced player in the history of professional football. Werblin had gotten nervous the week before the game. He had heard that the Saint Louis Cardinals were preparing to raise their offer to Joe, and he hinted that he would like to have Namath's signature before the game—secretly, of course.

Bryant asked him if Joe had agreed to the terms.

Werblin said, "Yes, but that's all I have. There's nothing on paper."

"Sonny, you have his word," said Bryant. "That's all you need."

The day before the game, Namath stopped by his hotel room to reassure the man who was emerging as a powerful force in the new American Football League. Later, Werblin would say: "I offered him a Coca-Cola, and he refused. He said Coach Bryant told him he was not to accept a damned thing until the game had been played."

It was fun to be young when Joe Namath was young, to watch him during the years of the llama-skin rug and the Fu Manchu mustache and the hostesses waltzing through a revolving door. And, of course, there was the miracle of 1969, the win over the Baltimore Colts in the Super Bowl that would become pro football's greatest upset.

I got to know Joe through those years and we hit it off fine, because he knew me as Coach Bryant's friend. That label opened a lot of doors in football. It was like being a Mason, or something.

But his dealings with the press were mixed. He went through a period of being bored with interviews and avoiding reporters. His differences may have begun on the flight from Miami to New York the week of the Orange Bowl. A New York writer happened to be across the aisle, and he began the conversation by asking: "Tell me, Joe, is it true that you majored in basket-weaving at Alabama?"

"No," replied Namath, "basket-weaving was too tough, so they put me in journalism."

Of course, Namath was a marked man. The press asked itself, if this guy can get into trouble in Tuscaloosa, what can he do when they turn him loose in New York?

Joe did fine. He had a magical year, and a brave career supported by two bad legs. And he revealed a wry sense of humor. In one game, he handed off to a veteran running back named Abner Haynes, and when the blocking broke down and Haynes saw three or four Oakland linemen bearing down on him, he pitched the ball back to Namath. They buried him. Later, asked if the pitchout surprised him, Joe replied: "Have you ever had an egg jump out of the pan at you?"

His style and skill made Namath a star. But five words helped make him a Hall of Famer: "We'll win. I guarantee it." It is acceptable in sports to boast if you back it up. Joe Willie did it in the third Super Bowl against the Colts.

I did not even consider that boast to be Namath's best line of the evening. During a round of after-dinner speeches, Larry Grantham, the solid and serious Jets' linebacker, had asked the audience to applaud the players' wives, who had sacrificed so much during the season.

Then Namath went to the mike and asked for a hand for the single girls of New York, "who sacrificed just as much and complained a helluva lot less."

Out of that 16–7 win over the Colts, Namath became a symbol of pro football's glory days. No other player, including Red Grange and O. J. Simpson, was marketed more effectively. Deep in his gypsy soul, Joe wanted to think that material things didn't matter. But he made a ton of money, enjoyed it and—for what he gave back to the sport—earned every dime.

He threatened to retire once, when the commissioner asked him to sell his interest in his club, Bachelors III, after reports were made public that gamblers were among the clientele. Joe finally did. One of those who urged him to do so was Bryant, in a phone call from Tuscaloosa.

"Joe, if those so-called friends gave a damn about you," said Bear, "they'd tell you to sell."

He defended his friends and said he had to do what he thought was right.

There was a pause on the line and then Bryant said, "Joe, have you gotten so big you've forgotten how to pray?"

"No, coach," he answered. "That's about all I have been doing for the past week."

He grew in taste and class. Traded to the Rams, Joe didn't play a down the last two months of what turned out to be his last season, 1978. He never complained, never stirred the kind of trouble that one in his position could easily have done.

In August 1986 Joe Willie Namath, who shook from his white shoes the coal dust of Beaver Falls, who made headlines as a rebel, a playboy and a quarterback, although not necessarily in that order, was inducted into pro football's Hall of Fame at Canton, Ohio.

His presence there is the final verdict on his career as a professional. We can only guess at what he might have done on two sound legs. You tend to feel the same way about Mickey Mantle. On ailing legs, Mantle made it to the Hall of Fame. With healthy wheels, he might have joined Ruth and Cobb as three of a kind.

Namath cannot be judged only on the record. You had to see him, his style, the dart-gun release, the way he ran a team and raced a clock and brought a crowd to its feet.

He did not look much older, as he walked across the field to receive his plaque, than the freshman who climbed the tower his first day at Alabama.

The suit was smartly tailored, the hair razor-cut and styled, somewhere between the crewcut he wore in college and the mod length of his New York rebel days. And in the middle of a brief talk thanking the people who needed to be thanked, a television audience across the country heard his voice crack when he said:

"Coach Bryant, Mrs. Bryant, wherever you are, we miss you."

Chapter 10

The '60s: High Tide

On the heels of Trammell, Namath and Sloan came Ken Stabler, the latest in a list of quarterbacks who blossomed under a coach noted for his defensive instincts. How different they were: Trammell, cleancut, scholarly, a future doctor; Namath, who entertained us around the clock with his arm and his lifestyle; Sloan, quiet, religious, steadfast; and Stabler, the good ole boy from the Redneck Riviera.

But one way or another Bryant reached them. Whatever went into the compactor, what came out was a winner.

As a sophomore, Stabler was a defensive back on the 1965 national championship team, maybe the most satisfying of all Bryant's champions. They would have to come from way back to get it, after opening the season with a loss to Georgia (17–16). After five weeks Alabama was unranked, tied by Tennessee and with a one-point win over Ole Miss. Bear was debating whether to stick with Sloan or switch to his young left-hander, Stabler. He stayed with Sloan, who responded with a big finish.

The day Tennessee tied them at Birmingham was the day Stabler threw the ball out of bounds to stop the clock, at the two-yard line, then realized it was fourth down. And Bryant knocked the locker-room door off its hinges with his shoulder.

He was angry with himself, not his players. He blamed the blunder on a substitution he had made and told the team that if he'd had it to do over he would have stayed home and they would have won without him.

It may have started out only as a ploy to sharpen the team's competitive edge. But Bryant began telling them they still had a shot at the national title. They won their last five, scoring 30 or more points in each of the last three, and week by week they gained ground in the polls. When the season ended they were fourth, behind only Michigan State, Arkansas and Nebraska.

This was the first year the polls would not close until *after* the bowl games; the change was the result of Alabama winning the 1964 crown in spite of the loss to Texas. So now they had a chance to have it both ways.

Bear went to the blackboard one day and showed the squad how it could happen: He picked UCLA to upset Michigan State in the Rose Bowl, and LSU to knock off Arkansas in the Cotton. And that night, in the Orange Bowl, the Crimson Tide would face Nebraska with everything on the line.

And just like the tumblers clicking in a wall safe, the bets came in: UCLA upset Michigan State, 14–3. It was LSU over Arkansas, 14–7.

And under the lights in the Orange Bowl, Alabama went for broke. A touchdown underdog, and outweighed up front by 48 pounds a man, the quick-striking Tide completed a screen pass off a tackle-eligible play on its first possession and went on to demolish Nebraska. The game was not nearly as close as the final score, 39–28, made it seem.

Ray Perkins had an all-America year at end, and the star of the defense was Jerry Duncan, who had been recruited as a halfback, and played tackle at 190, or less.

Alabama had done it, had come from 10 weeks behind to finish first in the nation. But a Bryant-coached team would never again have the advantage of sneaking up on an opponent. For the rest of his career, they would be favored perhaps 90 percent of the time. This was not a role he preferred. When the hunters are loose, no one wants to be the hound, least of all Paul Bryant.

It was hard for him now to sell the idea of his little "narrer-butted boys"—meaning narrow, or skinny—going up against the goliaths every week. But he tried.

His dire predictions and woeful references grew thin and even Bear began to play it for laughs. Thus the stage was set for an annual series with Clemson starting in 1966, pairing him against a coach just as Southern and cranky and colorful, Frank Howard.

It was Howard who rejected the idea of adding rowing to the varsity calendar, because "Clemson will never subsidize a sport where the athletes sit on their ass and go backward."

Howard had attended Alabama and, in the words of Charley Thornton, "was as big a poormouther as Coach Bryant. And they were good friends. Frank was beloved by the media, and he couldn't resist taking off on 'ole Beah down theah lyin' about those skinny little boys of his, all suppose to weigh 180.'

"The week of the game in sixty-six, the Clemson publicity man, Bob Bradley, came to town and the two of us dropped by Coach Bryant's office. He decided he had to do something to get back at Frank and the three of us decided to rig the scales, the one we actually used to weigh the players.

"Coach Bryant had the scales set back about thirty pounds. Then he had me take our roster to a notary public and have her sign it. Well, hell, all that means is that she witnessed your signature, not that the figures are right. But we sent a photocopy to Frank and he just howled.

"On the Friday after Clemson worked out, we had Bradley bring Frank to the dressing room. He knew he was being set up but he didn't know how. Coach Bryant said, 'Now, Frank, this is where we weigh all our players and I want you to satisfy yourself that our figures are right. He turned to Bradley and asked him what he weighed. Bob just subtracted the thirty pounds and said, 'Aw, Coach, I don't know. The last time I got on a scale I weighed 137 or so.' He hopped on the scales and sure enough he was maybe a pound off. Then it was my turn, and I said, 'Oh, 132.'

"Now everybody looked at Howard. We had a photographer there, and he snapped a picture when Frank got on the scales. That needle quivered and stopped between 220 and 225. Hell, Frank Howard hadn't weighed 220 since he was in the eighth grade. He turned around and said, 'Goddam, Beah, I owe you an apology. Them scales are right on the money.' "

One year Bryant and Howard were invited to be the opposing coaches at a Texas high school all-star game. In the car driving to the stadium, Frank pointed out that there was no reason for either of them to be embarrassed by a one-sided loss. He suggested that if the score started to get out of hand, the losing team's coach would take out his handkerchief, and that would be the signal to call off the dogs.

Bryant agreed. And here Thornton picks up the story: "Both benches were on the same side of the field. Coach Bryant's team had gone ahead a couple touchdowns and was moving for another in the fourth quarter. Howard pulled out his handkerchief and gave it a discreet little wave, trying not to be too obvious. Coach Bryant folded his arms and stared straight out at the field.

"Now Frank is just flapping his arms like a seal and Bryant won't look at him. Frank is yelling at him, 'Beah! Hey, Beah!' And Carney Laslie walks over and tells him Howard is trying to get his attention. But Coach Bryant just loved the idea of getting Frank upset.

"And now his team is getting ready to score again, and Frank just throws that handkerchief to the ground. The teams lined up and for an instant the crowd noise stopped and you could hear Howard halfway up the stands: 'Beah, you lyin' son of a bitch, *look at me!*' But it worked out fine, because Frank got a lot of mileage out of that story on the banquet circuit."

Bryant's disciples were moving out across the land in the 1960s, some of them just in time to get swept up in the cross currents of that decade: the antiwar movement, the drug culture, the sexual revolution, long hair, the kinds of rebellion that had avoided football and the people who coached it.

Bryant had waited 10 years before one of his assistants had been hired to head his own staff. That was Jim Owens, at Washington, where he replaced Darrell Royal after the 1956 season.

By 1964, Jerry Claiborne had taken over at Virginia Tech, Charlie Bradshaw at Kentucky and Phil Cutchin at Oklahoma State. And the closing of the circle, in a sense, took place in December of that year, when the Texas Aggies hired one of Bryant's Junction Boys, Gene Stallings, as their new head coach.

Stallings replaced Hank Foldberg, whose teams had won only five conference games in three years. Foldberg had followed Jim Myers.

In my story in the *Houston Post*, I described contacting Bryant by phone in New York, where he was attending the Hall of Fame dinner:

Asked his reaction, The Bear showed that he had lost none of his dramatic flair. "It's the first time I've cried in twenty or thirty years," he said, "and believe me, I really did. I cried because I'm so proud that one of my little Junction boys is going back there to take over. And, secondly, I cried because I'm so upset over losing him. Shoot, with Stallings gone I may have to go back to work."

Stallings was an all-conference end at A&M who recorded in a notebook nearly everything Bryant told his players. As early as his senior year, Bryant was predicting that someday Bebes—his nickname since childhood—would be a head coach.

"A&M could go back to Rockne," declared Bryant, "and they could not have picked a better man. He will be the best football coach the school ever had, and that includes father."

The last reference was to himself. In his mellowing older age, with his former players branching out into head jobs of their own, Bryant has adopted a kind of daddy image.

The story had a funny sequel. Months later, a free-lance writer named Bob Curran told me he walked into Bryant's hotel room during our phone interview. He said he noticed that Bear's voice was husky and he thought he saw some moisture around his eyes.

"What's wrong with Paul?" he asked a mutual friend.

"He just lost an assistant coach," the man whispered.

"How old was he?"

"Twenty-nine."

"My God," exclaimed Curran, "that's awfully young. How did he die?"

"Oh, he didn't die," the friend assured him, "he just went to Texas A&M."

In the next three years, while Alabama was winning one national title, just missing another and losing a total of three games, the

Aggies were struggling to regain their respectability. The break-through came in 1967. The Aggies lost their first four games, and with Stallings's job not exactly secure, finished the season with six straight victories. They started their winning streak when quarter-back Edd Hargett scrambled for the touchdown that beat Texas Tech as time ran out. A victory over Texas, on Thanksgiving Day, gave them the conference title and a trip to the Cotton Bowl.

Alabama, once-beaten (by Tennessee) and once-tied (by Florida State), was picked as the visiting team, setting up the most fraternal postseason football game Dallas had ever seen.

Stallings was just a pup out of Bryant. He walked like him and talked like him and quoted his teachings as though they were scriptures. On recruiting: "Coach Bryant didn't tell you how to load the truck, he just told you to load it." And on overcoaching: "I was running around before the kickoff one day and reminding players of their assignments. He grabbed me and said, 'If you can't coach 'em during the week, you sure as hell can't coach 'em at one o'clock on Saturday.' "

The Aggie players had heard so many stories about Bryant, the coach who coached their coach, they must have thought they had played for him in another life.

At their daily press conferences, Bryant and Stallings tried to out-poormouth one another. Bryant usually won. Stallings had commented that he thought the Aggies had recruited well that year, then added: "Of course, we recruited a bunch of kids who couldn't play for Alabama."

And Bryant retorted: "Well, hell, Bebes, we still have some you recruited and they can't play for Alabama, either."

There was an honest and open affection between them, but being at a bowl game was clearly a bigger adventure for the Aggies than for the Crimson Tide. So evident was Stallings's allegiance to the Bear, and so closely crafted were the teams in the style of football they played, one writer asked jokingly if the Aggies used the same postgame prayer as Alabama. "Yes, we do," Stallings replied. "It's called the Lord's Prayer."

Each day brought a new test of one-upmanship. Stallings came to one interview right from the practice field, wearing a maroon jacket and his coaching cap soiled and set low on his forehead. His khaki pants were muddy and he had on high-topped hunting boots.

Bryant wore a checked blue sport coat, charcoal slacks, a charcoal tie with blue stripes and alligator cowboy boots.

Bear muttered something that sounded like "Ol' dingy cap," and then said he was surprised that Stallings would appear in public in his work clothes.

"You taught me to work," said Gene. "I can party after the game." When they sat down and Bryant crossed his legs, you could read the letters embroidered on the sides of his boots. They spelled out, TEXAS AGGIES. Bryant ran a hand over the leather and said, "I'm rather proud of them. Some Aggie ex gave 'em to me after we won the title in fifty-six. Stallings and those fellows earned these boots for me."

You could feel the fun Bryant was having, the pleasure in seeing the Aggies in the Cotton Bowl, reenacting the game that wasn't played in 1956. And he could not resist chiding his protégé about his "overnight" success.

"When I first came to Texas A&M," the Bear recalled, "I had been coaching for twelve years, and I came here from Kentucky and Mother and I were invited to a party in Dallas at the home of some rich oilman, maybe Clint Murchison. When we were ready to leave, Mary Harmon couldn't find her claim check, but the fellow we were with said we didn't need it, and he told the girl in the cloak room she wouldn't have any trouble finding it, 'It's the only cloth job in there.'

"Now I had been coaching twelve years. The next day I went down to Houston and borrowed some money from Doc Doherty, an Aggie friend of mine, and bought Mother a fur coat." At this point, Bryant turned and addressed Stallings directly: "Now, Bebes, you been a head coach for three years, and my question is this: Where was Ruth Ann today when we tried to phone her all afternoon?"

"She was out buying that fur coat," said Stallings, with the grin of a man who knew he was being had.

"*What?*" exclaimed Bryant, with mock astonishment. "After just three years?"

"Well," said Stallings, "one championship at Texas A&M and you can afford it. You ought to know that. You got those boots."

The Aggies upset Alabama, 20–16, as Edd Hargett threw touchdown passes to Larry Stegent and Tommy Maxwell, and Wendell

Housley ran 20 yards to produce a 20–10 lead in the third quarter. The Aggies were holding on at the end, when Curley Hallman intercepted Kenny Stabler's last pass with 22 seconds to play.

Hallman was an Alabaman, once rated the fifth-best high school quarterback in the state. Bryant had recruited the first four, so Curley signed up with Stallings and was moved to safety. He grew up in Northport, on the other side of the bridge from Tuscaloosa. "Everything you hear about Alabama, and the way they love Coach Bryant, is true," he said after the game. "They make jokes about him feeding ten thousand people with a Coke and a bag of potato chips."

When the gun sounded, 75,000 spectators and the viewers watching on television were treated to the kind of showman's gesture seldom seen in a game of any importance. Bryant made his way through the crowd to reach Stallings. Instead of the traditional handshake, he hoisted his gangly pupil awkwardly to his shoulder and carried him toward the lockers, a most unsteady equestrian. You had the feeling that a grinning Stallings got down as quickly as he could, without being rude.

On the Aggie sideline that day, rooting against Paul Bryant for the first time in their lives, were some of the veterans of the '56 season—John David Crow, Jack Pardee, Loyd Taylor, Bobby Marks, Charlie Krueger, Dennis Goehring. The Cotton Bowl had been one joyful family feud. There was no way to know that the locusts were coming to A&M again, and that 18 years would pass before they would return, and then under another Bryant student, Jackie Sherrill.

At Alabama, when the coaching staff voted 10 to 1 to give Joe Namath a second chance, Stallings was the one who voted to suspend him. Actually, there were two such votes if you count Bryant, and most people did. The next spring, Joe Willie returned to the team, led the Tide to 10 victories and then signed the contract with the Jets that made him rich and famous.

Stallings never recaptured the magic of the 1967 season. One year he dismissed from his team the best athlete he ever coached, Mo Moorman, who went on to become an all-pro lineman at Kansas City. Moorman was kicked off the team for cutting classes, a reason as rare then as it is today.

The A&M job was still as tough under Stallings as it had been under Bryant. The state schools in Texas still did not recruit blacks. There were no girls on campus, and no multimillion-dollar athletic dorm. Young Americans were getting killed in a place called Vietnam, and football prospects were not exactly charmed by A&M's rich military traditions.

So the Aggies didn't win and Stallings was fired in 1972, a stigma hard to shake. You could go back to D. X. Bible in the 1920s without finding a coach who was ash-canned by A&M and ever again commanded his own team.

Stallings showed up the next year coaching the defensive backs at Dallas. And there he stayed, twice turning down head coaching offers because he felt the timing was unfair to his employer. It takes a certain kind of class and security to turn down the only thing you have ever wanted, for a reason as old-fashioned as loyalty.

He was hired as head coach of the Saint Louis Cardinals in 1986, coming to them with a mighty handsome pedigree—12 years as a player and coach under Paul Bryant, 13 as an assistant under Tom Landry.

Cardinal owner Bill Bidwell interviewed Gene three times. "I checked you out," Bidwell said, "and a lot of people think very highly of you." Stallings looked him in the eye and said, "That's good, because I checked you out, too." The cool, detached influence of Landry was a valuable balance to the earthy, hard-nosed approach he learned from the Bear.

Stallings has a retarded son, Johnny, who was not expected to live past his sixth birthday. He was 23 when he heard the news that his father had been hired by the Cardinals, and he told him, "I'm proud of you, Pop."

So were a lot of other people. Namath had to wait only a few months for his second chance. Gene Stallings waited 14 years.

In the summer of 1967, Ken Stabler reenacted the Namath drama. He was thrown off the team, for reasons he explained:

"I'm not your basic conformist, and Coach Bryant was tough on me for my own good. I don't know where I'd be if it wasn't for him. I needed guidance.

"At the end of my junior year, I had a knee injury and had been kept out of spring practice. I got frustrated, started running around and chasing ladies. One thing led to another, and I ended up in

Foley, my home town. He sent me a telegram that said: 'You have been indefinitely suspended. Signed, Coach Paul W. Bryant.' "

A few days later, he received another wire, just three words long: "He means it," was the message, signed by Joe Namath.

"I enrolled in summer school," said Stabler, "and every week I had to report to Coach Bryant. It was one of the hardest things I ever had to do. I'd go in and see him. He looked like he weighed about five hundred pounds sitting across that desk. He never said anything until the end of the summer. Then he looked at me and said, 'You don't deserve to be on this football team.' I didn't say anything at first. But I was kind of stubborn, like him. Finally, I said, 'Well, I'm coming out there anyway.' One of the assistant coaches told me later that was what sold him on me. Then I went out and bought a case of beer and drove back to Foley, throwing away the empties at every stop sign. I was happy.

"I cussed him a thousand times in practice. Not to his face. I'm not crazy. I smoked cigarettes, but never in front of him. Figure that one out. If he had ever called me on a Monday and said he needed help, I would have been on the first plane to Birmingham. Sunday would have been tough [during Stabler's pro years]. But I'd have gone. That would never have happened, though, because of the kind of man he was. He wouldn't have called me on a Sunday no matter how much he needed me. He would have waited until Monday."

I was not a part of Bryant's Alabama years, and will not attempt to recreate them here, except in a general way, or through the eyes of those who were.

In 1980, I had a chance to get to know Stabler, after he had been traded to Houston by the Oakland Raiders, in return for Dan Pastorini. It was that year's most publicized trade, the first time starting quarterbacks in the NFL ever had been swapped one-for-one. Stabler was coming to a team coached by a man who also bore the Bryant imprint, Bum Phillips.

The Network was still going strong.

On the night the trade was made, Stabler happened to be in a crowd attending a banquet in Mobile, where Bryant was the speaker. Recalled Kenny: "The news came over the wire late that afternoon.

I just barely had time to shake hands with Coach Bryant and ask how he was doing. Bunch of people around him. During his speech he stopped right in the middle of it. Somebody had slipped him a note about the trade.

"Coach Bryant looked around the room and asked, 'Is Kenny Stabler still here?' I stood up and said, 'Yeah, Coach.' He said, 'You have to be the luckiest man in the world. You're going down there with all those cowboys and you'll be playing football for Bum Phillips, who is one hell of a man.' "

Later, Phillips would say: "I didn't exactly go into that trade blind. I knew a little about Kenny. I called Coach Bryant. He said, 'Don't believe all you've heard. He's a great kid. He'll do whatever you ask of him. He's a winner.' "

By now, the kid was 34 years old with flowing, salt-and-pepper hair and a full beard, and he looked older than Phillips, though possibly not as old as Bryant. There was also a serene and spiritual quality about Stabler. Even when he was holding a can of beer in his hands, or a football, he had the air of a prophet waiting to be handed the tablets.

Instantly, Stabler decided that Bum reminded him of the Bear. "If he [Bum] said something, you could write it down as the truth. They were both full of one-liners and most of 'em were based on common sense. I think a great deal of Houston's success was due to the fact that the players cared an awful lot about Bum."

I found Stabler impressive in an unexpected way. There seemed to be absolutely no tension in him and no evasiveness. He was not afraid to reveal himself—a sharp and refreshing change from many professional athletes.

"People always thought my lifestyle would ruin me," he said, the first time we talked. "Yeah, I like to get out and get after it. So what if I go out and drink, shoot some pool, chase women, stay out late, don't come home. All the time I'm doin' that I'm bein' nice to people. I go into bars and sign autographs and shake hands and shoot the bull. What's wrong with that?"

I learned that Stabler amused himself in his spare time by writing country and western songs. He had composed a total of three. Either he did not have a lot of spare time or he did not rush himself when the creative juices were flowing.

Kenny had never exposed his work to what he called "a real

singer," although he was well acquainted with several. His shyness was understandable. After all, Willie Nelson had never jogged up to him in the huddle and offered to show how far he could fling a football.

Most country music is based on universal themes: pain, weakness, love, whiskey, pickup trucks, good- or bad-hearted women and moving on down the line. Stabler's compositions were no exception. His favorite, he said, was one he had written "about hangin' out in honky-tonk bars and meetin' some lady, gettin' to know her and saying good-bye the next morning. Pretty soon it gets old. Everybody gets tired of that lifestyle, sooner or later."

The song may or may not have been autobiographical. But you did not have to be a bartender to enjoy Stabler's trust. He seemed to offer it automatically to anyone who had not crossed him. One day, at the Houston Oilers' training camp in San Angelo, in that summer of 1980, I sat with Jim Dent, a Dallas writer, in Stabler's room in the team dormitory. The talk was about Bum and country music and what Waylon Jennings called the basics of life. Out of the blue, Dent asked him what kind of dreams he had. Now, you can sometimes tell if an athlete has any imagination by how he responds to an unexpected or whimsical question. You ask some athletes what kind of dreams they have and they will pitch you out the nearest window.

But Stabler's eyes lighted up. "I had one the other night," he said. "I dreamed that I was on this river in Alabama with my friend Randall Watson. He and I are pretty close. And we're up there in this place where we can get away from people. And we're sittin' and fishin' and all of a sudden, Dan Rather pops out of the woods. Honest to God! And he's wearing a coat and tie and tennis shoes. He came up there and shot the bull with us. And I kept waitin' for a camera crew to come out of the woods and ask about my tax return."

(I had helped Rather with a book a few years earlier. I was able to assure Stabler that, in all probability, Dan would have hunkered down and asked him if he ever listened to Floyd Tillman records. Rather grew up in Houston, in the Heights, in a house where the radio was always tuned to the kind of music that Stabler's generation thought it discovered. Tillman's big hit was "I Love You So Much It Hurts Me.")

After he finished describing his dream, Stabler leaned back and said, "Boy, I really like these questions. Got any more?"

It occurred to me that Stabler must have been a puzzle to Paul Bryant much of the time. But he and Bum Phillips were soul brothers.

"Right after the trade," he recalled, "I came to Houston and went into his [Bum's] office. He was propped up with his cowboy boots on the desk. He had on ragged Levis and an old cowboy shirt. His hat was cocked back on his head and he was spittin' tobacco juice into a Coca-Cola cup. He was just an unpretentious cowboy who happened to coach football."

There was, as Stabler noted, a lot of Bear Bryant in Bum Phillips, certainly in the way they cared about their players. The main difference was that Phillips seemed willing, and able, to show his interest and his affection even before they finished their careers.

Bryant could appear ruthless in his decisions, cutting or suspending a player. And yet he could be thoughtful and considerate in an almost manic way. He might spend days trying to land a job on a Canadian football team for a player he had just fired for conduct he considered distasteful or disloyal. Only one point mattered: that the job was needed.

Of all the Bear watchers, of the hundreds who played for him and coached under him, I don't believe anyone understood what made him tick as well as Bum did. He explained once why so many of Bryant's disciples had mixed records as coaches. "They wanted to coach like Bryant," said Bum. "And they couldn't. For one thing, Coach Bryant didn't coach the way they thought he did. He didn't treat everybody alike. And he made exceptions all the time. He just didn't talk about it. And he didn't do it in a way that embarrassed them."

There was a revealing encounter in 1978, the first time the Houston Oilers played the Dallas Cowboys on national television, on Thanksgiving Day, with both teams bound for the playoffs. The Oilers had never played the Cowboys when the outcome meant anything.

In the Dallas squad meetings, Ermal Allen gave the scouting report on Houston. Ermal had coached under Bryant at Kentucky. Also on the Dallas staff were Jim Myers and Gene Stallings, former Aggie coaches with links of their own to that particular legend.

Allen, a jut-jawed, stiff-backed figure who parted his hair down the middle, told the Cowboys: "Bum Phillips used to work for Bear Bryant, and he's a disciple of that philosophy of coaching. Very fundamental; he tailors his game to the personnel he has to work with." Allen turned to his blackboard and chalked in the Oiler offense. "More and more this year, the Oilers have put four receivers on the field. The only set back is Earl Campbell. Now you can see, from this formation, there are very few things they can do. The quarterback hands off to Campbell, who hits straight ahead or slides outside. He can pitch out to Campbell going wide. Or he can fake to Campbell and pass. Unless they start a receiver in motion, nothing else is possible. The Oilers *show* you what they are going to do— and they just challenge you to stop it."

The Oilers had never beaten Dallas in the regular season. With a minute left, the game came down to this: the Oilers had a six-point lead and faced third-and-five in their own territory. If the Oilers didn't make the first down, here again would come Roger Staubach. The words of Ermal Allen brought the matchup into focus. Disguising nothing, the Oilers broke the huddle with Campbell the only running back. He took the handoff from Dan Pastorini, skittered along the line of scrimmage, for an instant bolted free, then skidded into the arms of a Dallas tackler.

A gain of seven yards. The game was won. The Houston bench exploded in celebration. Bum Phillips bellowed a rodeo whoop and walked around with both fists high in the air. In the Oiler locker room, a reporter reminded him that he had been saying all week that this was just another game. "Yeah," he admitted, with a grin, "but I lied."

Bum's introduction to football was not so different from Bryant's. He grew up in the East Texas towns of Orange and Beaumont during the Depression. His father, a truck driver, made the run to Houston twice a day, six days a week. His father liked baseball, but considered football a dangerous and pointless sport. "I came home late one night and he asked me where I'd been," said Bum. "I told him football practice—this was high school—and he said, 'You quit that; you'll get your leg broke.' The next night I came home late again and he asked me where I had been. I told him football practice and he wore my butt out good. Next night, the same thing. He told me to lay down on the bed and he wore me out some more. Next night, same thing. But this time he said, 'Okay, but if you get your leg broke just remember I told you so.' Daddy was like a lot of country people. All you were supposed to do was work."

In many ways, listening to Bum was like listening to Bear, the main difference being that when Bryant paused it was for effect, and when Bum paused it was to spit tobacco juice into a cup.

However, when Phillips put himself down you suspected there was a strong coil of truth in what he said. For example, on his career as a 185-pound guard in high school: "I thought I was real good until I saw one of my old films. Most disappointing experience I ever had."

On joining the Marine Corps at 18: "I learned my lesson. I never joined anything else the rest of my life. I went in as a private and thirty-one months later I came out as a private. The Marine Corps was real spit 'n polish. I wasn't."

Bum had the spit but not the polish. He was not offended when people were surprised that he could coach, and that he had a nice touch with a phrase. "Two kinds of football players ain't worth a damn," he once said. "The one that never does what he's told, and the other that never does anything *except* what he's told." And, although he did not push the point as far as Bryant did, he felt that the nature of football required a willingness to play hurt, or when ill. "Flu doesn't keep you from playing football," he said. "It just makes you uncomfortable. If you're sick, you can always call time out, throw up, and keep on playing."

And: "I've always said the things I say now. But when I was coaching at Nederland High School, nobody came around to write them down."

Phillips coached the Oilers to 33 wins in three years, took them to the playoffs three times and twice came within one win of the Super Bowl. He was fired after the Oilers lost to Oakland in the first round in 1980, and his gamble on Stabler did not pay off. They teamed up again in New Orleans two years later, both having been dismissed by the Oilers.

There was no reason to wonder why Stabler, at 36, still wanted to hang on as a player. It wasn't money or boredom or a hunger for revenge or redemption. "It must not be easy for people to understand," he said, "but for me playing football is fun. Being on the field, that's the part I need. It's fun. That's all."

George Blanda had still been hanging on, in his late forties, when Stabler reported as a rookie to the camp of the Oakland Raiders. He was the team's third-string quarterback, a kid not much older than Blanda's own son. They were out of the same bloodline, having played for Bryant 19 years apart.

They played golf together and sat on the bench together and second-guessed the starting quarterback, Daryle Lamonica. That was the year, 1970, that Blanda thrilled the Geritol generation by coming off the bench to win three games and tie another with his passing and kicking.

It was an effort for Stabler not to call Blanda "sir." Fresh out of Alabama, he had short brown hair and plump cheeks and you can't imagine him ever being that young. Blanda was 49 when the Raiders finally released him, the third and last team to do so.

Bryant's players had a tendency to get there early and stay late. Of course, this is a social problem that applies to the pros, not the colleges, and to the players, not the coaches.

Few coaches are allowed to overstay their time, to doze past their bus stop. One who didn't was Bum Phillips, who retired after the 1985 season, giving up the last year of a contract that was worth close to $300,000. He had been unable to get the Saints over .500 in his five seasons there. It wasn't the pressure to win that wore him down, just the not winning. The fans booed Earl Campbell in his first game after coming over from Houston, and once Bum had beer poured on him as he reached the tunnel at the end of the field. He said it wasn't fun any more, and he quit.

Bryant had always said he would do the same, quit if it stopped being fun. I have letters dated as far back as 1962, in which he would give himself another year, two at the most.

But winning was his addiction. There were tough times that didn't last. His lawyers beat up the *Saturday Evening Post* lawyers. And he created Alabama football in his own image. For all the turbulence of the 1960s, they had won three national titles in five years. His 1966 team deserved one, but didn't get it, in spite of 11 straight wins, six of them shutouts. They played Nebraska again, this time in the Sugar Bowl, and drubbed them even worse than the year before, 34–7.

But the voters voted Notre Dame the number 1 team that year, and the choice rankled Bryant. That was the year the Irish elected to run out the clock and settle for a tie with Michigan State, creating a demand for buttons and bumper stickers that read, TIE ONE FOR THE GIPPER. Bryant thought it was sinful, giving the title to a team that had played for a tie.

As a junior, Stabler had what Bryant called the best year any of his quarterbacks ever had. He was a lefthanded Namath, and he could run then, well enough to earn his nickname, Snake.

"Stabler had ability coming out of his ears," said Bryant. "He had a great touch passing, he could run the ball outside and he was quick as a cat."

This was a decade of quarterbacks at Bama—Trammell, Namath, Steve Sloan, Stabler and then Scott Hunter. The Tide won 90 games, the best 10-year record of any team in America. But something was happening, a glitch in the assembly line. Alabama was about to stumble off the mountain top.

Bryant said later that he thought his problems began in 1967, that team discipline had possibly suffered because he failed to impose a stricter penalty on Stabler. The Snake was on the bench, still on probation, when Alabama opened the season against underdog Florida State. The Seminoles jumped into a 14–0 lead in the first quarter, and now Stabler entered the game. They struggled to earn a wild 37–37 tie.

An hour documentary on Coach Bryant appeared that fall on ABC, and it led off with action from the Florida State game. I wrote a review of the special in the paper the next morning:

> The opening sequence was a grabber. You see this Florida State lad streaking for the goal line, his golden helmet gleaming under the artificial light, and then the camera cuts to the Alabama bench, where the air is rent by what at first sounds like the death call of a wounded buffalo.
>
> You quickly established, however, that the noise came from one Paul (Bear) Bryant, and what he actually said was: "What the hell is happening out there?"
>
> It was real. It was vivid. It was effective.
>
> But after that, ABC's hour-long special—"Coach Bryant:

Alabama's Bear"—seldom lived up to its promise. The first mistake the boys in the ABC think-tank made was in admitting that the show had been seven months in the making. Right away, this cost them the sympathy vote.

Secondly, if a viewer wants to see 10 minutes of game action, he can tune into any of a half dozen coaches' shows in Houston alone, and watch until his eyeballs bulge. Granted, the Alabama-Florida State scuffle must have been a dilly, and 37–37 ties are not exactly as common as crabgrass. Still, one doubts that this particular episode will be listed among the Great Games of the Century.

Yet ABC bored us with all that footage—it seemed even longer than 10 minutes—on the pretext that the viewer would see "Bear Bryant in action." What we got was some classic back-of-the-head shots, a frantic conversation with his quarterback about calling 50-go-and-release, several pained facial expressions and a lot of gibberish. One was almost prepared to believe it when a worn, subdued Bryant told his team in the locker room: "I sure didn't help you any from the bench. It was just confusion over there."

. . . The best part of the show was Bryant himself:

Indoctrinating his new players, saying that he expected them to be clean, neat, scrubbed, to write home to their mothers, attend church and smile, which is asking a lot of any young man.

A film clip of the Bear going on television to deny "with every force at my command" a story that he had contrived to rig the outcome of the Georgia game.

The Bear, recalling how he used to finish the chores and then sit for hours, watching the trains pass through Fordyce. And how he would dream of riding that train out of town.

. . . We are indebted to ABC on at least one account. The mystery of what coaches say to a trailing football team at halftime has been revealed at last. A hidden camera and microphone caught Bryant's pep talk to his players. "This is perfect," he almost whispered. "We're behind. They're all fired up. If we got any class, we're going to find out right now."

The column touched on what worked and what did not, and a few days later a letter arrived, postmarked Tuscaloosa. It was dated November 3, 1967—the Friday before Alabama was to play Clemson.

Dear Mickey,

After reading your column someone sent me, for the first time I realized just what I thought of the television thing. I honestly could not even explain to Mary Harmon what I thought was missing. You did it for me. I know I was disappointed they did not have more of my former players and shots from some of our big games rather than that opening thing.

. . . This old goat would listen to anybody about now if they could tell me how to get people to tackle and strike some blows. We have been doing a lot of catching the entire year, and consequently have had more injuries than I can remember. It is easy for me to use that as an excuse, but the cold, hard facts are that we have not been hitting people like you are supposed to when wearing that red jersey. We did start a little of it in practice this week. If we can get eleven on the field really trying these last few games, I believe we will begin looking like Alabama is supposed to and, in that event, we might be seeing you down your way when the season is over.

The letter was dictated but apparently not signed and mailed until after the weekend. There was a postscript in ink at the bottom. *"We are still piss poor."*

Alabama had squeaked past Clemson, 13–10.

But the reference to seeing us after the season, I knew, was to the Cotton Bowl feelers he had already received. Alabama won its last five and then lost to the Aggies on New Year's Day in Dallas.

With Scott Hunter at quarterback, the Tide finished 8-and-3 in '68, the beginning of what Bryant would call a three-year slump.

At the end of the decade, 1969, the bottom nearly fell out. They won six and lost five, what amounted to a losing season in Alabama. To compound the grief, they were buried by Auburn (49–26) and by Colorado in the Liberty Bowl (47–33). Those who knew Bryant covered their ears and waited for the large explosion that was sure to come.

Chapter 11

Pen Pals

Over the years, Coach Bryant had gotten it into his head that my stories had somehow helped him climb the coaching ladder, even contributed to his image. I thought not. I accepted the sentiment as the compliment he meant it to be. But if it were true, which I doubted, it was incidental to my job. I worked for the *Houston Post*, not Coach Bryant or Texas A&M.

The idea was so illogical to me that I could not even feel modest about it.

But he had said as much to Jones Ramsey, in so many words, and Darrell Royal, and more than a few writers. It made as much sense to me as Babe Ruth thanking the official scorer at Yankee Stadium for his home runs.

But there it was. He touched on this notion when he inscribed a copy of his autobiography to me; and when he could not remember if, in fact, he had sent the first one he mailed a second, so that I had the message in writing not once but twice:

To Mickey,

. . . Were it not for you this would never [have] been written 'cause I'd have never escaped the Brazos. Warmest personal regards—always—

Paul "Bear" Bryant

The next one was dated three weeks later, April 30, 1975, and the inscription expanded slightly on his original thought:

. . . Were it not for you I'd still be on the Brazos. I have and do treasure your friendship. Always know Mary Harmon and I love the entire family.

Sincerely,

Paul "Bear" Bryant

He was generous that way, in giving people credit they did not deserve and often did not want. Never mind that the reference to A&M made it sound like an escape from the Planet of the Apes. I knew what he meant. I also knew I had no more to do with his success at A&M than, say, a tuba player in the Aggie marching band. Nor did I encourage the long-standing desire of Alabama to bring him back. All he was doing, really, was thanking me for being on his side.

I believe Coach Bryant felt he owed me. For what, I am not sure. I was not naive about the fact that we used each other, and together we turned out reams of good copy. He gave me the colorful and descriptive lines. I tried to report them faithfully, sometimes building a story around one nice phrase. Nearly everything he said then seemed fresh or original. When he said that the Aggies won "because they had good mamas and papas," it was more than a harmless piece of flattery to the parents of his players. He was reminding them, the players, that they came from decent homes and that he, Bryant, was working with the values and character they had brought with them. "Good mamas and papas" was one of the phrases he wore out at Alabama, but back then it sounded fine, and was widely circulated.

We did help each other. I became a better-known writer because of him, and I would like to think my stories enabled the readers to find the soft center beneath the hard outer shell. Some of this had to do with the contract that exists between the writer, the subject and the reader. I often worried, still do, about whether we treat the people we write about fairly, and as fully dimensional figures. Do we owe them more sympathy, or none?

Bryant made my job easy. It was not just that he was a complex and interesting piece of work, but that he held back very little. He took me into his confidence, and once there I found it hard to get out.

Possibly I am making the attachment, and the tradeoff, more equal than they were. But at some point in those years we made a leap in our relationship, from hero worshiper and worshipee, to good friends. When I twice left Texas for jobs in New York, once with the American Football League and again to edit a sports magazine, he always called if he found himself in the city. I knew I had moved out of that paternal circle that had previously defined our friendship the first time he played one of his practical jokes on me.

My secretary at the American Football League was a sweet and circumspect young woman named Joan McCook. She buzzed me on the intercom one day and in an almost trembling voice told me I had a call, but the man would not give his name and she did not think I wanted to talk with him. "Exactly what did he say?" I asked her. There was a pause and I heard her take a deep breath: "He said, 'Just tell the little son of a bitch that it's the guy whose wife he has been running around with.' "

I assured Joan it had to be a joke. With more than passing curiosity, I picked up the phone and said hello. He had been on hold for nearly a minute, had a sense of what was being said, and greeted me with a deep and hearty laugh I recognized instantly. "Goddam, Coach," I said, "you shocked the hell out of my secretary."

"Yeah," he said, with satisfaction. "I hate it when they ask if they can say who's calling."

I have only vague memories of that night, of the people who moved in and out of Coach Bryant's hotel suite; how we started out in two or three cabs and wound up with one, leaving one club for another and having dinner late at a fine German restaurant then on 11th Street, called Luchow's. But I cannot forget the date—December 7, 1966—or the dark mood it triggered for one of his friends, long after the coach had gone back to his hotel, leaving me to guide them. I had been in New York a few months. It was the perfect example of the blind leading the blind.

The friend—I will call him Dixie—had gotten Bryant involved in one of the business deals that would eventually make him a wealthy man. Good for the coach, and good for the business.

Dixie had fought in World War II and that night, in the German restaurant, where a large group of Japanese tourists had taken a table near ours, after too many drinks, a lot of old and bitter feelings surfaced. We had to grab him and half push him toward the door to avoid a scene with the Japanese, who never noticed, who were laughing and chattering and enjoying the robust German music that filled the room.

By the time we reached a bar below street level in the Village, the rest of the group—however many there had been of us—began to disappear. We were down to three, Dixie, his date, an airline hostess based in Birmingham, and me. He started talking in the cab about the war and was still going strong in the bar, when I looked at my watch and realized it was nearly 4:00 in the morning. She was still listening to him when I left.

What had triggered the sudden mood swing, it became clear, was a visit a few weeks earlier to his office by two Japanese executives, top people in the company's Tokyo plant. He described how he and his wife had entertained them with dinner in his home, and after a while he had said to them: "I'd like to ask you a personal question. Our countries fought against each other. Some of my friends died. Maybe yours. Now you have been in my home, shared my food and my whiskey. What I want to know is, if we were at war again, could you kill me?"

He said his guests looked at each other, possibly puzzled by the question, but responded only with smiles and shrugs. He excused himself, went upstairs to his bedroom and returned a few moments later with a Japanese army pistol.

As his guests examined it, he told them: "I took it off a dead Jap on the beach at Okinawa. Then I urinated on his body."

That was when I left.

I called Coach Bryant's rooms around noon the next day, and the airline hostess picked up the extension. She was the only one awake. I asked her if I had missed anything and she said I had.

She and Dixie had watched the sun come up, she said, and he recalled how he had been a law student at Columbia when the Japanese bombed Pearl Harbor, and a week or so later he enlisted in the Marines. He never made it back to law school. After the war he returned to Alabama, went into business, not a glamorous one but profitable. He became an executive and had stock in the company.

When they caught a cab out of the Village that morning, a Saturday, he realized they were only a few miles from the Columbia campus and he had a sudden hankering to see if his old dormitory was still standing. It was. He told the taxi driver to wait and he got out and went inside, found his old room and knocked on the door. The time was a little after seven. A very sleepy student opened the door and Dixie apologized, explaining how he had once occupied that room, twenty-five years earlier, was in the neighborhood and had an urge to see it. He took a quick look inside, thanked the young man for letting him impose and left.

"Do you know what?" the hostess said, finishing the story. "The boy who had Dixie's old room was Japanese."

I did not get a chance to call back until later in the day, and by then I was told Coach Bryant and his party had checked out and flown home to Alabama. There were to be many such visits, always with one or more friends, some more interesting than others.

Once he called wanting a favor. Charlie Finley, the controversial owner of the Oakland A's, had told Bryant he had the inside track on a National Football League franchise in Birmingham. He wanted Bryant to come in as his partner, with the titles of general manager and head coach. Finley had engaged Bryant's interest by talking huge numbers. Bryant did not want his interest made public. He asked me to call Pete Rozelle, the NFL commissioner, and find out how Finley stood with the league.

I checked with Jim Kensil, who was then Rozelle's top aide. Kensil called back within an hour. The message was blunt: There were no plans at that time to expand into Birmingham. If there were, Finley would not be regarded favorably as a prospective owner. Jim made a point of adding that the presence of Coach Bryant would be regarded as a plus for any group seeking a franchise, but he ought to steer clear of Finley. I passed that information on, and Coach Bryant said: "That's all I wanted to know. I like ol' Charlie, but you can't always count on what he says."

During those years, after he had left Texas and I was in and out of New York, we stayed in touch. One of the unexpected things about Bryant was how consistently he did so, with former players, other coaches, and friends of long or casual standing. He returned calls and answered letters. He kept up with how the kids were. He knew if the career was going well, or poorly, and if the family had been good, or bad.

I never made copies of the letters I wrote him. It never crossed my mind that it would have been an interesting thing to do. Nor was there a pattern to the letters of his that I saved. In many of them he wrote about his football teams, usually in a gloomy way. Once in a while he offered a nice insight into the sport as it was then played, or the details of a particular game. Sometimes he wrote with word of a mutual friend.

I made a reference to his having felt a kind of debt to me. Whether he really felt this way, or why, is unimportant. But before he left A&M he brought up the idea of writing his autobiography. I don't think he ever asked me if I wanted to work with him on it. He took it for granted that I did. And this became an understanding between us. It was also, I think, my payback.

While the idea excited me, I was never able to tell Coach Bryant that I liked talking about it far better than the idea of doing it. Too much time has passed, and my feelings were too complicated, to be really honest with myself about it now. But I had not yet written a book, knew that I was still too much in awe of him to do the objective work that was needed, and had a powerful fear of letting us both down.

But Bryant made occasional references to his book—"I'm gonna have to put that in my book"—as though it were in progress, and he dropped my name in connection with it. I still have in my files a telegram dated July 16, 1961, from Earl Burton, of *Sports Illustrated*:

UNDERSTAND YOU ARE DOING A BOOK ON BEAR BRYANT. DO YOU
THINK THERE IS ANYTHING IN IT THAT WOULD BE SUITABLE FOR
EXCERPTING? COULD WE ARRANGE WITH THE PUBLISHER TO TAKE
A LOOK AT THE MANUSCRIPT OR GALLEY PROOFS?

That expression of interest impressed us both, and while it did
nothing to generate any pages of manuscript, the coach and I talked
more earnestly for several months about the book.

Apparently, we had even begun to kick around dates for getting
together and taping some interviews. Houston had been awarded a
team in the National League, and I was assigned to cover it in 1962
and for several seasons thereafter. In January, Bryant had written

. . . I have nine additional clinics over and above my own
schedule and I simply will not be here more than three days
at a time until July. If we cannot get together before then, I
will make it a point to get someplace this summer, where
your baseball team is, and we can begin our little background
for our story. My thinking on this is that we could go ahead
and be preparing the book and have it written and go on sale
when I retire from coaching. I believe by doing that we could
put things in it that otherwise we could not include. I don't
think it would be very long, either, couple years, maybe even
sooner. Anyway . . . I will be in touch with you and we will
get together some way, somehow.

It was certainly wonderful to see you in New Orleans.
Glad to see your pretty wife. Please give her and the children
our love.

Cordially,
Paul

The reference to New Orleans meant the Sugar Bowl, won by
Alabama over Arkansas, 10–3. The highlight of any Sugar Bowl
week is always the New Year's Eve party on Bourbon Street, in the
historic restaurant called Antoine's. There is a ritual where the rival
coaches don the tall white chef's hats and white aprons, and stir the
brandy and strong Louisiana coffee that becomes café brulôt, top-

ping off the rich six- or seven-course dinner. Also, as part of the tradition, the presidents of the two schools offer up some flowery words about the greatness of their coaches.

And I remember Bryant walking up to the microphone, turning to his younger colleague, and saying: "Frank, about that business of loving you just as much whether you win or lose, I just want to say one thing: Don't believe a damned word of it."

I could always count on seeing him two or three times a season, and usually at a bowl game. Two years earlier, in 1959, I was in New Orleans with another *Post* writer, Jack Gallagher, whose style differed sharply from mine. Jack was tough, crusty, cynical, but he had taken a liking to Bear after a slow start.

Alabama had lost to Penn State in the Liberty Bowl the week before, and Bryant had stopped off to watch the Sugar Bowl and bet on the horses. After first encountering the Bear at the Fair Grounds, watching the ponies run with Dizzy Dean, Jack wrote of "a tearful reunion in the circular bar of the Monteleone Hotel." (This is a clear example of a writer taking literary license.)

> When Bryant coached Texas A and M and Herskowitz, then as now, covered the Aggies for the *Post*, they became fast friends. "Where's brother Mickey?" was the first question Bryant asked at the tracks.
>
> Brother Mickey was back at the hotel writing a story, and in the evening Bryant came around to visit him.
>
> "You know, Bear," said Herskowitz, who has become so bold that he has dropped the reverent "Coach" in addressing the Alabama headmaster, and now calls him by his nickname, "I heard some people this year say that your team couldn't score, and I defended you. I said that you considered scoring a sign of weakness."
>
> Bryant smiled tolerantly and admitted that the sons of Alabama's mommies and poppies crossed the goal in 1959 about as often as their coach picked winners at the race track.

Now is as good a time as any to correct the record. I saw myself gaining in maturity, and one way to show it, I thought, was to be less formal. I went through periods of trying to call him Bear, and once or twice I went with the even more intimate Paul. I had some success at using Papa, a term he liked and used himself and whose sound appealed to me as Hemingwayesque. But in the end, I never felt comfortable referring to him other than as Coach Bryant, as nearly all his players did. Where I have used Bear on these pages, and I have done so frequently, it was for convenience or the rhythm of the sentence or to avoid repetition.

It is probably a conservative guess to say that 90 percent of what I wrote about him over the years has been uncritical. Except for the anecdote about Charley Milstead, the one he misjudged, I really took him to task only once, and then in stories that ran for a week or more. My sympathies were completely against him, and I found his actions faulty and unfair.

In 1957, as athletic director, he had fired the Aggie basketball coach, Ken Loeffler. Charges of recruiting violations in basketball had been partly responsible for the sanctions not being lifted after the football team won the conference title in '56.

Bryant had hired Loeffler in the first place. Loeffler had been determined to make the Aggies a national power in basketball, and had begun to enlist the support of some rich exes who previously had concentrated their loyalties on football. This was where the trouble began. But Loeffler was also a brilliant and outspoken fellow, a law professor, who spoke Latin and could quote dead poets for hours.

He had won national titles at LaSalle and developed Tom Gola, a three-time all-American. People were stunned when Bryant, seeing that a change was needed at A&M, went out and hired a basketball coach of Loeffler's stature. He had resented Rupp's power at Kentucky, but he was secure now, and eager to show that he wanted a championship basketball team, too.

It did not work out that way, of course. Loeffler (pronounced LEFF-ler) was a captivating character who had an opinion on everything: Texas politics, the pace of integration in the South, sex, the absurdities of sports and higher education. He had a theory that the oil powers in Texas would not let A&M go coed, preferring that most Aggie students jump in their cars each weekend and drive across the state to visit their girlfriends.

Loeffler campaigned in all his booster club appearances to make A&M coeducational, to admit blacks and, in a somewhat less serious vein, to put the basket on the floor "so the little man can dunk the ball, too."

Loeffler wore bow ties, played the piano by ear, and could, as one writer said, "recite Homer with all the original gestures." Bryant was proud of him, and enjoyed his quotes and his antics, right up to the moment his long reach in recruiting brought the NCAA back to the campus.

So Bryant fired him. That day I drove up from Houston and sat with Ken and his wife for hours in their living room, all of us cursing the Bear. My stories were filled with sympathy for the fired coach, and unsparing of the athletic director, concluding that Bryant had undone the good impression he created when he upgraded the basketball team.

Bryant never mentioned the articles to me, never defended his action, never gave any indication that he expected me to react in any other way. I kept up a correspondence with Loeffler, who gave up coaching and went back to teaching law, at Montclair College, in New Jersey. We met once, by accident, a few years later, and over drinks in a hotel bar he told me he had no ill feelings toward Bear. He laughed and said, "You know, if he walked in here right now, he'd sit down and put his arm around me and tell me just what he said the day he fired me: 'I'm sorry, Ken. I like you. But you're fucking up my program.' "

Now the 1960s were flying by, Bryant was enjoying the kind of success and recognition coaches dream about, and enormous changes were taking place across the country. On the campuses, students were tearing their T-shirts and screaming about causes and justice and social unrest. It was a time in which they were particularly, after many years of acquiescence, calling to question the importance of athletics, especially football.

And so perhaps related to these times, perhaps not, Bear Bryant kept making references to his retirement. It became a habit with me to drop him a note before the start of a new season, and when he answered on August 30, 1963, he said:

". . . We are about to get underway, so I will be brief and to the point. I believe we should think of the book in terms of a date two years from now, possibly immediately following the '64 season. This is *strictly, strictly, confidential*, but if everything went right, what would you think of the possibility of a movie autobiography type of a thing? If this has any possibility, we should do it before John Wayne gets too old because he would probably be the only guy who could do the job."

The underlines were drawn by him. He scribbled another of his postscripts at the bottom of the page, and to this day I am not certain what it says. I think the sentence reads: "Mick, things [look] tough all way. Next couple years publicity should determine if go or not."

I did not have the foggiest idea what he meant, whether he was referring to the coming season or even hinting at the conflict just ahead of him involving the *Saturday Evening Post*. I put the letter away, planning to ask him about it at another time. I never did. I had a hunch though that his California friends were chatting him up about a movie. Of course, he was right about John Wayne.

After the back-to-back national championships in 1964 and 1965, Bryant was without argument the most distinctive coach in college football. I have been careful not to say the best, although I thought he was, nor the most famous, even as his nearest competitors were dropping out or falling behind. He had been less known than Frank Leahy or Red Blaik. They were gone now. He had passed Bud Wilkinson and Duffy Daugherty and Bobby Dodd. John McKay and Woody Hayes were in the running, but they didn't have the aura.

It kept getting back to me that Bryant had changed, turned mellow, since his Aggie trials. I don't think he changed, so much as he simply allowed more people to see his softer, funnier, more human side. But he had changed as a coach, and with the times.

He touched on this in one of his letters, undated, with a kind of wistful tone to it: "The day is gone when you could take a two-fisted little Aggie, make him mean, and just out-gut somebody." I read this as a lament for a game he knew had passed. In an era now gone, you pushed and the other side pushed back, and whoever pushed the hardest won.

In early 1966, *Sports Illustrated* assigned John Underwood to write a five-part series on Bryant's career and life, under the headline, I'LL TELL YOU ABOUT FOOTBALL. The first one appeared in August, and it was just a wonderful job by the two of them; Bryant being himself and John capturing the texture of him. I would have felt that way even if the first paragraph of the first article wasn't about me and the time I drove up to A&M to ask Coach Bryant if there was dissension on the team.

In September, we exchanged letters, and I must have picked up an item in the paper that the Ethics Committee was looking into a complaint, otherwise unidentified, because his reply left little doubt that he was upset:

> In regards to Ray Graves and the Ethics Committee statement, I would have blasted him good, but I did not think it was worth dignifying his comments. I had a letter from him the following day which I did not even bother to answer. To hell with the Ethics Committee, him and the whole outfit. I would be glad for their committee, the NCAA, the United Nations or the Foreign Relations Committee to investigate our program, or me!
>
> It was good seeing you this summer and I look forward to that more often. I might mention, however, that it might be well to make those trips to Miami very seldom, because . . . no one can keep up with Dick Fincher and his gang around the Bonfire. If you doubt that, think of what happened to Clure Moser. Seriously, they are good people; of course, I wish that I was young enough to move in their circles myself—on the other hand, if I was young enough, I couldn't afford it.
>
> I am not sure whether the *Sports Illustrated* thing hurt or helped me. I know that we got tremendous coverage out of it. I had much mail from all over the country and, with one exception, it was very good. I understand people around Atlanta are bitter, and I am sorry about that because I really did not mean to develop any new opponents, enemies, what have you. Anyway, it is water over the dam and there isn't anything I can do about it now.
>
> Paul, Jr., was married last Sunday and Mother and I are old and alone. One of our neighbors is going out of the country and is leaving their teenager with us for a couple of weeks, so that should take up a little of the slack. May even make us happy that we do not have the responsibilities.
>
> Anyway, I showed Mary Harmon your letter and she asked to be remembered to you and the family.

A little translation may be in order. I believe the problem with Ray Graves, a former coach, and the NCAA had to do with Bryant's admission in the *Sports Illustrated* articles that he had "bought" players at A&M and Kentucky. His point was that he no longer had to do so at Alabama. He was the only coach I knew who ever admitted to such acts, nor did he apologize for them. It was his proud boast that "We never had to outbid anyone. We just met the competition."

The reference to the Bonfire in Miami will arouse memories for a certain circle of sports diehards. The club was one of the country's great hangouts for jocks and fanatics. Dick Fincher was a Miami car dealer, once married to the actress Gloria de Haven. Clure Moser had been a controversial sportscaster who died of a heart attack earlier that year.

The series in *Sports Illustrated* was eagerly received by Bryant fans and critics. My own feelings were mixed. It did not take a genius to know the material for a book had been collected. Sure enough, a week after the first article was on the newsstands Bear called and said that *Sports Illustrated* wanted to expand the series into a book, and how would I feel about working with Underwood?

I had known John when he was with the *Miami News*, liked his work and respected him. I also envied him in a way, because I felt that as a professional he started even with Coach Bryant. It was a grown-up friendship they had.

There was no contest to be Bear Bryant's best friend, and I don't want this to sound as if there were. I doubt that his friends worried much about where they ranked. I wouldn't trade my place, whatever it was. But I met him at 19, while I was still in college, and felt I would always carry some of that "Little Mickey" baggage.

In fact, I had worked five nights a week, and had three kids and a diploma in four years. The day I graduated from the University of Houston, I received a telegram: UNDER THE CIRCUMSTANCES IT TOOK SOME GUTS. I'M PROUD OF YOU. PAUL W. BRYANT.

Now I tried to explain that most of the work had been done, the heart of the book was in the articles, and John would not need my help. Bear said he had a commitment to me. I said no, he did not. He said if there was no way for me to be involved, he would not do the book.

My guess was that he had already signed a contract and had no reason not to go ahead. But some of the fun would be gone if he thought he had broken a promise. I had to convince him that I didn't mind and wasn't hurt. Mostly what I felt was relief, at not having to attempt a book for the first time with someone I could never be neutral about, whose respect I so wanted.

Underwood had spent three months traveling with him, preparing the series. They taped some of their sessions at a cottage in the Florida Keys owned by one of Bryant's TV sponsors. "Paul," said Underwood, "relaxed on the patio in Bermuda shorts and gave free rein to his memory, which is remarkable—names, dates, places, scores, triumphs, embarrassments—he knew them all and they checked out. He even corrected my spelling."

We continued the conversation on a trip I made a few weeks later to Birmingham. I told him it just wasn't the kind of situation that required two writers. He asked if I couldn't help with the research. I answered that the research was already done. "Well, dammit," he said, "you and I been talkin' about this book for ten years."

I said that was okay, if he ever retired he could do another, and I would work on that one. His features relaxed and he grinned. "That's a deal," he said, and we shook hands on it.

The book with Underwood, *Bear, The Hard Life and Good Times of Alabama's Coach Bryant*, did not appear until the spring of 1975—the ways of the publishing business are sometimes strange. But it was a rich and revealing and authentic book, as I knew it would be, and sold well, especially in Alabama.

Underwood was with Bear for a speaking engagement at Pepperdine College when the question of his health made news for the first time. They had come from Las Vegas, where Bryant had played hard, slept too little and drunk too much.

He was just starting his talk when sweat popped out on his forehead. With a calmness and a clarity that could only have confused his audience, he said, "Excuse me, gentlemen, but is there a doctor in the house?" Then he keeled over.

As he was being lifted into the ambulance, he handed John his wallet. It was stuffed with $100 bills he had won at the crap tables in Vegas. Underwood had been with him, watching Bear roll the dice and whoop it up, when the man next to him suddenly "pitched forward into the chips. What propelled him was Bryant. The man's right hand was gripped in Bryant's bear-like left." He had discovered it a split-second earlier in his coat pocket.

Bryant was in the hospital only a day, and the verdict then was simple exhaustion, the remedy a few days' rest.

He did not imagine his illnesses, when he had them, but his friends kidded him about being a hypochondriac. In the late fall, at A&M, he always had a bottle of cough syrup on his desk. One week we both had colds, each with his own tonic. The Bear twisted the cap off his and drank it like soda pop. He stared at me while I fumbled with a spoon. I saw the look he gave me, and slipped it back into my pocket. I think of that as the day Bryant taught me to drink cough medicine from a bottle.

In my house we all learned from him. When his team got off to a shaky start in 1969, in what would be his worst season at Alabama, I mentioned in one of my letters that my son Steve had made his junior high team as a defensive end. This time I did not receive a reply from Bryant. Steve did.

The letter was addressed to Master Steve Herskowitz:

Dear Steve,

It is refreshing to hear that some young men still like to play defense. Most prefer to play quarterback. Loving to hit is the big part in playing defense. Remember, when you are playing defensive end, you always try to make good tackles and try to keep the ball carrier from getting around you. The main thing is to go full speed ahead and try to win every play.

Steve, good luck to you and your team for the remainder of the season.

Sincerely,

Paul Bryant

Four years passed. I saw Coach Bryant at the 1973 Sugar Bowl. He asked about the children and, in particular, how Steve was doing with his football. I said, "Well, I wasn't going to brag, but he made all-conference at middle linebacker in the Texas Prep School Conference, and he's only a junior." His team, Saint John's High in Houston, had lost one game that year.

There was a flicker of interest in Bryant's eyes. As long as I had known him, no lead was too obscure if it involved recruiting. "All-conference," he repeated. "Only a junior. Middle linebacker! How big is he?"

Proudly, I answered, "He's five-five and weighs 145."

The light went right out of Bear's eyes. He walked away, chuckling.

I yelled after him: "Boy, you sure have gotten picky at Alabama. He could have played for you at A&M."

There were times when I may have overdone it, preaching the Bryant gospel. The summer he was eight, Brian, the one named after Bear, joined Steve at Big State baseball camp, at Irving, a suburb of Dallas (where the Cowboys later built their stadium).

I had doubts about Brian being old enough to cope with six weeks away from home. By the time I had driven back to Houston and pulled my car into the driveway, the phone was ringing, proving me right. It was Brian. He wanted to come home. He had just heard the rules: Had to make up his bed. No television. A shower every day, whether he needed it or not.

I made a special trip back to Irving for the sole purpose of informing Brian he could not come home. I would not let him quit. And I proceeded to repeat the words of every sign I could remember from Bryant's locker-room walls. A winner never quits and a quitter never wins. The time not to quit is the first time. There is no disgrace in being down, the disgrace is in not getting back up. It isn't the size of the dog in the fight, it's the size of the fight in the dog.

We were sitting on his cot in the dormitory facing each other. I asked him if he understood what I was saying. He shook his head. I said, "I'm telling you we have already paid for the full six weeks and you can't come home. You don't ever have to come back. But I won't let you quit. You have to stick it out. Once you quit, you will be tempted to quit whenever the going gets tough."

And I left him there. We received tearful letters two or three times a week. One night Steve called and offered to pay Brian's bus fare back home. But I made him stay. When the six weeks were finally up, I was on an assignment and Sue had to drive alone to Irving to pick up the boys. She told me later what happened.

When the bell rang, releasing the campers, Brian was the first one out of the building. He threw open the rear door of the car and pitched in his glove, his cap, his duffel bag. Then he plopped himself in the front seat, turned to his mother and said, a grim expression on his round, eight-year-old face:

"Mom, you can tell Dad for me I'm not a quitter. *I haven't quit wanting to come home since I got here.*"

He may not have captured the exact spirit of Bear Bryant's teachings, but he had stuck it out.

Chapter 12

The '70s: Flood Tide

The '60s had been a rebellious period and some of the turmoil spilled over into the next decade. Bryant was trying to come to terms with it. The times had changed. People had changed. The country had changed. Not even football was the same. Not even at Alabama.

He was still smarting from the results of the 1969 season, when Alabama lost to Vanderbilt—good grief, Vanderbilt was practically in the Ivy League—and suffered a 41–14 thrashing by Tennessee, among five losses.

And the next year, 1970, was not going to be any better. It began with Southern Cal climbing all over them by a score of 42–21, and a black fullback named Sam (the Bam) Cunningham scoring three touchdowns on Bear's skinny little white boys. The line out of Tuscaloosa later was that Sam Cunningham did more to integrate Alabama in 60 minutes than Martin Luther King did in 20 years.

Bear eventually said so himself. But memory can be a con man. It wasn't so much Cunningham who helped break the color line at Alabama, as a halfback named Clarence Davis, who also ran wild, scored a couple of times and, more to the point, had been born in *Birmingham*.

It was going to be a touchy year all around. Before the season, a student activist group demanded Bryant resign for failing to recruit black athletes. He was no bigot. In his final years, he would find it easier to relate to some of the black players, who came out of poverty not much different than his own, than to the sons of prosperous white families.

Bear might have integrated his teams as early as his Kentucky years, and had long lamented the loss of Alabama blacks to the Big Ten and the West Coast. But the pace of integration in the South was determined by politics, not by football coaches.

At some point prior to 1970, he was called on in his office by a delegation from the NAACP. To their surprise, Bryant agreed with them when they said the time was long overdue that the university's sports teams were integrated. He opened his desk drawer and removed a sheet of paper. It was a list of the 15 best black football players in the state. The governor might not be ready. The regents might not be ready. But Bear was. He told his visitors that if they could get any name on that list to enroll at Alabama, he would have a scholarship for him.

None did. But the barrier was coming down.

Coaches all over the country felt besieged. There were divisions along racial lines, and players wanting to grow their hair long, join protest marches and smoke funny cigarettes. Bryant looked older than his years and for the first time a few rumbles were heard among Alabama exes, who wondered if the game was passing him by. He was 57, and aged beyond his years.

Yet whenever I spoke with him, or received a letter, his mood seemed almost chipper. He was confronted with a challenge, and that was all he needed, an additive for his engine.

Ole Miss threw something at him he didn't expect—48 points— and Rebel flags waved far into the night. Then Tennessee did it again, beating him for the fourth straight year, this one a 24–0 shutout. He was chain-smoking and taking pills to sleep and he was right where he needed to be: fighting mad.

No school had ever defeated a Bryant-coached team four years in a row, and the shutout was the first the Tide had suffered in 115 games. That game seemed to typify the entire season. It was so uncharacteristic, they attempted 51 passes and Tennessee picked off eight. In the huddle, wide receiver David Bailey suggested to Scott Hunter that he try throwing one to a Vol linebacker, "and I'll see if I can intercept it."

In September, Smokey Harper, his faithful trainer at Kentucky and A&M, died in a Tuscaloosa Hospital at 73. Smokey had moved to Alabama after his retirement, and Bryant had created a job for him looking after the team's film library.

A letter from the Bear arrived a few weeks later, with the Tide struggling at 3-and-3. "I really need Smokey now to tell me what a great coach I am," he said. "Believe me, I miss him in many ways.

". . . Our group is just as bad as we sound, but if we survive we should improve and just could have a ball club before this year is over. We have the best sophomores we have had in some time and are playing them. We will continue to stick with them regardless, in an effort to build another team. You would be surprised at how low I let this thing sink. It is amazing when you know that I am one guy who knows you had better go get some horses, which we haven't done recently."

Bear could not be blamed for thinking his team had struck bottom. But there was more to come. They blew a 17-point lead and lost to Auburn for the second year in a row, 33–28.

Remarkably, with a 6–5 record, Alabama was invited to appear in the Bluebonnet Bowl, in Houston, against Oklahoma, whose credentials were not much gaudier at 7–4. But inviting Alabama to a bowl game was as automatic as asking Judy Garland to sing "Over the Rainbow."

On New Year's Eve 1970, in the Astrodome, with people wearing funny hats and blowing on paper horns, Alabama and Oklahoma played to a 24–24 tie. Some writers compared Alabama to a great old entertainer whose show used to be watched by millions. Now he was reduced to working in lounges, still trying to knock them dead with songs from the '50s.

But that night, and that game, would be a turning point for Bryant and his team. In his postgame interview, Bear lamented, "Oklahoma ran up and down the field on us. Looks like Alabama didn't know much about stopping the wishbone."

On Alabama's return flight from Houston, Bear sat in his usual seat at the front of the plane. He had his briefcase open and he was diagramming plays. He hardly looked up the entire flight. He was, in fact, looking ahead instead of back. He was wondering how the wishbone would look in Alabama crimson.

The Tide had stayed with the I and wing-T formations and even pro sets. But teams like Texas, Houston and Oklahoma were ringing up telephone numbers with the wishbone. "I knew after spring training," he said, "that we couldn't win with dropback passing. We couldn't win the year before with a pro-style passer. Or the year before that. We could move up and down the field, but we couldn't get it in the end zone."

After spring practice, Bryant went back to school—to the University of Texas campus—to study the wishbone-T with Darrell Royal, whose staff designed it. This was the second time he had called on his young friend for help, the sign of a man reasonably secure with his own legend.

The first visit had been in 1954, when Bryant's quarterbacks at A&M were having problems getting the snap from center. Royal was then in his first head-coaching job at Mississippi State. Bryant brought Jim Owens along and spent three days.

"He wanted to talk about our center," recalled Royal. "We had a great center by the name of Hal Easterwood. He was an all-American that year. We used a three-point stance for our center, with one hand on the ground and the other on the ball. Bear hadn't seen that stance before. We felt he could fire off the ball and block a little more effectively.

"I remember we got out our films and went over it in detail. He watched Hal Easterwood block for a reel or two and then said, 'That's it, shut it off. I've seen all I need to see.' That was the way he was. Once he made up his mind there wasn't any need to spend more time on it. He knew he could use it.

"Then in seventy-one he called about the wishbone, and asked if I would spend some time with him. I said, yeah, I'd be glad to, and he said, 'No, I mean *real* time. Can we get a projector, go somewhere and not have any phone calls or interruptions?' "

The Royals happened to be remodeling their home and living at the time in apartments near the campus. Bryant moved in with them and Darrell had a projector sent over and they went to work.

"It was very much like the time he wanted to see what our center was doing. We spent one morning looking at films and had just started again that afternoon. He said, 'Well, you can shut that damned thing down. I've seen all I need. I've decided to go the wishbone.' Then he said, 'What I need now is your promise that I can call you during two-a-day practices.' I said, 'Coach, you can call me any time I'm not on the field.' He said, 'I won't keep you long. The call will be short. I'll have something specific in mind that I want to ask about.' "

Royal agreed to bring his offensive coaches to Tuscaloosa for a clinic later that spring. Bear and Darrell would go off together, leaving the assistants on both staffs to visit. In the fall, Bryant called as often as five or six times a day.

He would tell people later that Royal had saved his career, a statement Darrell regarded as a tad strong. To show his thanks, Bear tried to pay for a room—a den or a bedroom—in the home the Royals were remodeling. Darrell wouldn't let him.

Jones Ramsey, who had moved over to Texas in 1961, found Bryant sitting on the step outside the athletic offices one morning around 8:00. He had been there since 6:30, not wanting to disturb the still sleeping Royals, but looking for someone with whom to visit. "Hell, Jones," he demanded. "Doesn't anybody around here work?"

That season, Bryant and Royal exchanged game films each week and were on the phone constantly. "If we ran into anything new defensively," said Royal, "that people were doing against our offense, we'd call each other immediately." It was like a crisis hotline. They kept it up until Royal retired in 1976.

Bryant studied his notes and looked at films and drew diagrams all summer. Four days before fall practice, he announced to his staff that they were going to install the wishbone. "We're going to sink or swim with the Texas stuff," he said. "This isn't a trial, it's a commitment."

His best athlete that year was Johnny Musso, the tailback who became known as the Italian Stallion. Musso recalls the team's shock: "Here it was three weeks before the opener with Southern California and Coach walks into the squad meeting and says we're going to put away the passing game and put in the wishbone."

This is not the way football teams usually operate. Nobody changes an offense in late August. A coach who is going to install an entirely new system does so in the spring, so the team will have that time to work out the wrinkles and all summer to think about it. But here was Bryant, not renowned as an adventurer, telling them they were going to change all the blocking assignments, put three backs behind the quarterback, and run the triple option. What was more incredible, they were going to do it in three weeks, just in time to play a team that had humiliated them the year before.

"If I didn't think you could do it," said Bear, "I wouldn't ask you to try."

Bryant's enthusiasm was apparent to the entire team. He closed the team's practices to the press and the public and the move was kept secret. The day the conference press tour flew into Tuscaloosa, he had the Tide back in its old pro set, running the same plays and pass routes. The visiting writers were not impressed.

Now the excitement level among the players kicked into another gear. They had faked out the sportswriters, put on an act and pulled it off. Southern Cal was next.

"Coach Bryant called me from Los Angeles," says Royal, "on Friday night before the game. I asked if he thought USC had any idea he was gonna run the wishbone. He said he didn't think so. He thought they were prepared to defend against what Alabama had run last season and in the spring. He said, 'I think we'll surprise 'em. If we do, maybe we can play 'em respectable.' "

Alabama upset Southern Cal, 17–10, with Terry Davis as their original wishbone quarterback, and Johnny Musso scoring twice. It was a magical day, Bryant's 200th coaching win. Back in Tuscaloosa, students paraded around the quad and some swam in the fountain in front of the administration building.

They went on to sweep the regular season, winning 11 in a row. Musso ran for four touchdowns against Florida, following the blocks of John Hannah, who would go on to become the best offensive tackle in pro football. Only once in the last 10 games were they held under 30 points. Nebraska, that year's national champion, pounded them in the Orange Bowl, 38–6. But the word had gone forth:

Alabama was back.

In the process, Bryant had dealt with two other problems, one a distraction (hair), the other major (race).

The opposition to signing black athletes still existed in the state, but the political and social pressures no longer carried the same force. Yet the challenge for Bryant was a delicate one. There was no stampede by blacks to play at the university whose governor, George Wallace, had in 1963 stood in front of a schoolhouse door to defy segregation. And Bryant, in some ways, must have seemed a quintessential white Southern coach.

Again, it was Southern Cal that offered a breakthrough. John McKay had enjoyed considerable success recruiting in Bryant's backyard. During one of their regular visits, after the 1970 season, McKay mentioned that the best prospect on his list was a junior college player, a defensive end from Mobile named John Mitchell.

In the past, Bear had recommended some players to McKay. And McKay, unaware that the whites-only signs were coming down at Alabama, had been pleased to take advantage of him. By the time Bryant could slip away to a phone he had forgotten Mitchell's name. He called his office and instructed them to find out what they could about a black defensive end from Mobile, who had played in 1970 at a junior college in Arizona.

Alabama's coaches had just signed Wilbur Jackson as their first black freshman recruit, out of Ozark. But Mitchell, as a junior college transfer, would be eligible to play right away—against Southern Cal, in the 1971 opener. And that was one of Bryant's selling points that day when he spoke to John and his mother on the phone. Within the hour, an Alabama recruiter had stopped by to see him.

Mitchell made the tackle on the kickoff in the upset of USC. In 1972, he became Alabama's first black captain and first black all-American, and later the first black to coach for Bryant.

Wilbur Jackson, 6′2″ and 210, spent a wasted year at flanker as a sophomore, wound up at running back and was drafted in the first round by the 49ers in 1974.

For as long as Bryant had been there, the hairstyles of Alabama football players would not have looked out of place at any Marine base in the country. Bryant had resisted pleas and individual petitions. Then, in 1971, the players had designated Johnny Musso to represent them in a new negotiation. Bear said he would think about it.

Then he sat down one Saturday to watch the Texas-Oklahoma game on television—Alabama was playing at night—and what he saw made him sit bolt upright. The Texas players had hair peeking out from under their helmets and, in some cases, touching the neckline of their jerseys. From time to time the cameras picked up a dignitary in the stands, at one point zooming in for a tight shot of Lyndon Johnson, the former president of the United States, whose hair was full and even swooped down over his collar in back. Another close-up revealed the Reverend Billy Graham with wavy blond-gray hair as abundant as Lyndon Johnson's. Bryant almost fainted.

That week Royal received a phone call. Bear said he noticed that the Texas players were wearing their hair longer, and he wanted to know if Darrell was going soft, or what?

Royal said, "Yeah, we've altered our attitude some. You know, Coach, the times have kinda changed. But I can tell you, it hasn't affected their play any. They work hard and they're playing great. Really and truly, I can't see that another inch or two of hair makes much difference."

At the time, Texas was in the middle of a 30-game winning streak.

That week, Bryant summoned Johnny Musso to his office. He asked him again, "Why in God's name do you want hair hanging out of your helmet?"

Musso replied, "It's important to us."

Bear sat silent a moment, then answered: "If it's important to you—and damned if I know why—then go ahead and let it grow. But keep it clean."

Of course, he knew why it was important to them. The girls liked it long. The players won their case when Bryant realized they had the support of Darrell Royal, Billy Graham and Lyndon Johnson.

During Bryant's years in Texas, and later, the one person I often heard him compared to was Lyndon Johnson, the almost stereotypical Texan. Everything about LBJ seemed magnified . . . his size, his drawl, his temper, his ego. Many of the labels and descriptions applied to Johnson seemed to fit Bryant as well.

Once, when Lady Bird Johnson was asked about her husband's reputation for flirting with other women, she replied: "Lyndon was a people-lover. I couldn't expect him to exclude half the people."

Darrell Royal was asked once to prepare the guest list of coaches to be invited to the White House for a presentation to be made by their association. "I had a limited number," he said, "and I was going over the list with Edith. She knew all the coaches. I wanted to invite some pals but I also wanted to get a mixture that would be appropriate. I got Jake Gaither in there [from Florida A&M]. I got Ara Parseghian for the Catholics. Abe Martin was president of the coaches' association that year, so he was on there. Then I started getting down to my pals and I said to Edith, 'Obviously, I'm going to ask Coach Bryant. The only thing that bothers me is how both Bear and President Johnson are going to fit in that Oval Office.'

"So it was really funny. We go in there and I'm introducing people to the president. Well, when we got down the line to Coach Bryant, Johnson turned and said, 'Now here's the guy I want to meet.' And the two of them just hit it off like that. It was just exactly like I predicted. Their personalities were so much alike. Both were awesome figures and they cast a big shadow. They had a kind of an aura about them. But they were both capable of great kindness and thoughtfulness, and they were both tougher than hell. I mean, you could see both sides of them. And they showed both sides. They didn't try to hide either one—the tough side or the emotional, soft side."

There was even a Bryant parallel to the famous scene in which Lyndon Johnson insisted on showing reporters the scar from a gall bladder operation.

Years after Bear had rebuilt his empire at Alabama, he checked into a Birmingham hospital for a minor and discreet surgical procedure, believed to be a circumcision. Clearly, this was not an occasion that required publicity, but Bryant seemed pleased at having the operation, given his age. One of his visitors was Benny Marshall, the sports editor of the *Birmingham News*, a popular writer and an old friend.

Bryant asked Marshall if he wanted to see the result of the surgeon's skill. Benny politely declined. But Bryant insisted, raised the sheets and waited for his friend's reaction. "What do you think?" he said.

"Well, Coach," said Benny, suppressing a laugh, "I have to say I'm disappointed in the size of your tallywacker."

Everything came together in the 1970s—the switch to the wishbone-T, the arrival of the black athlete, a renewal of his recruiting vigor, even Bryant's accommodation of his players' grooming preferences—for the greater glory of Alabama football. They became the first team in college history to win over 100 games in a decade.

They added three more national titles, depending on which polls you believe, in '73, '78 and '79. In nine years, the Tide lost four conference games, three by a field goal or less. The numbers were awesome: 11–1, 10–2, 11–1, 11–1, 11–1, 9–3, 11–1, 11–1, 12–0.

Notre Dame kept them from one undisputed title and knocked them out of another in back-to-back bowl games. The '73 team, quarterbacked by Richard Todd, was a monster, rated by some the most explosive of all Bama teams. No opponent got closer than two touchdowns, as the Tide scored 66 points on California, 44 on Vanderbilt, 42 on Tennessee, 43 on Miami.

Then came Notre Dame. The Tide went into the Sugar Bowl rated number 1, the Irish third. In one of the finest games ever played for such stakes, the Irish won, 24–23, protecting the lead with a daring pass completion from their own end zone.

"We all cried," said Sylvester Croom. "We were on the verge of greatness. I still don't feel the best team won that night."

The 1974 season was almost a replay. Todd scored from punt formation to win the opener over Maryland, and again Bama reeled off 11 in a row. This time they met Notre Dame in the Orange Bowl, and down the tubes went another national title, the Irish winning it, 13–11, in Ara Parseghian's last game as coach.

To compound the pain, Bama had not won a bowl game in eight appearances.

At some point, in those seasons, Bryant dealt with a drug threat that was creeping across the country's locker rooms. He didn't think it could happen at Alabama, and didn't recognize the signs until a couple of his model citizens underwent radical personal transformations and dropped out. Then he dealt with it the only way he knew how: head-on. He gave a blanket warning to any users to kick whatever they were on, and served notice that there would be no second chances for those caught with drugs.

Then one day Bryant and his coaches made a sweep of the dormitory. Seven players were dropped from the team. From then on, drugs were not a team issue at Alabama.

Bear may or may not have been in the room the night a group of coaches discussed the severity of the problem, and compared their approaches to it. When someone asked Eddie Robinson, of Grambling, who would later exceed Bryant's win total, how he handled it, he replied, "I don't. Every fall when the team reports,

I make a speech, and I tell the new players to leave those drugs alone, they kill your sex drive. And we've never had a problem."

On Saturday's scoreboards, Bryant's problems were few and far between. His successes had carried him to another dimension, and more than once in the '70s rumors were afloat that he was being courted for political office. It seems clear that he could have run for governor, had he wished.

He went along with it once, as a gag, and I happened to bump into him that week in Las Vegas. It made for a nice column for a light news day:

Las Vegas—He walked into the coffee shop at Caesar's Palace the way he walks across a football field, his head erect, his gait slow and deliberate.

Paul (Bear) Bryant was on the second leg of his campaign swing, having announced the night before in Phoenix, at a banquet, that he was running for president. Las Vegas had reacted calmly to the news that a presidential candidate had come to town. It was not yet noon, meaning that most of the natives were still asleep, and only the really serious tourists were in the casinos, beating the hell out of the slot machines.

Bryant sat now with Jimmy the Greek, the eminent odds-maker, and a couple of Texas friends. The big oil interests are expected to rally behind the candidacy of the Alabama football coach, who believes he can solve the energy crisis by making the whole country turn out for two-a-day workouts.

Bryant looked across the table at Jimmy the Greek. The rich, deep voice rumbled out of his throat like a freight train out of a tunnel. "Jimmy," he said, "I want to know the odds on my being elected president. Can you do that?"

The Greek said, "That's easy, Paul. What do you want the odds to be?"

A writer, one of the most brilliant political analysts on the scene today, remembered that Bryant's name had been placed in nomination at the Democratic convention in 1968, for vice president, by a delegate from Alabama. The move caught the imagination of all America. "You got three votes," I reminded him, for it was I.

Bryant nodded. "That's why I decided to run," he said. "I may be the only Democrat left who can still get three votes."

Everything about Bryant is distinctive, the walk, the voice, the Mount Rushmore face, the way he squints as though the sun were always in his eyes. The idea of running for president came to him, he said, when he realized that, at 61, he was getting too old to coach, and the only other thing he was qualified to do was run the country.

He had his cabinet already in mind, and his choices reflected the seriousness of his campaign. "I want Bud Wilkinson to take Kissinger's job," he said, referring to the suave former Oklahoma coach. Wilkinson is a born diplomat and a splendid selection, though not as inspired as Bryant's next one. "I want Woody Hayes for secretary of war," he said, "and Joe Namath will be my secretary of social affairs. I'll make Ara Parseghian my secretary in charge of bowl games or my ambassador to Arabia, I'm not sure which."

This was a wry reference to the fact that on the last two New Year's Days, the now retired Notre Dame coach cost Bryant's Alabama team a clearcut national championship. The Bear also said he would find a cabinet job for Darrell Royal, but one not as good as it might have been if Texas had beaten Auburn, his old rival, in the Gator Bowl. Bryant's standards are high.

"I'd also like to include Gerald Ford," he said, in the generous spirit we have come to expect of our statesmen, "but I'm going to have to talk to him. He's never been on a winner, you know. The team he captained at Michigan won only one game."

Bryant listed several other possible appointees, such as Howard Cosell, secretary of bad mouthing, and others in that vein. We took them to be of a frivolous nature and hardly worth repeating.

At one point, Jimmy the Greek suggested that Bryant might need someone experienced at making odds and taking polls. I recognized this for what it was, a pitiful attempt to attach himself to a man of destiny. It pleased us when the candidate said nothing, pursing his lips to indicate that he was thinking.

"Have you thought of anyone for press secretary?" I asked, casually, ducking my head and flashing the shy smile that so often has been described, to my amusement, as boyishly charming.

"Yep," said Bear, "I'm putting Muhammad Ali in charge of press relations. I thought about Charlie Finley, but decided he was too controversial."

I asked the candidate how he stood on the most pressing issue of our time: lie detector tests for football coaches. "I like it," he said, heartily. "Good idea. I even tried talking our people, our conference, into doing it."

Gazing directly into his eyes, we paused to weigh what he had just said. He must have meant it. Would Bear lie about a thing like lie detectors?

It was pointed out that certain Southwest Conference coaches felt the talk about using such devices had cost them dearly in the recruiting battle with Oklahoma. "That's why I wanted it," he said. "I know on the last signing day, Oklahoma went down to Miami and picked off our good ones we wanted. I'd like to see some folks take a lie detector test about that."

Whether or not he wins the presidency, and frankly we think the country needs him, Bryant indicated that he will retire as Alabama coach after the 1975 season. "People have said I'd coach until I died," he said. "But that thought doesn't appeal to me much anymore. The only thing that kept me at it this long was all the deals I have that depended on my coaching."

Not long after that, Paul Bryant and his entourage rose and left the coffee shop. When last seen, the candidate was seated at the roulette table, trying to finance his campaign.

In some ways, of course, Bryant's interest in politics was a serious one—as it related to Alabama football. In 1978 Bryant was honestly disturbed by the prospect of the state electing a governor, Fob James, who had been a great player at Auburn. He feared that

Auburn people would use the office to help them recruit, a practice not unknown in states where football was considered a major industry.

James had been a registered Republican, but switched parties to run for governor as a Democrat. That worried Bryant even more. At a rally in Mobile, he had once presented a houndstooth hat to Gerald Ford, when Ford was president, as a favor to friends. Angry mail poured in from his fellow Democrats across the state.

But the more Bryant thought about an Auburn man in the governor's chair, the less he liked it. And in the middle of the football season, at one of his weekly press conferences, he endorsed the Republican, Bill Baxley. He said he had nothing against Fob James personally, didn't know him, felt sure he was a fine man. But he was from Auburn, and that could not be good for the University of Alabama.

He knew he would catch hell for taking such a stand and he did. Even the Alabama faculty was upset that their football coach would use his stature to get involved in an election.

What was worse, Fob James won the race. Meaning that an Auburn man was now an ex officio member of the Alabama board of trustees, and in the usual custom would be invited to crown the homecoming queen.

Meanwhile, Fob James was not unconcerned about his relationship with a coach who had become nearly a mythic figure in the state. A meeting was arranged, the night before the homecoming game, at the motel in Tuscaloosa where Bryant sequestered his team. The governor went to Bryant's room, knocked on the door, and heard a deep, growly voice say, "Come in."

The door was unlocked. Fob James walked in and there was Bryant, lying in bed, fully clothed, his head propped up on a pillow, his legs stretched out, watching the sports channel on television. James said, "Hello, Coach." Bryant gave him his steely-eyed look and said, "How old are you?"

James said, "Forty-four, sir."

Bryant started grinning, eased himself out of the bed, and said, "Well, then, you're old enough not to believe all that shit you read in the newspapers, aren't you?"

The newly elected governor of Alabama burst out laughing. Bryant started toward him with his arms open and they embraced each other, in the middle of a motel room in Tuscaloosa.

Charley Thornton heard the story from Cal James, the brother of the governor. "It just shows," he said, "the knack Coach Bryant had for kind of neutralizing a difficult situation."

By the end of the decade, Bryant stood alone as the dominant figure in college football. I sat beside John Underwood in the press box at the Sugar Bowl, New Year's Day of 1979, waiting for the collision between the number 1 and 2 teams—Penn State and Alabama. On the TV monitors located overhead we kept seeing a replay of the scene from the Gator Bowl, in which Woody Hayes, the Ohio State coach, slugged a Clemson linebacker, Charlie Baughman. No matter how many times you saw it, the images did not seem real. Baughman intercepted a pass, and had been driven out of bounds in front of the Ohio State bench. It was the classic example of being in the wrong place at the wrong time.

Underwood's eyes were still on the screen. "It's a shame," he said, "that football could not have been fun for Hayes, the way it is for Bear."

There had been snickers in the Sugar Bowl press room that week after Bryant had sadly taken note of the firing of Hayes by the school he had served for 28 years. Bryant had said, "He is a class person who has dedicated his life to college football."

To some, that sounded like Jimmy Carter overpraising the Shah of Iran. But Bryant genuinely liked and admired Woody Hayes, who at the time was the only active coach of a major college within 50 victories of Bryant's total (of 284).

Alabama made a glorious goal-line stand in the fourth quarter to defeat Penn State, 14–7, after an eight-yard run by Major Ogilvie had broken the tie.

It was an oddly fraternal scene that unfolded down on the goal line, pure Reb-Yank stuff. The Lions had been stopped on third and one, and had called a time-out facing fourth down, needing so little for the touchdown that could tie or win the game and produce a possible national championship. Their gifted quarterback, Chuck Fusina, walked over to measure the ball, but his view was blocked by the crimson-shirted Marty Lyons.

Fusina cocked his head and grinned at the big Alabama tackle. He asked, lightly, "How far is it?"

Lyons spread his hands and said, "'Bout that much."

"Ten inches?" estimated Fusina.

"Yeah," agreed Lyons. "You better pass for it."

Penn State elected to run, right at them, and by 'bout that much, maybe 10 inches, failed to score, failed to win, and lost the national championship.

After the Crimson Tide had yanked the Superdome rug out from under the Nittany Lions, a writer wondered, half-jokingly, if Bryant had asked Joe Paterno for his vote in the poll that would settle all earthly matters.

"No, I didn't," rumbled Bryant, "and I wouldn't ask for yours." But there was no doubt where Bear's vote would go. The same place as his heart. "I will proudly cast it for Alabama," he promised, "because today I think we have the best football team in America."

As Bryant goes, so went half the country. The two major wire services gave us co-champions, the coaches (UPI) picking Southern Cal and the news folks (AP) lining up behind Alabama. That there existed any question at all reflected the unpredictable nature of the college polls, and the need for a national playoff. After all, number 2 Alabama had knocked off number 1 Penn State on a day when none of the bowl games was decided by more than a touchdown.

As the nation's football fans had dangled from the chandeliers, waiting for the results to be announced, the Alabama players remembered the previous year. On New Year's night of 1978, Bryant had told them exactly how the cow would eat the cabbage.

Recalled Barry Krauss, the linebacker: "Last year, everything Coach told us turned out to be right—except the vote. He said we had to beat Ohio State convincingly [which they did, 35–6]. He said Oklahoma would lose. Michigan would lose. And Notre Dame would beat Texas. We just looked at him, feeling it couldn't happen like he said. Damned if it didn't.

"Man, I was driving home, sure we would be the national champions. Then we go and get ripped off."

After the bowl games in '78, Notre Dame leaped from fifth to first. At least in 1979 Alabama only got half ripped off.

It was Charley Thornton, after thumbing through the records one day, who casually mentioned to Bryant that he was within reach of Amos Alonzo Stagg's record for most victories in a career. Thornton saw the record as an incentive that might be valuable after a decade of unparalleled success. The Bear saw it as a way of resolving the question of when he would retire, an uncertainty other schools had used against him in recruiting.

And that was how the public learned of his game plan, through a 17-year-old high school senior. "A prospect in South Florida asked me if I was going to be his coach for four years," recalled Bryant. "I told him I would be. He was the first person I had told. It was recruiting time and so I thought I'd clear the air."

In keeping with the vagaries of sport, and fate, the prospect who won Bryant's pledge dropped out of school after his freshman year.

Bryant had preached a form of Toughlove long before it became a social therapy. Meanwhile, even as younger coaches dropped out all around, he continued to search for new ways to reach his players. What other coach would have written Ann Landers for help, as Bryant did, in August of 1982?

He asked the advice columnist to reprint a column about a fictional teenager who dies in an automobile accident. The column was written from the point of view of a 17-year-old who drives the family car too fast, crashes and sees himself being declared dead and buried. ". . . Most of these boys [his players] are seventeen and eighteen years old," wrote Bryant. "I hope it does something to them. It might save somebody some day."

His players may or may not have appreciated him. But thousands of Ann Landers fans did.

By then his secretary was processing 6,000 requests a year for signed photographs. No one could count the letters that kept coming, mostly from children. After a win over Missouri, by 38–20, he received a thank-you note from a convict at the Missouri State Prison at Jefferson City, grateful to Bear for beating the point spread. He wrote that he had won "seventy-four packages of cigarettes, nine bags of coffee, three street shirts, ten packs of razor blades" and, "best of all, another man's Sunday-morning eggs for a month."

Bryant reckoned that the legend business was getting a little hard on the spirit. "I encourage my players to come in and see me if they have a problem," he said. "But the young ones, they don't. I wish they would. They would flatter me if they came in. I may not be helpful, but I'd surely listen."

Of course, the Bryant you saw now was Father Flanagan compared to the one who had taken on those earlier, rugged, rebuilding tasks. The players of A&M, Kentucky and Maryland might have hesitated to say, in the heat of a season, as Barry Krauss did: "I love him. The biggest thrill is that I can walk in and talk to him, and he knows and cares about me."

He had, indeed, changed with the times, able to coach with equal success players of different eras, from those who wore crewcuts to those who used hair dryers in the locker room.

The 1979 season was to be his Mona Lisa. They swept the table, 12 straight wins, this time a number-1 ranking in all the polls. Every week brought a new achievement. Alabama made 28 first downs against Georgia Tech, kept the ball for 93 plays against Baylor, gained over 600 yards on Vanderbilt, held Florida to three first downs.

Major Ogilvie scored twice in the first period and Billy Jackson rushed for 120 yards as Arkansas fell in the Sugar Bowl, 24–9. The perfect season was Bryant's third at Alabama. Now he was coming up to 1980 and his 35th year as a coach.

"Thirty-five years makes a long time," he reflected. "A lot of good, a lot of bad, some things you did that were smart, some things you did that were plain stupid. Thirty-five years makes a lot of changes."

Chapter 13

The '80s: Paper Chase

Now the countdown had begun in earnest. Saturday after Saturday, win by win, Paul Bryant closed in on the record of Amos Alonzo Stagg. In the process, he was rounding out the legend as well.

Alabama had returned to Dallas to meet Baylor in the Cotton Bowl on New Year's Day 1981. His opposing coach this time would be Grant Teaff, a solid, straight-arrow type who had given supporters of the Baptist school their best season in years.

At their final joint press conference, Teaff began with: "I want to dispel a rumor that I heard today. The rumor was that when I heard that Alabama had accepted the invitation to play in the Cotton Bowl, I almost decided to give up coaching and go into the ministry.

"The word was that I would rather bear the cross than cross the Bear."

"Yeah," Bryant retorted, "I'm the one that started the rumor. I told people he'd gone out and got drunk and the school had run him off."

From my seat in the gallery, I asked what Bryant thought his chances would be of lasting 35 years if he were starting out in coaching today. "In the first place," he said, "if I were starting out today I sure as hell wouldn't go into coaching."

He did not explain what he would have done instead. Possibly he would be with the circus, still wrestling the bear that made him famous—in the first place.

I was in Dallas to cover the game and for a more personal reason. I wanted my youngest son, Christopher, to meet him. I am not sure what it was about Coach Bryant that made you want to introduce your children to him, but you did. My daughter Robin was two or three when I drove her to College Station for that ritual. She was a wispy little thing, blond and blue-eyed, totally unimpressed with the purpose of the trip. But on many a Sunday I had held her on my lap, telling her we had to watch Bear's TV show before I would consider her plea to be taken outdoors.

We were waiting by the gate to the practice field when he emerged from his office and I said, proudly: "Robin, this is Coach Bryant. Go to Coach Bryant, honey." He squatted like a baseball catcher and held out his arms to her. Whereupon she wrapped herself tightly around my legs and, to my great embarrassment, began crying her little eyes out.

Finally, Bryant grinned and gave an understanding shrug and went off to join his team. I headed for my car, Robin running to keep up, begging: "Pick me up, Daddy. Pick me up." I told her no, that I was unhappy with her. When she asked why, I explained because she had refused to go to Bear.

"Bear? *That* was Bear?" she said, with honest puzzlement in her two- or three-year-old voice. "I didn't know that was Bear."

It dawned on me then that in the privacy of our own living room, she had never known him as Coach Bryant.

I was especially anxious for him to meet Christopher, who was then eight, tall for his age and a natural athlete. We adopted Chris a few weeks before his third birthday, so I could brag on him because he did not inherit his talent from me. He was this kind of kid: the first time he picked up a basketball, he knew how to dribble. The first time he put his hands on a football he threw a spiral. And, at seven, playing third base in tee-ball, he could backhand a hard grounder and make the throw across the diamond.

There were people all around us, but Chris and I were on Bryant's immediate left as we walked down a long hallway. I was partly making conversation, and partly curious as to what he would say: "Coach, Chris can throw a football with either arm and kick one with either foot. What should I do with him?"

Without turning his head, Bear said, "Wait till he turns pro and then charge double for him."

I laughed. But as we continued walking, I made an uneasy discovery. Bear was *leaning* on me. The hand he had placed on my shoulder was not just a gesture of friendship. He was using me to steady himself, to support his weight.

There was nothing feeble about him. His was still a big, powerful presence. But now the thought sank in: He has grown old. A sadness swept over me that was not for him alone. It was for all of us, and for the good years that were gone and would not come again.

I have forgotten who said it, whether it was then or later, or where. But I still hear a voice asking, "Do you realize Coach Bryant is three years *younger* than President Reagan?"

And another voice responded, "Yeah, but Reagan ain't drunk near as much whiskey or run around near as much as Coach Bryant."

In August of that year, his doctors had ordered him into a hospital. He suffered from swelling in his joints and fluid in his lungs. There was grave talk about the risk of congestive heart failure. They put him on medication and didn't let him out of bed for six days. He lost 21 pounds and was back on the practice field in time to open his 36th season as a head coach.

He was taking 11 pills a day and complaining that "I don't know what any of 'em are for." He walked two miles a day, usually after practice. He wore an odometer on a belt loop of his pants to make sure he didn't shortchange himself. At home, he swam laps in his heated pool.

He didn't look well. His step was slower and two deep lines ran from each side of his mouth down to his jaw, giving it the appearance of being hinged, like a puppet's.

A headline in the *Dallas Times-Herald* read: THE OLD GRAY BEAR ISN'T WHAT HE USED TO BE.

On his doctors' orders, he had stopped drinking, except for a minor slip, the night after Alabama lost to Notre Dame, 7–0, one of their two losses in the 1980 season. He had one shot of whiskey with his steak and went to bed. He had cut back his smoking from two packs of unfiltered Camels a day to 8, maybe 10 cigarettes. He would no longer jump in a plane to speak at a Touchdown Club somewhere, or even to visit a prospect. He had virtually quit recruiting, unless his coaches told him it was absolutely essential ("At my age it just seems undignified," he said, "for me and the young man").

He kept aw-shucksing about the record, but no one doubted that it was this goal that kept him going. At team meetings, the players said, he talked about life at least as much as football. He told them stories, drawn from his own experiences and the wisdom of his thousand years. Charley Thornton begged to be allowed to tape record those team meetings, but Bear wouldn't let him.

"Coach Bryant has taught me that you have to work hard to get anywhere," said Major Ogilvie, "and that you're always on a plateau. You either go uphill or you go downhill. He cares about the welfare of his players and his people."

In fact, for someone who put such a store by meanness and toughness most of his career, Bryant no longer raised his voice. The man who once drove his players to unconsciousness under the Texas sun hired experts at Alabama to teach him about fluid intake and heat-humidity ratios.

Unlike the pros, who adapt their material to fit the system, Bryant always shaped and molded and sculpted his teams to fit his personnel. The 1980 team had no franchise player, but the talent ran so deep that Bear sent them out in waves—a true Crimson Tide. In the opener against Georgia Tech, he used 11 running backs in a 26–3 romp.

In October, the Tide coasted past Kentucky, 45–0—a trip through the time jungle there—for his 300th victory. After Bama mauled Baylor in the Cotton Bowl, 30–2, the total had reached 306, meaning he needed 8 to tie Stagg and 9 to pass him.

Baylor went into the Cotton Bowl featuring the best offense in the Southwest Conference, the best the school ever had. The Tide rolled up five times as much yardage. Ogilvie led his team in rushing and scored on a plunge from the one, making him the first player ever to run for a touchdown in four bowl games. Peter Kim kicked three field goals and middle guard Warren Lyles was voted the MVP.

*   *   *

Analyzing Bryant now became a new national pastime. There was no collective effort to turn him into some kind of Wallace Beery character, but he had outlasted or outcoached his critics.

That craggy road map of a face made the cover of *Time* magazine. His trainer, Jim Goosetree, had been with him since his second coming at Tuscaloosa, and observed a subtle change: "There is a degree of fear motivation still present in his personality. It's the fear of failing to live up to his expectations. He has recognized that the values of young people are different from what they were at one time; but, in a fatherly way, he still demands a degree of discipline that is high."

It all had something to do with what Hemingway called "the bonding of men." Darrell Royal, who was an Oklahoma quarterback when they first met, who coached against him and played golf with him and enjoyed his company, said: "The greatest testimony that any coach can have is those guys who have long since been out of the program. You go ask them how they feel about Bryant, and it's great right down the line. Charisma alone doesn't do it."

Bear had never been very big on introspection. But he tried: "My mama wanted me to be a preacher. I told her coachin' and preachin' were a lot alike. I don't think she believed me."

As the record drew near, Bryant no doubt could see the closing of the book, and beyond it. "I'm just a plowhand from Arkansas," he said one day. "But I have learned over the years how to hold a team together. How to lift some men up, how to calm down others, until finally they've got one heartbeat, together, a team."

This thought was as poetic as Bryant ever allowed himself to get, and how important you judge this as an accomplishment depends on where you place such things as football in the planetary order. Bryant himself was not above admitting to an occasional doubt.

"I've had a full life in one respect," he told Herschel Nissenson of the Associated Press. "But I've had a one-track deal in another respect. My life has been so tied up with football, it has flown by. I wish it wasn't that way, but it has gone by mighty fast. Practice, recruiting and games; there hasn't been anything except football."

Oh, maybe there were one or two other interests, if the record and certain rumors were to be believed. He was astute enough to know that his financial security would not depend on his salary as a coach. One survey in the early 1980s pegged his annual earnings at $450,000—his base pay accounting for less than a fourth of that figure. Radio and television benefits, speeches and endorsements accounted for most of the rest. No other coach was within a hundred grand of Bryant's income. Barry Switzer, of Oklahoma, was rated the runner-up at $270,000, followed by Jackie Sherrill, the new head coach at Texas A&M ($240,000), Lou Holtz, then with Arkansas ($226,000), and Jerry Claiborne, Kentucky, rounding out the top five at $152,500.

Sherrill and Claiborne, it was interesting to note, had played and coached under Bryant.

He had become a self-made millionaire years earlier, of course. Exactly how rich is hard to say. But no other football coach donated $300,000 to his school, as Bryant did, for scholarship and building funds.

You tend to believe he would have done well investing on his own. "The second thing I look at in the paper every morning," he said, "is the stock-market tables. First thing is Ann Landers, usually on page six."

But the brother-in-law deals helped, made available by the friends and admirers who were always there. "I always thought Coach Bryant had a sort of lonely life," says Charley Thornton, "and to some extent I'm sure he did. But he developed deep ties to a few individuals. At A&M there were people like Bob Bernath and his wife Kate who played bridge with Coach and Mary Harmon every Thursday during football season, just to get his mind off the game."

(Of this recreation, Mrs. Bryant once said: "He doesn't like 'visiting' bridge. He wants to bid and win and skip the talk.")

At Alabama, his usual business partner and sometimes hunting companion was Jimmy Hinton. "But half the time when we go hunting," said Hinton, "he never fires a shot. He mostly just likes to ride a horse and watch the dogs work." There was always a group he could count on, said Thornton, and among them were Julian Lackey, whose family was in funeral homes, and Preacher Franklin, the Coca-Cola distributor, both dead now; and Sloan Bashinsky, whose potato-chip company sponsored his TV show. One of his advisers was an Auburn ex, Neil Morgan, who made his pile in the construction business.

At A&M, the deals often had to do with oil, and his advisers included Johnny Mitchell, Herman Heep, Maggie Magee and Doc

Doherty. Others like Gordon Edge and Clarence Jamail kept a low profile but were always around to help. Some, such as Pat Morgan, the Alabama grad who settled in Houston, were on call wherever he went.

"He was such a great people person," said Thornton. "One on one, he could have taken the worst enemy he had and, if he spent a day with him, I guarantee you they would have wound up as friends."

Like Lyndon Johnson, Bryant was not indifferent to half the people. There were rumors at one time of a romance with a former Alabama beauty queen. The story, if true, never received much circulation, in or out of the state. A friend was asked how Mrs. Bryant dealt with the episode. "In exactly the right way," he said. "Like it never happened."

Such discretion was not always the rule. Mrs. Bryant loved him so, and was secure enough, that she could at times talk proudly of her husband's attractiveness to other women. At Kentucky, the daughter of one of the state's wealthy horse breeders fell in love with him. Mary Harmon asked him to break off the relationship and he stalled.

Then one day the young lady called on her at home and asked, point-blank, "How much would it take for you to let him go?"

As she herself told the story, Mrs. Bryant said firmly, "I am sorry, but he is not for sale," and showed her to the door.

I asked him once, after one of his periodic hospital stays, what the doctors had said was wrong with him. "They say it's eighty-five percent smoking, poor diet and the pressures of coaching," he replied, "and fifteen percent booze and other things."

He reflected for a moment and said, softly, "I wish it had been eighty-five percent booze and the other things."

Once, when we were visiting in Birmingham, he excused himself to go for one of his long doctor-ordered walks. I offered to keep him company and he declined. I took it for granted that he had a lot on his mind. After he returned, he explained, "When I take my walk, it's the only time I can smoke without someone lecturing me."

Drinking may or may not have been one of Bryant's demons. But at some point he thought it was, and he sought help in a way and for a reason that was typical of him. He thought a friend in Memphis had a more serious problem. Bear had donated money to a place in Shelby County, an old campground that had been turned into an alcohol rehab center, treating no more than five patients at a time. The friend was unwilling to go alone. So Bear agreed to go with him. Quietly he made the arrangements, and the treatment worked.

For years, Bryant rarely did any hard drinking outside of the company of close friends. But as he grew older, two drinks worked on his system the way five or six once had. He never let it interfere with football, and rarely did he embarrass himself in public. He did love the action in Las Vegas, and when he gambled he drank. He lost heavily one night in Caesar's Palace—the figure quoted was $50,000—and two friends had to put their arms under his shoulders and physically drag him out of the casino, at the request of the management. His heels left tracks in the carpet, and all through the lobby you could hear Coach Bryant shouting that they were all thieves and crooks.

The respect for him was such that his drinking inspired little if any gossip, in Las Vegas or in Alabama. No fuss was made when he took a cure, but those who knew admired him for it, and those who cared hoped his health would benefit.

It was late to undo the habits and temptations of a lifetime, but for the 1981 season Bryant had virtually gone into training. His doctor told me he was fitter than he had been in years. "I weigh 208 on my trainer's scales," he said, "and 199 on my wife's. I like my wife's scales."

The more he claimed to be bored with all the talk about the record, the more thought you suspected he was giving to it. But he said all the right things, including the essential tributes to Amos Alonzo Stagg. "Coach Stagg was the Babe Ruth of college football," he said. "To me, he is on a pedestal. You can't compare what he did years ago with football of today. In those days he didn't have a large staff. I've heard his wife scouted games for him and both of them mended uniforms. It was a completely different game then."

The only pedestal Bryant had been on up to then was his famous coaching tower overlooking Alabama's practice fields. He had been strictly a field coach until he went home to his old school, and I never heard the reason why he decided to climb the stairs. Homer Norton, the old Aggie coach, claimed to have been the first to use a tower back in the early 1940s, after his team had won a national title in 1939. He said it gave him a more commanding view of what was going on. In the end, it helped get him fired. When the Aggies began to lose, the exes grumbled that Homer should have been at ground level instead of up in the air with the pigeons.

Coach Norton's tower was constructed of wood and open to the weather. Bryant's was made of steel, had a flat roof and reinforced rails on all four sides, and came equipped with a bullhorn and a can of bug spray.

Watching Bryant shuffle across the field, you wondered how he could climb the 33 steps up the circular stairway. But his speed at getting down was an unending source of amazement to those players who committed some gross mental error, or failed to hustle.

In the spring of 1981, the legislature approved a special bill allowing Bryant to coach past 70, the mandatory retirement age for state employees. The measure was passed into law by his now good friend, Governor Fob James, the onetime Auburn halfback.

But controversy broke out as the state's teachers objected to this special privilege, and politicians to a man stampeded to line up on the side of Bryant. With all due respect, Bear was not so sure he wanted their protection. The issue, he said, had become "increasingly embarrassing to me. I was unaware the bill had been introduced . . . and had nothing to do with it being passed. I would like to ask that the entire matter be dropped."

The law stood, but Bear would deal with it in his own way, as everyone knew he would.

There was just a trace of suspense related to the record. This was not Roger Maris chasing Babe Ruth across the years, going down to the last games of a season with the home run mark in his gunsight. But if Alabama failed to deliver nine wins in 1981, the quest would carry over to another year. Who wanted that? Certainly not Bear.

Football is not a game played by a team of accountants working with pencils on paper. But anyone with a schedule knew that Alabama's ninth game was Mississippi State, and if the Tide did not lose any that was the week he would pass Stagg. This was the part Bear hated. *Unbeaten*? He could see five teams on the schedule better than his skinny-assed little boys.

Bryant was trying to be more grandfatherly, he said. But in the first days of fall practice several players, including a promising sophomore halfback named Linnie Patrick, could not run the mile in the prescribed time. He barred them from the squad until they could qualify. Meanwhile, linebacker Thomas Boyd was dropped from the starting lineup for the opener against LSU for disciplinary reasons. It was not the ideal way to begin a date with destiny, but down went the Bengal Tigers, 24–7.

The next week Georgia Tech brought off a shocker, 24–21, and after that loss Bryant suspended Boyd for missing curfew. Not only was there trouble in paradise, it became clear that the record was doing what Bryant had feared and predicted. It was psyching up Alabama's opponents.

More trouble. Patrick and another runner, Charley Williams, failed to report to the training room for treatment while the team was at Kentucky (winning, but not easily, 19–10). Bryant kicked them out of the athletic dorm. Williams later quit the team and then came back. In time, Patrick was allowed to return to the dorm.

The Tide blew away Vanderbilt and Ole Miss, but then the nearly unthinkable happened: unheralded Southern Mississippi fought them to a 13–13 tie. Of their first six games, they had won four. Alabama had to win all the rest to give Coach Bryant the record.

More bad news. The *Atlanta Constitution* quoted unidentified team members as saying the Tide had morale and racial problems, the result of Bryant's actions against Boyd, Patrick and Williams, all blacks. It was exactly the kind of storm a team with a goal, or a coach with a goal, could live without. Bear said the only thing he could, that he thought he treated his players fairly, no matter what their color. Boyd said his punishment was deserved.

In Houston, I read the stories and remembered how he had looked at the Cotton Bowl. I wondered if it really mattered, if being the coach with the most wins would be worth whatever the cost was going to be.

In the end, of course, only one opinion counted and that belonged to the man in the houndstooth hat. I remembered a scene from many years back, in that cramped and airless office under the stadium at Kyle Field, in College Station. Did I tell you how small his office was back then? Probably 10 feet deep by 12 feet wide, or not much larger than the desk in his spacious office at Alabama. I am not kidding. He had a file cabinet next to his desk and two metal folding chairs just to the right of the door as you walked in. If more than two people wanted to see him, someone had to stand. There wasn't room for another chair.

The challenge was so big, the hours so short, the visitors so few, I guess it didn't matter to him then, the size of his office. But I remember when Jones Ramsey and I squeezed in there one day while a writer from *Time* interviewed him, a pleasant fellow named Bill Rappleye who did not normally do sports. The Aggies were in the Top Ten, the legend was gaining, and Bill asked Bear why winning meant so much to him.

He gestured idly with his hands, then made two or three false starts, and finally thundered: "Hell, I don't know. All I know is, if you have on a different colored jersey than me, I want to beat your ass."

Whatever his health, age or the morale of his team, whatever his other problems, burnout was not going to be one of them in November 1981. I thought of all the younger coaches who had quit before their time. When Dick Vermeil left the Philadelphia Eagles, he announced that he wanted to find himself. In the past, all anyone had to do was look in the projection room.

Not many coaches quit because of the tension or because they are unwell, worn down, consumed. At least, this is not the reason they usually give. And many who do quit come back, having discovered that other pursuits are pretty dull compared to life in the pits. A heart attack didn't stop Bo Schembechler. George Halas made a comeback at 70 or 75, and finally turned in his clipboard when he discovered that his artificial hip prevented him from running up and down the sideline, screaming at the officials.

We do coaches an awful disservice, overpraising their success and treating their failures as though they had been caught burning down orphanages.

I did a lot of thinking that year about coaches, what makes them tick, what kind of people they are. I reached no new conclusions. I only knew that Bear Bryant would stay the course.

In early November, fullback Kenny Simon, another black, was

arrested and charged with a felony after police said he had fired a shotgun. Bryant conducted his own investigation and kept him on the team, saying Kenny was innocent "as far as we are concerned and I am proud to stick by him like any father would stick by his son." (In December, a county grand jury reduced the charge to "menacing," a misdemeanor.)

Meanwhile, the Tide had defeated Tennessee and Rutgers easily and squeezed by stubborn Mississippi State, 13–10. Penn State was next, and Bryant accepted the congratulations of Joe Paterno after a 31–16 victory, his 314th, tying Stagg. He looked good on the sidelines that day, wearing a turtleneck shirt and a crimson, V-necked sweater under his topcoat to ward off the chill. Under the hat, the face suddenly looked younger and healthier and the hair in back was longer than Bryant used to permit his players to wear theirs.

With the media pressure mounting daily, and only Auburn left on the regular schedule, Bryant dropped from the team two linemen, Bob Cayavec and Gary Bramblett, both white, for breaking training. The two were stopped at 1:30 A.M. by police, who ticketed Cayavec, who was behind the wheel, for drunk driving.

Bryant was willing to be a more benign and even patriarchal figure, if the players had let him. "I haven't forgotten the other way, either," he said.

So now it was back to the future. Down went Auburn's Tigers in the fourth quarter, 28–17, and Stagg went with them. Bryant stood alone in the dominion of college football, the possessor of 315 victories. In a footnote to the win, Linnie Patrick scored one of the touchdowns on a 15-yard run.

It was on to the Cotton Bowl, where Alabama would play a Texas team Bryant had never beaten in a bowl game, and only once (at A&M) in eight tries. The Texas coach was Fred Akers, like Bryant a native of Arkansas, who had played for the Razorbacks against Bear's Aggies in the late 1950s.

They were an interesting contrast: Akers, scrubbed, combed, picture perfect in an orange suede sport coat; Bryant, shoulders hunched, a gray jacket over gray shirt, no tie needed.

"Sure, it's special," said Akers. "It's an honor to be involved in a game like this, against someone like Coach Bryant. I've been with him before. I enjoy him, just like everybody else. I've admired him all through the years. We all admire him. He has been very gracious in giving us advice, sometimes when we didn't ask for it."

Bryant dismissed his team's disciplinary problems as nothing special. "No more than usual," he said. "There are always some. People say you shouldn't take borderline players, the ones who are likely to get into trouble. But you like to think you can help them. And if you don't try, they'll just play somewhere else and beat us. 'Course, I'd rather not have kids that are a problem. If I can't love them and pat them and brag on them, I don't want them. I tell 'em to go join the service or something."

He said his players were aware that Alabama had never beaten Texas "because they read the papers same as I do. But they're not feeling any great pressure. It's not like when we play Auburn or Tennessee. We had a coaches' meeting this morning and nobody puked."

Bear would not add to his total on New Year's Day, 1982. Alabama blew a 10-point lead against the Longhorns, who scored all of their points in the fourth quarter. Robert Brewer ran 30 yards and Terry Orr 8 for the touchdowns, and a 14–10 lead with two minutes and five seconds left.

Alabama needed a gigantic play to pull this one out. For a few wild seconds, it appeared that a 159-pound sophomore named Joey Jones would deliver it. He fielded the kickoff at the Alabama 1, veered to his right, weaved past the Texas bench and cut to the inside. "I ran around their kicker," he said, "and I saw lots of daylight. I figured I could beat those guys to the goal line."

Of all the great finishes in Bryant's years as a head coach, a 99-yard touchdown run by little Joey Jones might have been the Mona Lisa. But it didn't happen. He slowed down a tad to wait for his blockers, and a Texas tackler caught him from behind at the 30. It was a 69-yard kickoff return, the longest in Cotton Bowl history, but not quite long enough. Texas took a safety to protect the win, 14–12, and the game ended as so many others had—with a band playing "The Eyes of Texas" and the living legend walking slowly to the locker room, uniformed troopers on either side of him. He never looked back.

Bryant's teams finished 2-and-3 in the Cotton Bowl, but it is a hauntingly impressive fact that his first win (Kentucky over TCU) and his final loss came 30 years apart.

*   *   *

Before the 1982 season, Bryant retreated to the 3,000-acre farm of his son in Greene County and dropped out for two weeks. He was mending from cosmetic surgery—a minor facelift. He was talked into it by one of his former players, Dr. Gaylon McCollough, the center on the Namath teams and now a distinguished plastic surgeon. The deeper creases were smoothed out and the turkey wattle under his neck was removed. He looked better than he had in years. But when he reappeared in public, Bear never mentioned the operation to anyone, and if any of his friends had the nerve to ask, none admitted that he had. It became a nonsubject.

Alabama started the 1982 season as they had so many recent ones, with the look of eagles. They won their first five, four of them blowouts, ranked second in the polls and their fans were having visions of another national title. Then Tennessee, of the dreaded orange shirts, tumbled the Tide from the unbeaten lists, 35–28, in a tight one at Knoxville.

November, a month when Bryant's teams normally came of age, was a complete washout. LSU upset them, 20–10, and Bryant dropped broad hints that this season would be his last.

The team responded to the news in a manner remindful of the fadeout by his Texas Aggies in 1957. Pesky Southern Mississippi jolted them, 38–29, the first time Alabama had lost on its home field in Tuscaloosa in 19 years. The season ended bitterly, with a 23–22 defeat by arch-rival Auburn.

The Tide had finished with three straight defeats, four in their last six games: it added up to a 7–4 record, the poorest in 12 years. And on December 15, two weeks before his team would meet Illinois in the Liberty Bowl, Bryant made it official. When he read his retirement statement to the TV cameras, his voice stumbled, as though he could not read his own handwriting. He didn't seem sad or relieved or even sentimental . . . just tired. He would stay on as athletic director, but he had, in effect, fired himself as the coach because Alabama in 1982 had played, he said, only "four or five games like a Bryant-coached team should . . . whatever that is."

If we had learned anything over the years, we had learned what *that* is.

"There comes a time in every profession when you have to hang it up," he said, "and that time has come for me as head football coach at the University of Alabama."

At the same time, his successor was announced: Ray Perkins, one of his great Alabama players, a star receiver with the Baltimore Colts, most recently the head coach of the New York Giants.

Gaylon McCollough was one of perhaps three people who knew ahead of time when Bryant would reveal his retirement. Bryant had submitted a list of names to Dr. Joab Thomas, the new Alabama president, including three of his former players with head coaching experience: Perkins, Howard Schnellenberger and Gene Stallings. Out of loyalty, he added six names from his present staff, and among those interviewed were Mal Moore, Bobby Marks and Dee Powell.

Bryant had told Dr. Thomas that any of the candidates on his list would do a good job, and from that point on he did not want to be involved. The truth is, he did. He would have liked nothing better than to have been consulted on the final selection. Some close to him thought his choice would have been Stallings. But Dr. Thomas took him at his word.

The three front-runners were interviewed on the same day, a Sunday, for an hour and a half each. Then Dr. Thomas sent his board members home, telling them he would poll each one by phone the next day. Perkins received all five votes, and in 24 hours Ray had given his resignation to the Giants.

After the drama and excitement of the run for the record, the 1982 season had turned out to be an anticlimax for Bryant. But now the Liberty Bowl would take on a new significance—the Bear's last game.

He knew Alabama would go to a bowl. They were doing so for the 26th straight year. "If we win two games," he conceded, "some bowl somewhere would invite us." It was like asking Kate Smith to sing "God Bless America."

Memorial Stadium in Memphis was assured of a sellout crowd of over 54,000, and the match between two scarred teams emerged as a major attraction. It did not come easily or quietly, but there was no way Alabama would lose the Liberty Bowl.

The Tide won, 21–15, even though Tony Eason almost passed

them dizzy, attempting 55 passes and completing 35 for 423 yards, a record. The game was emotional and sloppy, with eight turnovers by the Illini and five by Alabama.

"We won in spite of me," said Bryant, in character to the very end. Alabama scored on drives of 76, 50 and 66 yards, with Jesse Bendross getting the middle touchdown on an end-around in the third quarter—one last trick from Bear's bag.

Mike White, the Illinois coach, held his chair as Bryant seated himself for the postgame interview, placing his houndstooth hat on the table in front of him. White sounded almost happy about getting beat: "I feel honored that I was the guy that got to play against you in your last game. We'll miss you."

When the final gun went off, White had crossed the field to give Bryant a hug. His players tried to lift the old man onto their shoulders, but his bulk or their nervousness didn't connect, and after a few fumbling moments they gave up and formed a tight cordon to escort him gingerly off the field. He strolled off into retirement with a record of 323 wins, 85 losses, 17 ties.

And behind them, the scoreboard lights blinked:

GOOD-BYE, BEAR, WE'LL MISS YOU.

Chapter 14

Epilogue

January 26, 1983

Paul Bryant did not have an unnatural interest in death, was not haunted by it. He was not a man of premonition. Nor did the subject appeal to him, darkly, in some abstract or metaphysical form. And it would be foolish, the worst kind of sports shtick, to think that he dismissed death as simply another opponent to be held off, if not defeated. He was a student of percentages. And he knew that three out of every three people do not leave this earth alive.

But he talked about dying enough, even in a half-joking way, to arouse questions. My guess is that this was so because he spent his life working against the clock. He knew the fullness of 60 minutes and the drama of 2, and he was always, acutely, aware of how much time remained.

At midafternoon on Wednesday, the 26th of January, 1983, I was sitting at a typewriter at a Houston television station, Channel 2 (KPRC-TV), preparing a script for the commentaries I sometimes did on the six-o'clock news. Ron Franklin, the sports anchor, appeared in the doorway and looked at me with a tentative, almost fearful expression. "He's gone," he said.

I didn't answer. The words did not connect with anything then on my mind.

"Bryant," he said. "It just moved on the wire. He's dead."

I went cold all over. I knew he had been taken to the hospital a day earlier, nothing new there. A wire story out of Birmingham had described his condition as good, the problem the usual one, exhaustion, his release expected shortly.

In a considerate, even apologetic way, Franklin asked if I would do an interview with him, talking about Bryant. I followed him down the hall to the studio, just feeling dazed and empty, but not teary-eyed, not that I was aware of. We taped the interview, and a clip from it appeared that night on the NBC news. I heard myself answer Ron's questions, and saw myself again that night, and still have no idea what was asked or what I said.

The next day, friends kept phoning to ask if I wanted to fly over to Alabama for the funeral. Pat Morgan and I talked about it. Johnny Mitchell said he would have a limo waiting at the Airport Hotel in Birmingham. If I got there before 9:00 A.M Friday, I could ride with the Mitchells to the morning service in Tuscaloosa. The burial, after a motorcade from the campus to Birmingham, would be at noon in Elmwood Cemetery. I didn't think I could go. The plane connections were spotty. I had stories to write and a TV special to tape. I wanted to go . . . and yet I did not.

It was after midnight when I finished my work. On impulse, maybe something a little stronger, I phoned for the ninth or tenth time and learned there was still a seat open on a Delta flight that left Houston for Birmingham at 2:25 A.M. I drove to Hobby Airport, bought a ticket and boarded the plane. Before I left my home that day I had packed a bag, just in case.

The flight was nearly full. With one stop, we would arrive in Birmingham around 7:00, in time to meet the Mitchells for break-fast.

One way or another, I determined there were 12 people on the plane flying to Coach Bryant's funeral. None of us knew each other. One burly fellow in a checkered sport coat turned out to be Al Kinkaid, then the head coach at Wyoming, once an assistant under

Bryant. Three of the passengers were part of a network television crew.

About the time we should have been landing, the pilot announced that Birmingham was socked in by fog and we would be diverted instead to Jackson, Miss. How long we would be delayed there depended, obviously, on when the fog lifted. There went Tuscaloosa. There went, possibly, the entire trip. I kicked myself, mentally, for giving in to my impulses.

One of the unfailing truths of air travel is that there are no happy passengers on a plane forced to make an unscheduled stop. While the others besieged the hapless agents at the counter, Kinkaid, the TV people and I spent the next hour checking out the numbers listed in the phone book for private planes. The list was not long, a couple were no longer in service, and only one of the rest answered. And his plane was engaged.

At 9:00 A.M. they called our flight. We had been cleared to continue into Birmingham. Kinkaid had given up, scribbled a note on the back of a business card and asked me to deliver it to Mrs. Bryant. I climbed back on the plane and an hour and 14 minutes later we were on the ground in Birmingham.

I checked into a room at the Airport Hotel and turned on my television set. Live coverage was in progress outside the church in Tuscaloosa where the memorial service for Coach Bryant was being held. Everything about the scene suggested nothing less than a state funeral: the hush in the voices of the announcers, the uniformly dark suits of the men who moved in or out of the church or merely stood by the door, the tearful or frozen faces of the people in the crowds who came to watch, or just to feel.

The small First Methodist Church, where the services were held, seated only a few hundred, meaning that even some of Bryant's former players and coaches had to stand outside in a crowd estimated at 10,000, listening to the eulogy over loudspeakers.

The eulogy was delivered by Steadman Shealy, a quarterback on the 1979 national champions who had gone into the ministry after a year on Bryant's coaching staff. Maybe, as Bryant had once tried to convince his mama, there wasn't all that much difference between coaching and preaching. You certainly could not disprove it by the crowds milling outside the church, or the 6,000 who earlier had passed by Bear's closed coffin, covered with red and white carnations, lying in state at the Memorial Coliseum.

One of the announcers quoted a few lines from the eulogy, but I missed it. Instead I thought of a story someone had told me on the phone before I knew I was going to Birmingham. A few days before Bryant's death, Shealy made an unscheduled visit to his office. He asked his old coach if he would kneel and pray with him. When it was time for Shealy to leave, Bear held the younger man's hand for a moment at the wrist, the way he did when he was sending a player into the game. He said, evenly, "You know, Steadman, in my own way, I bet I pray more than you do."

The story made me smile. He enjoyed the company, of course, but he was letting Shealy know that no one needed to lead him. Paul Bryant wanted to finish first, even in praying.

I read the paper, watched more television, and finally decided to catch a taxi to the cemetery. I really felt at loose ends, kind of lost. A motorcade of 300 cars would be leaving soon to make the 60-mile drive to Birmingham. The entire 1982 Alabama team, his last team, would be transported in three buses, leaving from the athletic dormitory, Paul W. Bryant Hall. The entire team had been named as pallbearers and eight had been chosen to carry the coffin.

The buses slowed to a crawl as they passed Bryant-Denny Stadium, the scene of so many victories, and the Memorial Coliseum, which housed the coaches' offices and had been built with the money from Bryant's successes.

I had forgotten the name of the cemetery (Elmwood), but the driver knew exactly where to take me. A few hundred mourners were already on the grounds, but the motorcade would not arrive for two hours and there was no crowding, no noise, no one even to restrict or regulate your movement. A wall of red and white carnations, thousands of them, had been arranged at the entrance to the cemetery.

The state police would later estimate the number of onlookers who lined the interstate from Tuscaloosa to Birmingham at 100,000. No one I talked with felt that figure was excessive. Many jockeyed for positions on the overpasses. They snapped pictures and held up handmade signs and banners: WE LOVE YOU BEAR, or WE'LL MISS YOU BEAR, or THANKS FOR THE MEMORIES, BEAR.

I did not have to walk around long before I began to bump into people I knew. Just a few steps inside the cemetery, I spotted Richard Gay, the Aggie fullback in 1957, with his son. We teamed up to look for the plot where Coach Bryant would be laid to rest. Along the way we encountered Jim Brock, the executive director of the Cotton Bowl, and Jimmie McDowell, with the National Football Foundation. Brock was the publicity man at TCU when he first met Bear. McDowell, known as "Mississippi Red," was a sportswriter.

The crowd was growing quickly. They came in brilliant sunshine, a day especially mild for January, not a topcoat in sight. We found the grave, under a canopy, and staked out a spot on a small rise on the other side of a path. The marker said Lot 57, Block 30. We could no longer see the narrow road that ran through the grounds. The motorcade, three miles long, would have to inch its way through 15,000 people. They were old and young, black and white, well dressed, most of them, and orderly. You could see them trying not to trample the grass or disturb the other graves.

We were blocked off when the buses carrying the team stopped in front of the grave, followed by the first of the long black limousines. We saw Mrs. Bryant and her daughter, Mae Martin Tyson, both wearing black dresses and veils, helped out of the car. They began to move to the canopy, followed by the Alabama coaches, the eight players, and school and state dignitaries, including Governor George Wallace in his wheelchair. Our view was completely blocked when I heard Gay say, "Let's go."

"Go where?" I asked.

"Just follow me," he said, and he grabbed his son's hand and plunged into the crowd. I jumped in behind him and the next thing I knew we were crossing directly in front of Wallace's wheel chair. He looked right at me. I sort of shrugged and said, "Excuse me, Governor."

When I pulled up next to Richard I realized we were right outside the canopy. We went through eye-lock with several of the coaches we knew who stood with the family: Sam Bailey, Dee Powell, Bobby Marks, one or two others.

Then it was over. The graveside service lasted only five minutes, at Mrs. Bryant's request. She did not raise her eyes as she was escorted back to her car. Richard wanted to walk over and say something, but I held back, feeling self-conscious and too aware of the crowd. I had just said no, I didn't think I would, when I looked up and saw Paul, Jr., at the door of the second car, motioning to us.

We walked over—Richard, his son and I. We hugged each other, and Paul said something about how his mother's phone had not stopped ringing with messages from Texas, from Aggies. They would never be able to return them all, "but when you go back tell the Aggies Papa loved them."

Then he turned to Gay, who had been his favorite player when Paul was 12 or 13, in the Aggie years. He took the palm of Richard's hand and held his own closed hand over it. "When Papa died," he said, "we took this off his finger. It was the only jewelry he was wearing." He opened his hand and let a ring drop into Gay's palm. It was the ring the Junction Boys had given to Coach Bryant at their 25th-anniversary reunion.

On my way out of the cemetery, without even thinking about it, I paused at the wall of flowers and picked a red carnation and a white one. As I walked to the car, I looked back, and saw hundreds of other mourners doing the same, so that the arrangement began to look pock-marked. I meant to take the flowers home, but I gave one to somebody's wife who asked for it, and left the other in my hotel room.

Many of his former players turned up at a reception—I don't think you would call it a wake—held later that afternoon at the Hyatt Hotel. I stopped by with Richard Gay. For the next few hours, I heard people say over and over, and heard myself say, that he was more than a football coach.

In truth, I am not sure what we meant by it, the phrase somehow suggesting that being a coach wasn't praise enough. As any coach who ever sat in a meeting with him or faced him from across the sidelines would tell you, no one knew more about football. As a game-day coach, at staying four or five plays ahead of the action, he had no equal. But what made him great, and possibly unique, was the way he reached people when he cared enough to try. And most of the time he cared. He used your fear and wanted your love, and what seemed an act to some was really the basic Bear Bryant, what John Underwood called that implausible combination of "ham and humble pie."

Of course, he was a motivator and one of the great communicators, in the old-fashioned way, without teleprompters or cue cards or index cards. Underwood told of attending a team breakfast one Saturday: "I sat next to an Alabama professor who had been invited along. Bryant curried faculty support by doing things like that, itself a form of communication. When he made his talk to the team, he barely spoke above a whisper. The players leaned forward in their seats, and one tipped over a glass of water. The spill hitting the floor sounded like Niagara Falls. When Bryant finished, the professor turned to me, awed. 'If I could reach my students like that I'd teach for nothing,' he said."

I found a clipping quoting a talk he made to his team at midweek, during the national championship year of 1964:

> After the game, there are three types of people. One comes in and he ain't played worth killing, and he's lost. And he gets dressed and out of there as quick as he can. He meets his girl and his momma, and they ain't too damn glad to see him. And he goes off somewhere and says how 'the coach shoulda done this or that,' and 'the coach don't like me,' and 'I didn't play enough.' And everybody just nods.
>
> And the second type will sit there awhile, thinking what he could have done to make his team a winner. And he'll shed some tears. He'll finally get dressed, but he doesn't want to see anybody. His momma's out there. She puts on a big act and tells him what a great game he played, and he tells her if he had done this or done that, he'd be a winner, and that he will be a winner—next week.
>
> And then there's the third guy. The winner. He'll be in there hugging everybody in the dressing room. It'll take him an hour to dress. And when he goes out, there is a little something extra in it when his daddy squeezes his hand. His momma hugs and kisses him, and that little old ugly girl snuggles up, proud to be next to him. And he *knows* they're proud. And why.

The laughter in that room, as his friends and players traded stories, was in contrast to the very real grief that gripped the state of Alabama. It is easy to say that such idolatry was misplaced, or out of proportion to what he was. But the fact remained that this was a loss to Alabama's pride. This line caught my eye in an obituary in *Sports Illustrated*: " . . . the news spread like stepping on an ant bed. Phone-in radio shows were deluged by callers who reached out for comfort, swapping accounts of personal encounters they'd had with the man and openly crying on the air in a sort of down-home version of the Islamic mourners' public wailing."

Over and over, I heard people try to describe what he meant to Alabama, to coaching, to the players who had indeed given him their bodies and souls and been molded by him. After all, this was a state that had been shamed in assorted ways over the past quarter century: by Wallace's stand in the schoolhouse door, and Bull Connor's fire hoses, and the next-to-last rankings in per capita income and teachers' salaries, just ahead of Mississippi. But Paul Bryant, and his teams, had elevated them.

Two points beg to be repeated. He was the most human of coaches, and the most Southern. One would blush to raise again the notion of football as mock war, but the comparison has been made by experts. Two Alabama historians, Grady McWhinney and Forrest MacDonald, concluded that football was to the Southerner what war was to the Celts, who 200 years earlier had helped settle the region. A Southerner whose age placed him between wars, they wrote, felt deprived of his manhood. "Football can fill that void. For Alabama, the Bear is the Robert E. Lee of this warfare."

All that day, and into the night, I learned more details of how Coach Bryant died, and it became more clear to me that he had known three years before that he was hastening his death, and that for reasons of his own he had taken the risk. He lived three weeks longer than he had given himself in that eerily prophetic, oft-repeated crack: "If I quit coachin' I'd croak in a week."

He suffered from coronary artery disease, commonly known as hardening or narrowing of the arteries. He survived a major attack in 1980, but his doctor, William Hill, prescribed a powerful stimulant and he was back on the practice field in about a week.

In 1981, according to Dr. Hill, Bryant suffered a light stroke with paralysis on the right side of the body. It isn't clear that anyone outside his family knew about this setback. Again, "after a week or two, he was back on the field."

"He made a remarkable recovery from the stroke," said Dr. Hill. "I was relieved when he announced his retirement."

On the early evening of Tuesday, January 25, Bryant felt violent chest pains. He was at the home of Jimmy Hinton, his partner in land and meatpacking deals, as well as in hunting, fishing and gin rummy. Bryant seemed to have a capacity for collapsing among friends, possibly one reason he lasted as long as he did.

He was rushed to Druid City Hospital, where tests disclosed no massive heart damage. He spent a restful night, and in the morning had a light, joking visit with Sam Bailey, his associate athletic director, and his successor, Ray Perkins. Bailey had been with him since his last season at A&M, 26 years earlier.

But at 12:24 P.M., Bryant's breathing became labored. Ten or 15 seconds later his heart stopped beating and a code-blue alarm sounded throughout the coronary unit. The medical staff swung into action to try to save his life. Nurses massaged his chest. A device was used to force air into his lungs. He was injected with an assortment of drugs, and Dr. Hill inserted a needle through an artery and into the heart.

For a few, brief moments they raised a weak heartbeat and then it was gone. At 1:30 P.M., Paul William Bryant was pronounced dead of a coronary occlusion—or blockage—brought on by hardening of the arteries.

And in the next several hours the news had spread "like stepping on an ant bed." At the cemetery, I was astonished by the response from people who never knew him, never attended Alabama, may or may not have been football fans. A black woman was there with four children tugging at her skirts, the oldest no more than six. She said: "They don't know who Bear Bryant is, but they will someday. I brought them so they could say that they was there for the passing of a great man."

Of course, I felt that way, always had. But football and matters related to it had been a part of how I earned my living. Such judgments may be better left to another time, but it was reassuring to know so many agreed with mine.

On the plane back to Houston, browsing through a Birmingham paper, I ran across an interview with a black man who ran a barbecue stand a block from the University campus. When he had no lunch meetings, Coach Bryant would walk down a hill and cross the road and sit there with him, on a barstool at the counter, under a corrugated tin roof, eating a barbecue sandwich on white bread and a diet soda, sometimes a beer. They would talk about fishing and hunting and dogs, mostly. Sometimes they talked about the way the times had changed. "One thing we never talked about," said the barbecue man, "was football."

I meant to save that newspaper, but I dozed off on the plane, was groggy when we landed, and left it in my seat.

The trip had not depressed me. I had nice memories of running into old friends, and even heard a few Bear Bryant stories that were new to me. But two weeks later, driving on a Houston freeway, alone in my car, going nowhere special, I had a flashback to that moment when Paul Bryant, Jr., dropped his father's Junction ring into the hand of Richard Gay. And I started crying. I can't say why, or exactly what I felt. But I cried for the next six exits, roughly a mile and a quarter. And then the tears stopped. I guess I had finally said my good-bye to Coach Bryant.

Of course, if he lived only in our memories, and sometimes on film, he lived nonetheless. A motion picture was released in August 1984 called, with suitable leanness, *The Bear*. I knew the producer, Larry Spangler, slightly, and I was aware that Coach Bryant's family had reservations about the film.

I had talked with Mrs. Bryant shortly after the announcement that Gary Busey was going to play her husband. Even with the honeysuckle in it, her voice was angry when she said, "Can you imagine that fat-faced, buck-toothed boy playing Papa. Papa was *handsome!*"

The remark was not meant to be taken personally. Busey is a shaggy, rumpled kind of fellow, whose portrayal of the late singer Buddy Holly won him an Oscar nomination. He is not unpleasant-looking, with a face soft and expressive, like a lemon meringue pie.

But he was not Papa. And though he gave an effort that might be described as gargantuan—he is rarely off the screen—Busey did not strike those who knew Coach Bryant as a very believable replacement.

The movie succeeded best with the scenes from Junction, where Bryant took his first Aggie team and where, out of the yellow dust and broiling heat, he created a legend and, in 1956, a championship team.

There was a nice, honest moment, at the end of the first week, when Bryant asked how many of his players would like to go to church with him on Sunday? Every hand shot up, the players sensing a way to get a day off.

"Good," said Bear (in the film), "that's very good. We'll leave for church right after practice. See you at breakfast at six A.M." The next shot showed the small church in Junction. A ceiling fan whispered as voices were lifted in song. The camera panned the room. Every Aggie player was asleep, his head resting on the shoulder of the person next to him.

It had happened exactly that way, in real life.

The week the movie was released, on August 26, 1984, Mary Harmon Bryant died of a cerebral hemorrhage in Druid City Hospital, in Tuscaloosa. A newspaper account of her death noted that she was a former beauty queen at the University of Alabama, and had been married to the legendary coach, her college sweetheart, for 48 years, until his death.

Eight months earlier, on January 23, 1984, Mae Martin's daughter, Mary Harmon Tyson, was married. The wedding took place almost a year to the day after her grandfather died.

In September 1985, Pat Morgan and I flew to Birmingham to see the Texas Aggies open their season against Alabama—me to write about the game, Morgan to kibitz.

The matchup was a hard one to resist. The teams were coached by former teammates under Bryant, and this is what the competition was all about: which young coach, and which team, could claim to be more Bearish than thou.

Ray Perkins's Alabama squad won the battle, 23–10, although the outcome was in doubt until the final five minutes. Jackie Sherrill, who would rally his team to a Southwest Conference title and a Cotton Bowl win over Auburn, boasted of the leg he broke, the blood he shed and the teeth he had lost on Legion Field 20 years earlier.

But Perkins had the edge there, too. During spring training of his freshman year, he collided head-on with a defensive back and was rushed to the hospital. The diagnosis was frightening. Three holes had to be drilled in his skull to relieve the pressure from a blood clot that formed in the brain. He was in intensive care for nine days and when he was pronounced out of danger, the first face he saw was Bryant's, hovering over him.

During the game, Alf Van Hoose, the sports editor of the *Birmingham News*, stopped by my seat. He was one of the writers who had Bear's confidence over the years. He asked where I was staying, and said he wanted to see me after the game.

We met Alf in the bar of the Hyatt. It turned out that he had nothing more on his mind than an urge to sit down with a kindred spirit and reminisce about Coach Bryant. I don't know if this is normal or healthy or silly or what, but we are like keepers of the flame, meeting without planning to, retelling our stories, waiting for the last surviving member of the club to drink the bottle of wine that must be stored away somewhere.

It was Alf who had persuaded James Michener to be one of the honorees at the Alabama Sports Hall of Fame dinner in 1976, about the time Bryant's autobiography reached the bookstores. Michener, whose best-selling works already included *South Pacific*, *The Source*, *The Drifters* and *Hawaii*, had passed through while researching a massive volume entitled *Sports in America*. He accepted the invitation, but specified that he would like another interview with Bryant. Alf assured him that could be arranged.

A press reception was held the night before the dinner, and Bryant arrived 30 minutes late, with his entourage. The moment he entered the room, the media circled him like fruit flies. "I told Michener," recalled Van Hoose, "to wait a moment and I would pull the coach away and get them some privacy. So I went over and said, 'I have someone who needs fifteen minutes alone with you and I'll keep the crowd away.' So I led Bryant to a corner and waved, and when he walked up I said, 'Coach, you remember Jim Michener, don't you?'

"Bear said, 'Oh, yeah, yeah.'

"Michener smiled and said, wanting to be gracious, 'Coach, you don't know what it does to an author's ego to come into a town with a book (*Hawaii*) and find that another author is outselling him three to one.'

"Bear just laughed and they chatted a few minutes and finally some TV station latched on to Michener and walked away with him. Bear turned to me and asked, 'Who did you say that fellow was?'

"I wanted him to feel good, so I said, 'Coach, that was Jim Michener, whose books have outsold any book ever published except the Bible. I mentioned his big sellers and added, 'That was a pretty good compliment he paid you.' "

Bryant thought about it for a moment and said, "Shit, it ought to have been fifteen to one."

Morgan, who had entered Alabama as Bryant was finishing, sat enthralled as we talked until the bar closed. He paid the tab and we walked into the lobby, in time to bump into Scott Hunter, former Tide quarterback, now a TV announcer. We resurrected the 1968 Bluebonnet Bowl, in which he appeared.

We stood in the lobby another 20 minutes or so, a bit brain-damaged but reluctant to leave the past. Then something I said about Coach Bryant reminded Alf of a friend of his, who had just retired from the army, having served three tours of duty in Vietnam. In the writing business, you hear possibly one fresh line a year. This one may have been it, for me, for 1985.

"The colonel was always talking about how tough his outfit was," said Alf. "So I asked him one day to tell me the truth, how tough was it? The colonel said, 'They were so tough, if Rambo had been in it he would have been the cook.' "

Tough outfit, I agreed. They could have played for Coach Bryant.

Afterword

On New Year's night of 1993, the Alabama football team accomplished the following:

Stuffed Gino Torreta, the Heisman Trophy winner, and ripped the heart and lungs out of favored Miami, 34–13, in the Sugar Bowl. In short, the Crimson Tide humbled Miami, a feat many students of human behavior considered impossible. Defeat them, perhaps; humble them, hardly.

Ended the '92 season with a perfect record, 13-and-0, and ran its winning streak to 23.

Won the school's first national championship since Paul Bryant's 1979 squad, thirteen years before. It was clearly the tasteful way to observe the tenth anniversary of Bryant's death — three coaches and one decade to the month.

Whether or not you conclude that Bama buried the ghost of Bear Bryant depends on whether you believe a symbolic burial was necessary, or even possible. Lean Gene Stallings did not and he should know, seeing as how he was the third coach hired to bring back the glory.

Not that Ray Perkins, a home boy, and Bill Curry, a classy intruder from Georgia Tech, didn't win. They just didn't win the way the Bear won, often, and with a growly certainty.

At the Sugar Bowl, Stallings was asked the question he had heard over and over again: Was he haunted, as Perkins and Curry were, by living in Bryant's huge shadow? His answer surprised the press.

242

"I kinda like it," he said, casually. "The players live in Bryant Hall. Right in front of my office is Bryant Boulevard, which leads to the Paul Bryant Conference Center, right beside the Paul Bryant Museum, down by Paul Bryant Stadium.

"That's the way it's going to be for a long time. It doesn't bother me one bit."

In a magic carpet kind of ride, Stallings won the Paul (Bear) Bryant Coach of the Year award, selected by the Football Writers of America. (Do we detect a pattern here?) Oddly, in the thirty-six years the trophy has been presented, Bryant never received one. The trophy was named after him in 1986.

There were special bonds between them. Stallings played for Bryant at Texas A&M from 1954 through 1956 and had been one of his famed Junction Boys. He was on his staff at Alabama from 1958 to 1964, before returning to Aggieland as a twenty-nine-year-old head coach. The Aggies won the Southwest Conference title in 1967 and went on to beat the Tide, and his mentor, in the Cotton Bowl.

"I won't ever be out of Coach Bryant's shadow," said Stallings. "In Alabama they loved him so much that they just tolerate the rest of us — as long as we win a few games."

All of which, the championship season, the awards, the memorial to Bryant's past, came together in a notable twist of timing. Bryant died of a heart attack in January of 1983, just weeks after his last team defeated Illinois in the Liberty Bowl.

This book first appeared in 1987, published by McGraw-Hill. It was a book Coach Bryant and I had planned to write together, and I had put aside the project after his death. A number of people helped revive it, and they are acknowledged elsewhere.

I said most of the things I wanted to say, and that needed saying, but at the end of the process I was left with one small regret. The original title for the book had been *The LEGACY of Bear Bryant.*

Instead, somewhere along the production line an innocent error was made, and the title turned into *The Legend of Bear Bryant.* In the larger scheme of things, I probably overreacted to this typographical accident. I thought the term "legend" was trite and overused, though few would argue that he qualified.

But legacy was the word I wanted, the one that best suited the theme of the book, the teams and players whose lives he changed and shaped.

It developed that 35,000 dust jackets had been printed and an effort to correct the title failed. A considerate and respected editor, Tom Quinn, tried to console me. "The difference really isn't that great," he said, "and besides, no one else will know that a mistake was made."

"Yeah," I said, "I understand that. But how do you think Margaret Mitchell would have felt if the publisher had changed the title of her book to *The Wind Blew Everything Away?*"

Of course, Quinn was right. No one noticed and, over the years, the legend deepened and has appeared in proximity to Bryant's name almost routinely.

We return now to New Year's night, 1993, when Miami, the defending national champion, was gone with the wind. Coach Dennis Erickson's team was considered invincible, as well as insufferable. A headline in *USA Today* asked: "Can Any Team Beat Miami?" It was meant to be one of those rhetorical questions.

This was Number 1 versus Number 2, a dream game between the two best teams in college football. "They never lose those kind of games," insisted *USA Today*. "Never."

Can we ever again believe what a newspaper tells us?

As great as Bryant's championship teams were, none of them had a season exactly like this one; with an offense so suspect, the Tide counted on their defense not only to stop the other team but to score points.

The Bama defense confused Torreta and took the starch out of his teammates. By the fourth quarter, the Hurricane players were no longer treating every tackle as a holiday, every pass deflection as a religious experience. They had stopped getting in the faces of the Alabama players, had stopped talking trash, had stopped taking a cheap shot whenever they could.

"It's a 'Cane' Thing," the Miami players kept assuring us, explaining their gangland idea of fun and intimidation. Alabama didn't buy a nickel's worth.

In a symbolic moment, the TV camera caught Miami's Lamar Thomas on the bench, hiding his head under a towel. He had gone nearly coast to coast with a pass, except that Alabama's George Teague ran him down at the 15-yard line and then stole the ball. He simply reached over Lamar's right shoulder, at full speed, and wrestled the ball out of his arms.

A five-yard penalty wiped out the play, but couldn't erase Miami's embarrassment. The Hurricane got the ball back, but 77 yards farther away from the goal line. Nothing erased the pass Teague intercepted earlier and returned 31 yards for a touchdown that put Alabama ahead, 27-6.

Toretta was intercepted three times, with two others, by safety Sam Shade and corner Tommy Johnson, setting up scores.

Alabama's game plan depended on the defense smothering Toretta and his swift receivers. The Crimson Tide went from one extreme to another — seven backs in the secondary, eleven players on the line of scrimmage. They flip flopped their two All-America ends, John Copeland and Eric Curry, and sometimes put them side by side.

Stallings gave Bill Oliver, his secondary coach, the credit for designing the schemes that shut down Miami's short passing game. The upset ranked among the all-timers, given the fact that the oddsmakers had made Miami a favorite by as much as 14 points.

Alabama's defense so dominated the Hurricane that the Tide stuck to the ground almost the entire game. Quarterback Jay Barker attempted 13 passes, completed four for 18 yards and had two interceptions. All year Alabama had been accused of being a one-dimensional team. "We are one-dimensional," conceded center Tobie Sheils. "Sometimes you only need one dimension."

The Crimson Tide does its share of mugging for the cameras, but this contest wasn't about style points. The rushing totals were so one-sided, Derrick Lassic alone outgained Miami by 87 yards. Lassic — rhymes with classic — finished with 135 yards on 28 carries.

Alabamans remember the Bryant years the way most people remember their childhood summers, a time of purity, all play with no falls. The Bear encountered his share of difficult times and difficult players, but the Tide, under Stallings, seemed to be tested week after week.

Under the new SEC format, Alabama had to slip past Florida to earn the conference title. After his team shut out Auburn, a quizzical Stallings remarked, "We've won 11 games, and we still haven't won anything." That oversight would be corrected a week later. Once again the defense never rested. With the clock winding down to three minutes, Antonio Langham intercepted a pass by Florida's Shane Matthews and returned it 26 yards for the winning touchdown. Alabama had won the SEC's first-ever playoff, 28–21.

The '92 team was faulted for not running up big margins against a schedule labeled non-violent. "We won the close games," said Stallings. "A lot of teams haven't."

Lassic, from New York state, twice had to be talked into staying in school, once after his girlfriend was killed in a car accident. She was driving from Montgomery to Tuscaloosa to see him. The coaches dragged him out of his room after he had secluded himself for a week, losing twenty pounds in the process.

Another story that received circulation at the Sugar Bowl involved a decision made nearly thirty years earlier. When Joe Namath was caught breaking the rules before the 1964 Sugar Bowl, Bryant let his coaches vote on whether to suspend him. The tally was ten-to-one to let him play. Stallings cast the only negative vote. Bryant agreed with him and Namath missed the game.

His hard line came back to bite him in 1993, when David Palmer, his fastest receiver, kick returner and occasional quarterback, was arrested twice in three months on charges of drunk driving. Times change. So do people. Stallings didn't turn to his coaches. He talked to three psychologists, who urged him to keep Palmer on the squad. He had come from a bleak background and football was his way out.

If anyone wanted to accuse him of going soft, Stallings shrugged it off. He suspended Palmer for three games and saw that he received treatment for his problem. "David needs the team," he was quoted as saying, "more than the team needs David."

The first time this book was released, Stallings was the head coach of the Phoenix Cardinals after fourteen seasons on Tom Landry's staff in Dallas. He wearied of fighting the front office in 1988 and resigned. In 1990, after Curry moved to Kentucky, he was hired as the head coach at Alabama.

Twice before, when the job was vacant, it was the wrong place or the wrong time. In his third season, Alabama went undefeated in thirteen games, won the national title and earned Gene Stallings the Bryant Award as coach of the year. Sometimes, you just have to believe in destiny.

BRYANT'S RECORD AS HEAD COACH

MARYLAND ERA
1945 (6–2–1)

60	Guilford	6
21	Richmond	0
22	Merchant MA	6
13	Virginia Poly	21
13	West Virginia	13
14	Wm. & Mary	33
38	VMI	0
19	Virginia	13
19	South Carolina	13

KENTUCKY ERA
(8 years, 60–23–5)
1946 (7–3)

20	Mississippi	7
26	Cincinnati	7
70	Xavier	0
13	Georgia	28
10	Vanderbilt	7
7	Alabama	21
39	Michigan State	14
35	Marquette	0
13	West Virginia	0
0	Tennessee	7

1947 (8–3)

7	Mississippi	14
20	Cincinnati	0
20	Xavier	7
28	Georgia	0
14	Vanderbilt	0
7	Michigan State	6
0	Alabama	13
18	West Virginia	6
36	Evansville	0
6	Tennessee	13

Great Lakes Bowl

24	Villanova	14

1948 (5–3–2)

48	Xavier	7
7	Mississippi	20
13	Georgia	35
7	Vanderbilt	26
25	Marquette	0

28	Cincinnati	7
13	Villanova	13
34	Florida	15
0	Tennessee	0
25	Miami	3

1949 (9–3)

71	Southern Miss.	7
19	LSU	0
47	Mississippi	0
25	Georgia	0
44	The Citadel	0
7	SMU	20
14	Cincinnati	7
21	Xavier	7
35	Florida	0
0	Tennessee	6
21	Miami	6

Orange Bowl

13	Santa Clara	21

1950 (11–1)

23	North Texas St.	0
14	LSU	0
27	Mississippi	0
40	Dayton	0
41	Cincinnati	7
34	Villanova	7
28	Georgia Tech	14
40	Florida	6
48	Mississippi State	21
23	North Dakota U.	0
0	Tennessee	7

Sugar Bowl

13	Oklahoma	7

1951 (8–4)

72	Tennessee Tech	13
6	Texas	7
17	Mississippi	21
7	Georgia Tech	13
27	Miss. State	0
35	Villanova	13
14	Florida	6

32	Miami	0
37	Tulane	0
47	Geo. Washington	13
0	Tennessee	38

Cotton Bowl

20	TCU	7

1952 (5–4–2)

6	Villanova	25
13	Mississippi	13
10	Texas A&M	7
7	LSU	24
14	Miss. State	27
14	Cincinnati	6
29	Miami	0
37	Tulane	6
27	Clemson	14
14	Tennessee	14
0	Florida	27

1953 (7–2–1)

6	Texas A&M	7
6	Mississippi	22
26	Florida	13
6	LSU	6
35	Miss. State	13
19	Villanova	0
19	Rice	13
40	Vanderbilt	14
19	Memphis State	7
27	Tennessee	21

TEXAS A&M ERA
(4 years, 25–14–2)
1954 (1–9)

9	Texas Tech	41
6	Oklahoma State	14
6	Georgia	0
7	Houston	10
20	TCU	21
7	Baylor	20
7	Arkansas	14
3	SMU	6
19	Rice	29
13	Texas	22

1955 (7-2-1)
0	UCLA	21
25	LSU	0
21	Houston	3
27	Nebraska	0
19	TCU	16
19	Baylor	7
7	Arkansas	7
13	SMU	2
20	Rice	12
6	Texas	21

1956 (9-0-1)
SWC Champions
19	Villanova	0
9	LSU	6
40	Texas Tech	7
14	Houston	14
7	TCU	6
19	Baylor	13
27	Arkansas	0
33	SMU	7
71	Rice	7
34	Texas	21

1957 (8-3-0)
21	Maryland	13
21	Texas Tech	0
28	Missouri	6
28	Houston	6
7	TCU	0
14	Baylor	0
7	Arkansas	6
19	SMU	6
6	Rice	7
7	Texas	9

Gator Bowl
0	Tennessee	3

ALABAMA ERA
(5 years, 50-12-6)
1958 (5-4-1)
3	LSU	13
0	Vanderbilt	0
29	Furman	6
7	Tennessee	14
9	Mississippi State	7
12	Georgia	0
7	Tulane	13
17	Georgia Tech	8
14	Memphis State	0
8	Auburn	14

1959 (7-2-2)
3	Georgia	17
3	Houston	0
7	Vanderbilt	7
13	Chattanooga	0
7	Tennessee	7
10	Miss. State	0
19	Tulane	7
9	Georgia Tech	7
14	Memphis State	7
10	Auburn	0

Liberty Bowl
0	Penn State	7

1960 (8-1-2)
21	Georgia	6
6	Tulane	6
21	Vanderbilt	0
7	Tennessee	20
14	Houston	0
7	Miss. State	0
51	Furman	0
16	Georgia Tech	15
34	Tampa	6
3	Auburn	0

Bluebonnet Bowl
3	Texas	3

1961 (11-0-0)
National Champions
32	Georgia	6
9	Tulane	0
35	Vanderbilt	6
26	N.C. State	7
34	Tennessee	3
17	Houston	0
24	Miss. State	0
66	Richmond	0
10	Georgia Tech	0
34	Auburn	0

Sugar Bowl
10	Arkansas	3

1962 (10-1)
35	Georgia	0
44	Tulane	6
17	Vanderbilt	7
14	Houston	3
27	Tennessee	7
35	Tulsa	6
20	Miss. State	0
36	Miami	3
6	Georgia Tech	7

38	Auburn	0

Orange Bowl
17	Oklahoma	0

1963 (9-2-0)
32	Georgia	7
28	Tulane	0
21	VAnderbilt	6
6	Florida	10
35	Tennessee	0
21	Houston	13
20	Miss. State	19
27	Georgia Tech	11
8	Auburn	10
17	Miami	12

Sugar Bowl
12	Mississippi	7

1964 (10-1-0)
National Champions
31	Georgia	3
36	Tulane	6
24	Vanderbilt	0
21	N.C. State	0
19	Tennessee	5
17	Florida	14
23	Miss. State	6
17	LSU	9
24	Georgia Tech	7
21	Auburn	14

Orange Bowl
17	Texas	21

1965 (9-1-1)
National Champions
17	Georgia	18
27	Tulane	0
17	Ole Miss	16
22	Vanderbilt	7
7	Tennessee	7
21	Florida State	0
10	Miss. State	7
31	LSU	7
35	South Carolina	14
30	Auburn	3

Orange Bowl
39	Nebraska	28

1966 (11-0-0)
34	La. Tech	0
17	Mississippi	7
26	Clemson	0
11	Tennessee	10

42 Vanderbilt 6
27 Miss. State 14
21 LSU 0
24 South Carolina 0
34 Southern Miss. 0
31 Auburn 0
Sugar Bowl
34 Nebraska 7

(10 years, 96–13–7)
1967 (8–1–1)
37 Florida State 37
25 Southern Miss. 3
21 Mississippi 7
35 Vanderbilt 21
13 Tennessee 24
13 Clemson 10
13 Miss. State 0
7 LSU 6
17 South Carolina 0
7 Auburn 3

1968 (8–3)
14 Virginia Tech 7
17 Southern Miss. 14
8 Mississippi 10
31 Vanderbilt 7
9 Tennessee 10
21 Clemson 14
20 Miss. State 13
16 LSU 7
14 Miami 6
24 Auburn 16
Gator Bowl
10 Missouri 35

1969 (6–5)
17 Virginia Tech 13
63 Southern Miss. 14
33 Mississippi 32
10 Vanderbilt 14
14 Tennessee 41
38 Clemson 13
23 Miss. State 19
15 LSU 20
42 Miami 6
26 Auburn 49
Liberty Bowl
33 Colorado 47

1970 (6–5–1)
21 Southern Cal. 42
51 Virginia Tech 18
46 Florida 15

23 Mississippi 48
35 Vanderbilt 11
0 Tennessee 24
30 Houston 21
35 Miss. State 6
9 LSU 14
32 Miami 8
28 Auburn 33
Astro–Bluebonnet Bowl
24 Oklahoma 24

1971 (11–1)
SEC Champions
17 Southern Cal. 10
42 Southern Miss. 6
38 Florida 0
40 Mississippi 6
42 Vanderbilt 0
32 Tennessee 15
34 Houston 20
41 Miss. State 10
14 LSU 7
31 Miami 3
31 Auburn 7
Orange Bowl
6 Nebraska 38

1972 (10–2)
SEC Champions
35 Duke 12
35 Kentucky 0
48 Vanderbilt 21
25 Georgia 7
24 Florida 7
17 Tennessee 10
48 Southern Miss. 11
58 Miss. State 14
35 LSU 21
52 Virginia Tech 13
16 Auburn 17
Cotton Bowl
13 Texas 17

1973 (11–1)
UPI National Champions
SEC Champions
66 California 0
28 Kentucky 14
44 Vanderbilt 0
28 Georgia 14
35 Florida 14
42 Tennessee 21
77 Virginia Tech 6
35 Miss. State 0

43 Miami 13
21 LSU 7
35 Auburn 0
Sugar Bowl
23 Notre Dame 24

1974 (11–1)
SEC Champions
21 Maryland 16
52 Southern Miss. 0
23 Vanderbilt 10
35 Mississippi 21
8 Florida State 7
28 Tennessee 6
41 TCU 3
35 Miss. State 0
30 LSU 0
28 Miami 7
17 Auburn 13
Orange Bowl
11 Notre Dame 13

1975 (11–1)
SEC Champions
7 Missouri 20
66 Clemson 0
40 Vanderbilt 7
32 Mississippi 6
52 Washington 0
30 Tennessee 7
45 TCU 0
21 Miss. State 10
23 LSU 10
27 Southern Miss. 6
28 Auburn 0
Sugar Bowl
13 Penn State 6

1976 (9–3)
7 Mississippi 10
56 SMU 3
42 Vanderbilt 14
0 Georgia 21
24 Southern Miss. 8
20 Tennessee 13
24 Louisville 3
34 Miss. State 17
28 LSU 17
18 Notre Dame 21
18 Auburn 7
Liberty Bowl
36 UCLA 6

249

1977 (11–1)
SEC Champions

34	Mississippi	13
24	Nebraska	31
24	Vanderbilt	12
18	Georgia	10
21	Southern Cal	20
24	Tennessee	10
55	Louisville	6
37	Miss. State	7
24	LSU	3
36	Miami	0
48	Auburn	21

Sugar Bowl

35	Ohio State	6

1978 (11–1)
AP National Champions
SEC Champions

20	Nebraska	3
38	Missouri	20
14	Southern Cal	24
51	Vanderbilt	28
20	Washington	17
23	Florida	12
30	Tennessee	17
35	Virginia Tech	0
35	Miss. State	14
31	LSU	10
34	Auburn	16

Sugar Bowl

14	Penn State	7

1979 (12–0)
AP National Champions
UPI National Champions
SEC Champions

30	Georgia Tech	6
45	Baylor	0
66	Vanderbilt	3
38	Wichita State	0
40	Florida	0
27	Tennessee	17
31	Virginia Tech	7
24	Miss. State	7
3	LSU	0
30	Miami (Fla.)	0
25	Auburn	18

Sugar Bowl

24	Arkansas	9

250